Statistical Fundamentals

Using Microsoft Excel for Univariate and Bivariate Analysis

First Edition

Alfred P. Rovai, Ph.D.
Azusa Pacific Online University

WATERTREE PRESS

Statistical Fundamentals: Using Microsoft Excel for Univariate and Bivariate Analysis

First Edition (Paperback)

Copyright ©2014 by Alfred P. Rovai

Published by Watertree Press LLC
PO Box 16763, Chesapeake, VA 23328
http://www.watertreepress.com

Trademarks

Microsoft® and Excel® are trademarks or registered trademarks of Microsoft Corporation, © Microsoft Corporation, in the United States and other countries. Use of this material does not imply Microsoft sponsorship, affiliation, or endorsement. IBM® and SPSS® are trademarks or registered trademarks of International Business Machines Corporation, registered in many jurisdictions worldwide. StatPlus LE® and StatPlus Pro® are trademarks of AnalystSoft, Inc.

Notice of Liability

The information in this book is distributed on an "as is" basis, without warranty. While every precaution has been taken in the preparation of this book, the publisher and author make no claim or guarantee as to its correctness, usefulness, or completeness for any reason, under any circumstance. Moreover, the publisher and author shall have no liability to any person or entity with respect to loss or damages caused or alleged to have been caused directly or indirectly by the information contained in this book.

Links to Web Sites

This book contains links to websites operated by third parties that are not under our control and are provided to you for your

Publisher's Cataloging-in-Publication Data

Rovai, Alfred P.
Statistical Fundamentals: Using Microsoft Excel for Univariate and Bivariate Analysis/ Alfred P. Rovai — First Edition
    p. cm.
  Includes bibliographical references, glossary, and index.
  Contents: Introductory statistical analysis using Microsoft
    Excel software — descriptive and inferential statistics,
    evaluation of test assumptions, and interpretation and
    reporting of statistical results.
  ISBN: 978-0-9911046-0-4 (pbk.)
  1. Statistical methods—Computer programs.
  HA32.R68 2014
  005.54—dc22

Library of Congress Control Number: 2013952448

Printed in the United States of America

Table of Contents

Preface

---

*"A judicious man uses statistics, not to get knowledge, but to
save himself from having ignorance foisted upon him."*

Thomas Carlyle, Scottish historian and essayist, 1795-1881

The purpose of this book is to provide users with knowledge
and skills in univariate and bivariate descriptive and inferential
statistics. It includes step-by-step examples of how to perform
various statistical procedures using Microsoft Excel's® native
operators and functions as well as automated procedures using
Microsoft Analysis ToolPak® and AnalystSoft StatPlus®.

Since the principles covered in this book cut across all
academic disciplines, undergraduate and graduate students in all
curricula can make use of this book. The examples are drawn
from across the social sciences and are meant emphasize the
generality of statistical theory across disciplines.

Using Excel's operators and functions, the learner knows
exactly how the solutions are obtained and is in full control of the
process, unlike some statistical software with sophisticated
graphic user interfaces in which the user has little knowledge
and flexibility regarding how the output is produced.

The examples included in this book were produced using
Microsoft Excel for Windows 2010 and Microsoft Excel for Mac
2011. The procedures also work with Microsoft Excel for
Windows 2013. Earlier versions of Excel, especially pre-2003
versions, have several issues with the statistical functions
dealing with inferential statistics and should not be used for the
types of scientific research described in this book where
precision of hypothesis testing results is important. Many
algorithm changes have been implemented, including renaming
functions and adding new functions, to improve function
accuracy and performance. Additionally, more recent versions of
the Excel Help file have been rewritten because earlier versions
of the Help file include some misleading advice on interpreting
results. All examples presented in this book were validated using

IBM SPSS®. In each case the solutions using Excel are identical to the solutions using IBM SPSS.

A major distinctive of this book is its affordable price. The concept of producing a deeply discounted textbook originates with Clayton Christiansen's work on disruptive innovation. Disruptive innovation is a term coined by Christensen to describe a process in which a product or service takes root initially in simple applications at the bottom of a market and then relentlessly moves "up market", eventually displacing established competitors. The intent is to apply this principle to college textbooks which, like tuition, have become very expensive.

This book also assists one in learning statistical concepts by applying appropriate formulas so one is fully aware of how solutions are obtained. The result is an affordable book that uses a spreadsheet program that is a standard feature of a popular office productivity suite that assists learning.

To use this book effectively one requires a personal computer, a recent copy of Microsoft Excel (Windows or Macintosh version), and basic skills in mathematics and Microsoft Excel. This book is intended primarily for two audiences:

　• Social science majors enrolled in introductory or intermediate statistics courses.

　• Professionals who have a need for a tutorial on how to conduct univariate and bivariate statistical analyses using Microsoft Excel and do not have convenient access to stand-alone statistics programs, such as IBM SPSS, or who desire the flexibility afforded using a spreadsheet program.

The examples in the book span a robust set of descriptive statistics, to include measures of central tendency, dispersion, relative position, normal curve transformations, and charts. It also includes a useful set of univariate and bivariate hypothesis tests to include the family of t-tests, one-way between subjects and within subjects ANOVAs, bivariate correlation and regression analysis, internal consistency reliability analysis using split-half and Cronbach's alpha models, and various alternative nonparametric procedures.

This book covers 23 different hypothesis tests to include a

description of the purpose, key assumptions and requirements, example research question and null hypothesis, Excel procedures to analyze data, a solved example using authentic data, displays and interpretation of Excel output, and how to report test results. Additionally, a companion website provides book users with supplemental resources to include Excel data files linked to the examples presented in this book. One can access this website at http://www.watertreepress.com/stats.

Included throughout this book are various sidebars highlighting key points, images, and Excel screenshots to assist understanding the material presented, self-test reviews at the end of each chapter, examples of Excel output with accompanying analysis and interpretations, and a comprehensive glossary. Included is a section on how to evaluate test assumptions such as univariate and bivariate normality, linearity, absence of extreme outliers, homogeneity of variance, and homoscedasticity. Underpinning all these features is a concise, easy to understand explanation of the material.

In addition to this paperback version, a Kindle version is also available. Users of either version are encouraged to provide the author with feedback at aprovai@mac.com to include recommendations regarding possible changes and additions to future editions.

Book Outline

Preface

Chapter 1 – Introduction to Quantitative Research

- Foundational concepts of quantitative research to include constructs, sampling theory, scaling, scales of measurement, and measurement validity

- Data ethics

Chapter 2 – Descriptive Statistics

- Excel fundamentals

- Measures of central tendency

- Measures of dispersion

- Measures of relative position

Appendix D – References

Index

I am particularly thankful to my former online statistics students who provided with valuable feedback regarding the learning process. I typically include weekly discussion forums in my course discussion boards and student identification of areas they least understood allowed me to go back to the textbook and elaborate various topics to improve understanding. These elaborations are included in this book.

Alfred P. Rovai, Ph.D.
aprovai@mac.com

Chapter 1: Quantitative Research

Quantitative research is the systematic investigation of social phenomena using statistical techniques. This chapter describes the basic quantitative concepts that underpin an understanding of subsequent chapters.

Chapter 1 Learning Objectives

- Explain quantitative research.

- Describe the differences between descriptive and inferential statistics.

- Understand the fundamental concepts of statistics including sampling, variability, distribution, scaling, and measurement.

- Contrast target population, sampling frame, experimentally accessible population, and sample.

- Match scales of measurement to variables.

- Understand the ethical handling, use, and reporting of research data.

1.1: Foundational Concepts

INTRODUCTION

Quantitative research is a type of research in which the investigator uses scientific inquiry in order to examine:

- descriptions of populations or phenomena

- differences between groups

- changes over time

- relationships between variables, to include prediction

The assumptions of quantitative research include the following considerations (Creswell, 2012):

- the world is external and objective reality is seen as one and therefore by dividing and studying its parts the whole can be understood
- phenomena are observable facts or events and everything occurring in nature can be predicted according to reproducible laws
- variables can be identified and relationships measured
- theoretically derived relationships between variables can be tested using hypotheses
- the researcher and the components of the problem under study are perceived as independent and separate (i.e., etic, an outsider's point of view

Quantitative research starts with the statement of a problem that identifies a need for research. It can be something to be explained, to be further understood, etc. The problem should address a gap in the professional literature and, when answered, should ultimately improve professional practice. It may address a present problem or one that is anticipated. It is a good idea as one formulates a research problem to seek the advice of experts in the field.

The problem statement produces one or more research questions. A good quantitative research question is one that is motivating for the researcher and has the following characteristics:

- Is specific and feasible. Must be answerable based on data from the study.

- Builds on previous research. Therefore, it is essential that the researcher conduct a thorough literature review prior to formulating any research question.

- Must respond to the problem statement and be worth investigating.

- Identifies the relevant variables/constructs and what one wants to know about them (e.g., differences, relationships, or predictions).

- Identifies the target population.

- Implies a statistical procedure (i.e., is testable using empirical methods).

The field of statistics is divided into descriptive statistics and inferential statistics as depicted in Figure 1.1 below (there are further subdivisions under each division that are discussed in subsequent chapters). Descriptive statistics are concerned with the collection, organization, summation, and presentation of data regarding a sample. Inferential statistics are meant to quantify data and generalize results from a sample to a target population of interest.

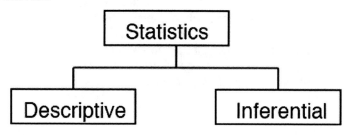

FIGURE 1.1
Divisions of statistics.

Below is a brief summary of the basic concepts of quantitative research starting with the concept of a construct.

CONSTRUCTS

A construct is a concept for a set of related behaviors or characteristics of an individual that cannot be directly observed or measured (Gall, Gall, & Borg, 2007). Its name indicates that it is a social construction. Sense of classroom community, intelligence, and computer anxiety are examples of constructs. They cannot be directly measured but rather are abstract concepts that are given concrete meanings by socially agreed upon definitions. Consequently, the researcher must first operationalize the construct in order to collect valid data. This operationalization is the development or identification of specific research procedures that result in empirical measurements of a variable argued as representing the construct of interest, e.g., measuring the variable grade point average when interested in the construct academic achievement. Operationalization defines the measuring method used and permits other researchers to replicate the measurements.

- The constitutive definition of a construct is a dictionary-like definition using terms commonly understood within the discipline (Gall, Gall, & Borg, 2007). It provides a general understanding of the characteristics or concepts that will be studied but must be complemented with an operational definition before the construct can be measured.

- An operational definition of a construct describes a measurement procedure that must be identified before actual measurement can take place; that is, it operationalizes the construct by describing how it will be measured. For example, an operational definition for student sense of classroom community could be sense of classroom community as measured by the Classroom Community Scale (CCS; Rovai, 2002) at http://www.sciencedirect.com/science/article/pii/S1096751602001021.

Operationalizing constructs is not limited to the use of test instruments. For example, American psychologist Edward C. Tolman operationalized hunger in a study that he conducted as the time since last feeding.

It is important in measurement planning and operationalizing constructs to avoid selecting instruments that result in range effects. Range effects are typically a consequence of using a measure that is inappropriate for a specific group (i.e., it is too easy, too difficult, not age appropriate, etc.). There are two types of range effects:

1. A ceiling effect is the clustering of scores at the high end of a measurement scale.

2. A floor effect is the clustering of scores at the low end of a measurement scale.

Looking for a test instrument to operationalize a construct? Check out ERIC/AE Test Locator at http://ericae.net/testcol.htm. Once a construct of interest for a study has been operationalized, it is time to formulate a data collection plan. Sampling is a key component of this plan.

SAMPLING

Sampling involves the collection, analysis, and interpretation of data gathered from a sample of the target population under study. The target population is the population to which the researcher wants to generalize study results; the experimentally accessible population is the subset of the target population to which the researcher has experimental access; and the sample is the group of participants from the experimentally accessible population who will participate in the research study and will be measured. To foster external validity of study findings, it is important that both the experimentally accessible population and the sample be representative of the target population. These terms are depicted graphically in Figure 1.2 that shows the sample is usually a subset of the experimentally accessible population and the experimentally accessible population is usually a subset of the target population.

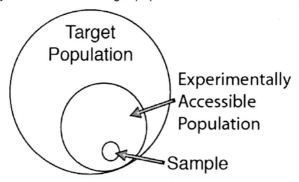

FIGURE 1.2
Relationship of sample to populations.

The sampling process consists of the following steps:

- identifying the target population

- obtaining a list of sampling units (see sampling frame below)

- specifying a sampling method for selecting units (cases) from the sampling frame

- determining the sample size (addressed in the next chapter)

• conducting the sampling

Sampling Frame

The sampling frame is the list of sampling units – which may be individuals, organizations, or other units of analysis – from the target population. Randomly selecting study participants from a suitable sampling frame is an example of probability sampling. A list of registered students may be the sampling frame for a survey of the student body at a university. However, problems arise if sampling frame bias exists. Telephone directories are often used as sampling frames, for example, but tend to under-represent the poor (who have no phones) and the wealthy (who may have unlisted numbers). If the researcher does not have a sampling frame, then he or she is restricted to less satisfactory samples that cannot be randomly selected because not all individuals within the population will have the same probability of being selected.

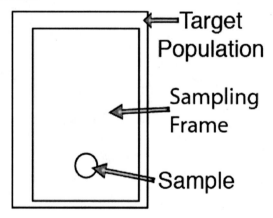

FIGURE 1.3
Relationship of sample to sampling frame and population.

Figure 1.3 depicts a sampling frame that does not include the entire target population. Consequently, the sampling frame as well as the sample may be biased thereby creating an external validity issue for the research findings.

Sampling Methods

There are two types or methods of sampling: probability sampling and non-probability sampling.

1. Probability sampling uses some form of random selection of research participants from the target population. Only a random sample permits true statistical inference to the target population thereby fostering external validity. Probability sampling includes several subcategories.

   • A simple random sample is a sample selected from a population in such a manner that all members of the population have an equal and independent chance of being selected. See the *Descriptive Statistics* chapter on how to generate random numbers using Microsoft Excel and use these numbers to randomly select a simple random sample from the sampling frame.

   • A stratified random sample is one in which the population is first divided into subsets or strata, e.g., a population of college students is first divided into freshmen, sophomores, juniors, and seniors, and then individuals are selected at random from each stratum. This method ensures that all groups are represented in the correct proportions.

   • A cluster random sample is a sample in which existing clusters or groups are randomly selected and then each member of the cluster is used in the research. For example, if classes of students are selected at random as the clusters, then the students in each selected class become participants in the research study. External validity is likely to be an issue if a sufficient number of sampling units – classes in this example – are not selected.

2. Non-probability sampling (purposeful or theoretical sampling) does not involve the use of randomization to select research participants. Consequently, research participants are selected because of convenience or access. External validity is an issue because the resultant sample may not adequately represent the population to which the researcher wants to make inferences.

   • A convenience sample is one in which the researcher relies on available participants. While this is the most convenient method, a major risk is to generalize the results to a known target population because the convenience sample may not be representative of the target population.

- A purposive sample is selected on the basis of the researcher's knowledge of the target population. The researcher chooses research participants who are similar to this population in attributes of interest.

- A quota sample is a stratified convenience sampling strategy. The sample is formed by selecting research participants who reflect the proportions of the target population on key demographic attributes such as gender, race, socioeconomic status, education level, etc. Research participants are recruited as they become available and the researcher assigns them to demographic groups based on their attributes. When the quota for a given demographic group is filled, the researcher stops recruiting participants from that particular group.

Sampling Error

Sampling error occurs when the researcher is working with sample data rather than population data. It assumes a probability sample and consists of two types: random error and systematic error or bias. Random errors tend to cancel each other out and have a minimal impact on overall statistical results. However, systematic error can impact statistical results.

When one takes a sample from a population, as opposed to collecting information from the entire population by way of a census, there is a likelihood that one's sample will not exactly reflect the characteristics of the population. Therefore, sampling error represents the variation between any sample statistic and its associated population parameter; that is, it is an error because the statistical computation (whatever it is) results in a value that does not coincide with the population parameter due to differences between the sample and the population.

Standard error of the mean (SEM) is frequently used as a measure of the effect of sampling error. If sampling includes other biases (such as non-sampling error), then SEM underestimates total sampling error for the mean. In most quantitative studies, a 5% error is acceptable. See the *Descriptive Statistics* chapter on how to calculate this statistic.

Non-Sampling Error

Non-sampling error is caused by human error and can result in bias. Biemer and Lyberg (2003) identify five potential sources of non-sampling error:

- Specification error occurs when the measurement instrument is not properly aligned with the construct that is measured. In other words, the construct validity of the instrument is weak.

- Coverage or frame error occurs when the sampling frame is a biased representation of the target population.

- Nonresponse error occurs when some members of the sample do not respond. A high response rate is essential to reliable statistical inference.

- Measurement error occurs when data collection is not reliable. Instrument reliability as well as inter- and intra-rater reliability are ways to help protect against measurement error.

- Processing error occurs as a result of editing mistakes, coding errors, data entry errors, programming errors, etc. during data analysis.

MEASUREMENT

Once the researcher has collected a sample and operationalized relevant constructs, measurement can take place. Measurement is the process of representing the construct with numbers in order to depict the amount of a phenomenon that is present at a given point in time. The purpose of this process is to differentiate between people, objects, or events that possess varying degrees of the phenomenon of interest. A measured phenomenon is referred to as a variable.

There are three basic types of measurement:

- Self-report measurement – One can measure a variable by asking participants to describe their behavior, to express their opinions, or to engage in interviews or focus groups in order to express their views. Alternatively, study participants can be asked to complete a survey. The self-report is the least accurate and most unreliable of the three types of measurements. Moreover, the least accurate type of self-report measurement is the retrospective self-report in which a person is asked to look back in time and remember details of a behavior or experience. Nonetheless, self-report measurements remain the most common type of measurement in social science research.

- Physiological measurement – Physiological measurement deals with measurements pertaining to the body. An apparatus can be used to take measurements; for example, a scale to measure weight, a tape measure to measure height, a device to measure heart rate, or a galvanic skin response sensor to measure anxiety.

- Behavioral measurement – Behaviors can be measured through observation such as recording reaction times, reading speed, disruptive behavior, etc. For example, the researcher defines key behaviors and trained observers then employ a count coding system to count the number of instances and/or duration of each key behavior. The employment of such a systematic approach to observation is important for the research study because, among its benefits, it promotes external validity by enhancing the replicability of the study.

Social scientists can better measure a construct if they look at it from two (or more) different perspectives. For example, behavioral measures of the construct of interest can be used to confirm self-report measures and vice-versa. This procedure is referred to as triangulation.

Triangulation is the use of more than one measurement technique to measure a single construct in order to enhance the confidence in and reliability of research findings. This concept can be extended to encompass the use of quantitative and qualitative methodologies in a single mixed methods research study to determine the degree to which findings converge and are mutually confirming. Additionally, triangulation can be used for behavioral measurement by using more than one observer to record the same session. In this way inter-observer agreement can be checked periodically throughout the data collection phase of the study.

A distribution is a list of the individual scores related to some measured construct; e.g., sense of classroom community scores. When one examines the interrelationships among these scores – in particular, how they cluster together and how they spread out – then one is examining this distribution. To help visualize interrelationships among the scores of any distribution one uses measures of central tendency, measures of dispersion, measures of relative position, and charts. These measures are discussed in later chapters. Common distributions include the following:

- Normal or Gaussian distributions model continuous random variables that form a bell shaped curve.

- Binomial distributions model discrete random variables. A binomial random variable represents the number of successes in a series of trials in which the outcome is either success or failure.

- Poisson distributions model discrete random variables. A Poisson random variable typically is the count of the number of events that occur in a given time period when the events occur at a constant average rate.

- Geometric distributions also model discrete random variables. A geometric random variable typically represents the number of trials required to obtain the first failure.

- Uniform distributions model both continuous random variables and discrete random variables. The values of a uniform random variable are uniformly distributed over an interval.

SCALING

Scaling is the branch of measurement that involves the construction of an instrument. Three unidimensional scaling methods frequently used in social science measurement are Likert, Guttman, and Thurstone scalings.

Likert Scaling

The Likert scale (pronounced Lick-ert) is a unidimensional, summative design approach to scaling named after its originator, psychologist Rensis Likert (Hopkins, 1998). It consists of a fixed-choice response format to a series of equal-weight statements regarding attitudes, opinions, and/or experiences. The set of statements act together to provide a coherent measurement of some construct. When responding to Likert items, respondents identify their level of agreement or disagreement to the statements. Likert scales are typically measured by a five- or seven-level scale and researchers typically assume assume that the intensity of the reactions to the statements is linear (i.e., equal intervals between item choices). For example, the choices of a five-level Likert scale might be *strongly disagree, somewhat disagree, neither agree nor disagree, somewhat agree,* and *strongly agree.* Individual statements that use this format are known as Likert items. see Figure 1.4 below for an example of a Likert scale.

Likert Scale

Directions: Each item has the following response set: Strongly Agree (SA), Agree (A), Neutral (N), Disagree (D), and Strongly Disagree (SD). Circle the best choice for each item.

1. I feel that students in this course care about each other   SA   A   N   D   SD

2. I feel that I am encouraged to ask questions   SA   A   N   D   SD

3. I feel connected to others in this course   SA   A   N   D   SD

FIGURE 1.4
Example of a Likert scale.

Alternatively, a semantic differential scale (a type of Likert scale) asks a person to rate a statement based upon a rating scale anchored at each end by opposites. For example, Figure 1.5 below depicts a semantic differential scale.

Semantic Differential Scale

All murders should receive the death penalty.

Strongly Agree   Strongly Disagree

| | | | | | | |

1   2   3   4   5   6   7

(circle level that applies)

FIGURE 1.5
Example of a semantic differential scale.

In summary,

- A Likert scale is a multi-item, summative scale, in which a score for the measured construct is obtained by adding scores across all Likert items.

- The range of responses should be based on the nature of the statements presented. For example, if the statements relate to estimates of time frequency, the responses may range from never to always.

- Likert scale items with less than five items are generally considered too coarse for useful measurement while items with more than seven items are considered too fine.

Odd-numbered Likert items have a middle value that reflects a neutral or undecided response. It is possible to use an even number of responses in which the respondent is forced to decide whether he or she leans more towards either end of the scale for each item. Forced-choice scales are those missing the middle or neutral option and forcing the participant to take a position. However, there are risks with this approach. Forcing a response may reduce the accuracy of the response. Individuals who truly do not agree or disagree will not like being forced to take a position, thereby reducing their likelihood to answer other items accurately. Additionally, forced-choice scales cannot be meaningfully intercorrelated or factor-analyzed (Johnson, Wood & Blinkhorn, 1988).

Likert scales can be assumed to produce interval scale data when the format clearly implies to the respondent that rating levels are evenly-spaced. However, researchers are not consistent on this point, as some researchers view Likert data as ordinal scale and others view the same data as interval scale. In particular, educational researchers tend to view these data as interval scale and health science researchers tend to view these data as ordinal scale. When in doubt, one should check the manual that accompanies the test instrument or check to see how other researchers in one's field use data generated by the test instrument in published research reports.

Guttman Scaling

The Guttman scale is a cumulative design approach to scaling. Its purpose is to establish a one-dimensional continuum for the concept one wishes to measure. Essentially, the items are ordered so that if a respondent agrees with any specific statement in the list, he or she will also agree with all previous statements. For example, take the following five-point Guttman scale (see Figure 1.6). If the respondent selects item 3, it means that he or she agrees with the first 3 items but does not agree with items 4 and 5.

Guttman Scale

Please check the highest numbered statement with which you agree:

1. One should not murder.

2. Murderers should be punished.

3. Sentences for murder should be severe.

4. More murderers should receive the death penalty.

5. All murderers should receive the death penalty.

FIGURE 1.6
Example of a Guttman scale.

Thurstone Scaling

The Thurstone scale also consists of a series of items. Respondents rate each item on a 1-11 scale in terms of how much each statement elicits a favorable attitude representing the entire range of attitudes from extremely favorable (a score of 1) to extremely unfavorable (a score of 11). A middle rating is for items in which participants hold neither a favorable nor unfavorable opinion. Numerical ratings for each statement are established by a panel of judges. Each statement on the scale has a numerical rating (1 to 11) from each judge. The number or weight assigned to each statement on the scale is the average of the ratings it received from the judges. The scale attempts to approximate an interval level of measurement. See Figure 1.7 below for an example of a Thurstone scale.

Thurstone Scale

Please check all those statements with which you agree:

_____ 1. All killers should be punished. (6)

_____ 2. Killing a person is OK in self-defense. (9)

_____ 3. Killing someone is never OK. (4)

_____ 4. All killers should receive the death penalty. (1)

_____ 5. Many killings are justified. (10)

_____ 6. Killing someone is rarely OK. (5)

_____ 7. Sentences for killers should be harsh. (2)

FIGURE 1.7
Example of a Thurstone scale.

This technique attempts to compensate for the limitation of the Likert scale in that the strength of the individual items is taken into account in computing the score for each item. The weights for the checked statements are added and divided by the number of statements answered. In this example, the respondent's average score for statements 1, 3, and 6 is 6 + 4 + 5 = 15/3 = 5.0 (i.e., dividing by the number of statements answered puts the total score on the 1-11 scale).

Variables

A variable is any characteristic or quality that varies. For example, if a group of people consists of both men and women, then group members vary by gender; thus gender is a variable. If students in a class achieve different scores on a test, then test score is also a variable.

Once a construct has been operationalized and measured, the resultant measurements represent one or more variables depending on the number of subscales generated by the instrument. For example, the Classroom Community Scale (Rovai, 2002), which uses a Likert scale, produces a total classroom community score as well as subscale scores representing classroom social community and classroom learning community. Each set of scores is considered a variable.

When the value of a variable is determined by chance, that variable is called a random variable. For example, if a coin is tossed 30 times, the random variable X is the coin side that come up. There are two types of random variables: discrete and continuous.

If a variable can take on any value between two specified values, it is called a continuous variable; otherwise, it is called a discrete variable. A discrete variable is one that cannot take on all values within the limits of the variable. For example, consider responses to a three-point rating scale that measures socioeconomic status (low, medium, high). The scale cannot generate the value of 2.5; therefore, data generated by this rating scale represent a discrete variable.

Discrete variables are also called categorical variables, qualitative variables, or non-metric variables. Quantitative (or numeric) variables are metric or continuous variables that have values that differ from each other by amount or quantity (e.g., test scores).

Scales of Measurement

An important factor that determines the amount of information that is provided by a variable is its measurement scale. Measurement scales are used to define and categorize variables. Specifically, variables are categorized as ratio, interval, ordinal, or nominal. Each has a decreasing level of measurement (from ratio to nominal) and each has a different mathematical attribute. These scales influence the statistical procedure one can use to analyze the data as well as the statistics used to describe the data. In general, one should use the highest level of measurement possible.

The four scales are described below in order of the level of information conveyed, from highest (ratio) to lowest (nominal).

Ratio Scale

Ratio scale variables allow one to quantify and compare the sizes of differences between them. They also feature an absolute zero; thus they allow for statements such as x is two times more than y. Examples of ratio scales are measures such as weight (in pounds), height (in inches), distance (in miles), and speed (in miles per hour).

Counting, greater than or less than operations, addition and subtraction of scale values, and multiplication and division of scale values are permissible with ratio scale data.

Interval Scale

Interval scale variables, like ratio scale variables, have equal intervals between each measurement unit. However, unlike ratio scale variables, interval scales have an arbitrary zero. Consequently, negative values are permissible. For example, temperature, as measured in degrees Fahrenheit or Celsius, represents an interval scale. The difference between a temperature of 100 degrees and 90 degrees is the same difference as between 90 degrees and 80 degrees. One can also say that a temperature of 100 degrees is higher than a temperature of 90 degrees and that an increase from 20 to 40 degrees is twice as much as an increase from 30 to 40 degrees. However, interval scales do not allow for statements such as 100 degrees is two times more than 50 degrees because the scale contains an arbitrary zero.

Counting, greater than or less than operations, and addition and subtraction of scale values are permissible with interval scale data.

Ordinal Scale

Ordinal scale variables allow one to rank order the items one measures in terms of which has less and which has more of the quality represented by the variable, but they do not provide information regarding how much less or more. In other words, the values simply express an order of magnitude with no constant intervals between units. For example, one might ask study participants to estimate the amount of satisfaction on a scale of 1 to 10. Resultant data are often considered ordinal scale data because the interval between rankings is not necessarily constant. This is most evident in the case of rankings in a horse race. The distance between ranks is not constant as the horse that came in second may have lost by a nose but the separation between other horses may have been greater. Many researchers consider IQ as an ordinal scale variable because the differences between IQ scores are not constant. Some researchers also consider Likert scale data to be ordinal.

Ordinal data can often appear similar to nominal data (in categories) or interval data (ranked from 1 to N). Ordinal data in categories are often referred to as collapsed ordinal data. An example of a collapsed ordinal variable is socioeconomic status (low, medium, high).

Counting and greater than or less than operations are permissible with ordinal scale data.

Nominal Scale

Nominal scale variables are unordered categories. Also called categorical or discrete variables, they allow for only qualitative classification. That is, they can be measured only in terms of whether individual units of analysis belong to some distinctively different categories, but one cannot rank order the categories. In other words, numbers are assigned to categories as names. Which number is assigned to which category is arbitrary. All one can say is that two individuals are different in terms of a categorical variable, but one cannot say which category has more of the quality represented by the variable. Gender (male, female) is an example of a nominal scale variable. The researcher could code male as 1 and female as 2 in Excel, or vice versa. Either way, the results will be the same.

Counting operations are permissible with nominal scale data.

Measurement Validity

Validity as discussed in this section refers to the validity of measurements. It does not refer to research design validity. Specifically, it evaluates how well an instrument measures a construct. The major types of measurement validity are summarized below (Gall, Gall, & Borg, 2007):

Face validity is an evaluation of the degree to which an instrument appears to measure what it purports to measure. It addresses the question: Does the instrument seem like a reasonable way to gain the information the researchers are attempting to obtain? It is often evaluated by the researcher.

It [face validity] refers, not to what the test actually measures, but to what it appears superficially to measure. Face validity pertains to whether the test "looks valid" to the examinees who take it, the administrative personnel who decide on its use, and other technically untrained observers. (Anastasi, 1988, p. 144)

Unlike content validity, face validity does not depend on established theories for support (Fink, 1995).

Content validity is based on the extent to which a measurement reflects the specific intended domain of content based on the professional expertise of experts in the field (Anastasi, 1988). Unlike face validity, it depends on established theories for support. It is frequently assessed using a panel of experts that evaluate the degree to which the items on an instrument address the intended domain.

Construct validity refers to whether an instrument actually reflects the true theoretical meaning of a construct, to include the instrument's dimensionality, i.e., existence of subscales (Fink, 1995). Construct validity also refers to the degree to which inferences can be made from the operationalizations in a study to the theoretical constructs on which those operationalizations are based. Consequently, construct validity is related to external validity and encompasses both the appropriateness and adequacy of interpretations. Construct validity includes convergent and discriminant validity.

- Convergent validity is the degree to which scores on one test correlate with scores on other tests that are designed to measure the same construct.

- Discriminant validity is the degree to which scores on one test do not correlate with scores on other tests that are not designed to assess the same construct. For example, one would not expect scores on a trait anxiety test to correlate with scores on a state anxiety test.

Criterion validity relates to how adequately a test score can be used to infer an individual's most probable standing on an accepted criterion (Hopkins, 1998). It is used to show the accuracy of a measure by comparing it with another measure that has been demonstrated to be valid. Criterion validity includes predictive validity, concurrent validity, and retrospective validity.

- Predictive validity is the effectiveness of an instrument to predict the outcome of future behavior. Examples of predictor measures related to academic success in college include SAT scores and high school grade point average.

- Concurrent validity is the effectiveness of an instrument to predict present behavior by comparing it to the results of a different instrument that has been shown to predict that behavior. The relationship between the two tests reflects concurrent validity if the two measures were administered at about the same time, the outcomes of both measures predict the same present behavior, and one of the two tests is known to predict this behavior.

- Retrospective validity refers to administering an instrument to a sample and then going back to others, e.g., former teachers of the respondents in the sample, and asking them to rate the respondents on the construct that was measured by the instrument. A significant relationship between test score and retrospective ratings would be evidence of retrospective validity.

1.2: Data Ethics

Ethics is the study of right and wrong. Data ethics represent the application of social and individual moral values and professional standards to collecting human subjects data, analyzing such data, and reporting findings. Adhering to ethical standards helps keep one not only moral but also within the law. Although the application of data ethics vary somewhat by profession, e.g., business, health services, and education, there are elements of commonality across all professions.

Researchers are obligated to protect the confidentiality of study participants. Research subjects have the right to expect that any personally identifying information will be limited to the authorized researchers and not be revealed externally (unless the subjects themselves authorize such exposure). Anonymity, where the identities of the participants are unknown even to the researchers, is not required for ethical research but certainly guarantees confidentiality. Additionally, researchers should take steps to ensure that all study-related data (e.g., papers, electronic files, etc.) is stored in a secure manner (e.g., locked cabinet, password-protected files) to preserve participant confidentiality.

It is relatively simple to manipulate and hide data, reporting only what one desires and not what the numbers actually communicate. To help guard against such behavior, integrity is viewed as the cornerstone moral value of statistics. Everyone involved in data collection, statistical analysis, and reporting must act with honesty, integrity, and responsibly as a professional at all times. Statisticians are especially vulnerable to conflicts of interest, such as conflicts that arise between personal/employer interests and the public interest that compromise professional judgments. For example, profits and promotion can sometimes take precedence over ethical behavior.

Of all the traits which qualify a scientist for citizenship in the republic of science, I would put a sense of responsibility as a scientist at the very top. A scientist can be brilliant, imaginative, clever with his hands, profound, broad, narrow—but he is not much as a scientist unless he is responsible. (Weinberg, 1978)

Responsibility manifests itself in many ways. A professional who is involved in statistics

- identifies and discloses conflicts of interest

- promotes quality by maintaining competency in statistical methods and uses only statistical procedures suitable for the data and obtaining valid results

- respects differences of opinion

- obtains Institutional Review Board review and approval of the research protocol before any data are collected

- obtains informed consent from all research participants prior to data collection

- maintains awareness of and follows applicable statutes and regulations; for example

  - individuals who work with educational data must know their responsibilities for the protection of student data under the Family Education Rights and Privacy Act (FERPA), the Individuals with Disabilities Education Act (IDEA), and the Health Insurance Portability and Accountability Act (HIPPA)

  - individuals who work with children (under the age of 18) must know that in addition to obtaining the informed consent of a child participant in research activities, it is generally also necessary to obtain parental permission

- acknowledges the contributions and intellectual property of others, e.g., by properly citing their works

- holds oneself and others accountable for the ethical use of data

- provides all of the information to help others judge the value of one's results to include reporting

  - the steps taken to guard validity

  - the suitability of the statistical procedures used to include an evaluation of statistical test assumptions

  - the statistical software used to analyze the data

• ensures confidentiality and protection of the interests of human subjects

• ensures data collection, analysis, and reporting reflect the unbiased search for truth

- guards against a predisposition regarding results

- collects data in an objective manner by avoiding leading questions and collecting data to support a viewpoint rather than discover the truth. For example, a biased survey of the Emergency Project to Support Col. North and the President's Freedom Fight in Central America conducted in the 1980s included the following item: Col North complained of Congress' failure to give consistent aid to the anti-Communist freedom fighters in Nicaragua. In September, Congress will be asked to approve such aid. Should Congress continue aid to the Nicaraguan Freedom fighters (a) Yes, they're battling for our freedom too (b) No, abandon Central America to the communists

- recognizes that the manner one asks a question in a survey greatly impacts its results, e.g., an NBC/Wall Street Journal poll asked two very similar questions with very different results: (a) Do you favor cutting programs such as social security, Medicare, Medicaid, and farm subsidies to reduce the budget deficit? The results: 23% favor; 66% oppose; 11% no opinion. (b) Do you favor cutting government entitlements to reduce the budget deficit? The results: 61% favor; 25% oppose; 14% no opinion

- avoids falsification, fabrication, plagiarism, and use of unorthodox methods

- clearly identifies all study limitations and weaknesses, such as failure to satisfy hypothesis test assumptions

- reports negative as well as positive results

- includes relevant information that challenges findings such as acknowledging conflicts with other results

- identifies and explains outliers

- avoids inappropriate charting or reporting that exaggerates small differences

- avoids including opinions as statistical conclusions

1.3: Chapter 1 Review

The answer key is at the end of this section.

1. What is a construct?

   A. A construct is any characteristic or quality that varies

   B. A construct is a categorization or concept for a set of behaviors or characteristics of an individual

   C. A construct is a method for making decisions about the target population

   D. A construct refers to how a characteristic is defined in a study

2. What is the most inaccurate and unreliable type of measurement?

   A. Self-report measurements

   B. Physiological measurements

   C. Behavioral measurements

   D. Parallel measurements

3. What type of variable cannot take on all values within the limits of the variable?

   A. Discrete variable

   B. Interval scale variable

   C. Ratio scale variable

   D. Quantitative variable

4. What scale of measurement is U.S.D.A. quality of beef ratings (good, choice, prime)?

   A. Nominal

   B. Ordinal

   C. Interval

   D. Ratio

5. What scale of measurement is used for number of events per minute?

A. Nominal

B. Ordinal

C. Interval

D. Ratio

6. What scale of measurement is undergraduate student status (freshman, sophomore, junior, senior)?

A. Nominal

B. Ordinal

C. Interval

D. Ratio

7. What scale of measurement are the numbers on the jerseys of players on a football team?

A. Nominal

B. Ordinal

C. Interval

D. Ratio

8. What scale of measurement is degrees centigrade?

A. Nominal

B. Ordinal

C. Interval

D. Ratio

9. In what scale of measurement is division and multiplication permissible?

A. Nominal

B. Ordinal

C. Interval

D. Ratio

10. What type of instrument validity is frequently assessed using a panel of experts that evaluate the degree to which the

items on the instrument address the intended domain, nothing less and nothing more?

A. Face validity

B. Content validity

C. Construct validity

D. Criterion validity

11. What type of instrument validity is associated with the degree to which an instrument appears to measure what it purports to measure?

A. Retrospective validity

B. Concurrent validity

C. Predictive validity

D. Face validity

12. What type of instrument validity is associated with the degree to which scores on one test correlate with scores on other tests that are designed to measure the same construct?

A. Retrospective validity

B. Concurrent validity

C. Convergent validity

D. Discriminant validity

13. What type of sampling occurs when participants are selected on the basis of the researcher's knowledge of the target population?

A. Probability sampling

B. Convenience sampling

C. Purposive sampling

D. Quota sampling

14. What type of sampling is a stratified convenience sampling strategy?

A. Probability sampling

    B. Convenience sampling

    C. Purposive sampling

    D. Quota sampling

15. What type of sampling is a sample selected from a population in such a manner that all members of the population have an equal and independent chance of being selected?

    A. Simple random sample

    B. Stratified random sample

    C. Clustered random sample

    D. Purposive sample

16. What type of sampling is a sample in which the population is first divided into subsets or strata and then individuals are selected at random from each stratum?

    A. Simple random sample

    B. Stratified random sample

    C. Clustered random sample

    D. Purposive sample

17. What type of sampling is a sample selected on the basis of the researcher's knowledge of the target population?

    A. Simple random sample

    B. Stratified random sample

    C. Clustered random sample

    D. Purposive sample

Chapter 1 Answers

1B, 2A, 3A, 4B, 5D, 6B, 7A, 8C, 9D, 10B, 11D, 12C, 13C, 14D, 15A, 16B, 17D

Chapter 2: Descriptive Statistics

There are two types of statistics: descriptive statistics and inferential statistics. Descriptive statistics, addressed in this chapter, are used to describe various facets of data to include central tendency, dispersion, and relative position. Also addressed are supporting charts and normal curve transformations.

Chapter 2 Learning Objectives

• Produce and interpret numerical summary statistics to include measures of central tendency, measures of dispersion, and measures of relative position.

• Summarize a dataset using the most appropriate measures of central tendency and dispersion.

• Describe a distribution in terms of symmetry, kurtosis, modality and outliers.

• Explain the properties of a normal curve.

• Define z-scores, T-scores, and NCE scores and convert from and to raw scores using Microsoft Excel.

• Create, modify, and interpret graphical summaries of quantitative data using Microsoft Excel.

• Evaluate a variable for normality using charts and descriptive statistics.

• Create tables and pivot tables using Microsoft Excel.

2.1: Introduction to Descriptive Statistics and Microsoft Excel

Descriptive statistics are used to describe what is or what the data shows. It is divided into the four subcategories shown in Figure 2.1 below.

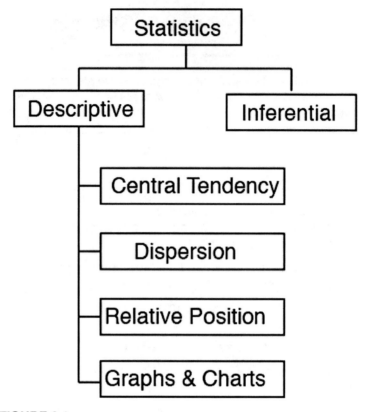

FIGURE 2.1
Divisions of descriptive statistics.

The first step in data analysis is to describe data using descriptive statistics. Descriptive statistics are a way to summarize large datasets and to detect patterns in the data in order to convey their essence to others and/or to allow for further analysis using inferential statistics.

> Key Point
> Descriptive statistics summarize data collected from a sample while inferential statistics reach conclusions that extend beyond the sample.

The shape of a distribution can vary greatly. A light-tailed distribution is one in which the extreme portion of the distribution spreads out less far relative to the center of the distribution when compared to the normal distribution. On the other hand, a heavy-tailed distribution is one in which the extreme portion of the distribution spreads out further relative to the center of the distribution when compared to the normal distribution. Light-tailedness and heavy-tailedness can be visually detected using a histogram.

A comprehensive description of data can also address the following distribution characteristics:

- symmetry (symmetrical, skewed positively, or skewed negatively)
- kurtosis (leptokurtic, mesokurtic, or platykurtic)
- modality (unimodal, bimodal, or multimodal)

It is customary to describe any dataset descriptively in any research report or journal article. Results sections of quantitative research reports describe the distributions obtained from measuring a sample on one or more variables by reporting, as a minimum, the sample size (N), group sizes (n), and the best measures of central tendency and dispersion for each variable. Additionally, charts are frequently used to display the shape of distributions. These terms are described in this chapter as well as the procedure used to generate relevant statistics.

MICROSOFT EXCEL FUNDAMENTALS

The examples in this book use Microsoft Excel for storing, organizing, and manipulating data as well as generating charts. Excel opens in worksheet view (see Figures 2.2 and 2.3 below).

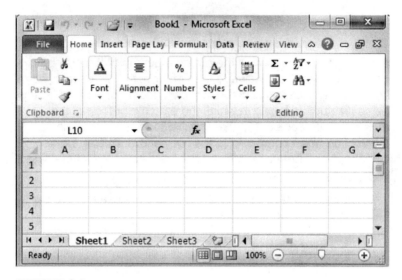

FIGURE 2.2
Windows version opening screen.

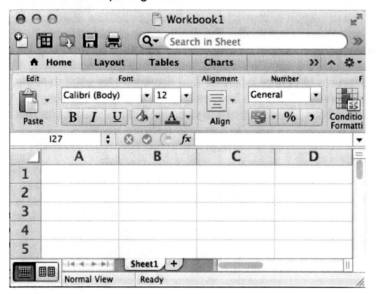

FIGURE 2.3
Macintosh version opening screen.

Excel uses what Microsoft calls a tabbed Ribbon system instead of traditional menus. The Ribbon contains multiple tabs, each with several groups of commands. These tabs (Home, Insert, Page Layout, Formulas, Data, Review, and View in Excel for Windows 2010 and 2013; Home, Layout, Tables, Charts, SmartArt, Formulas, Data, and Review in Excel for Macintosh 2011) provide access to a variety of tools. The default tab is the Home tab, shown above with basic tools allowing one to control general formatting such as font, font size, and cell alignment. The Insert tab (for Windows users) or the Charts tab (for Macintosh users) and the Formulas tab are especially useful in conducting statistical analyses (a portion of the Formulas tabs for the Windows and Macintosh versions are shown in Figures 2.4 and 2.5 below).

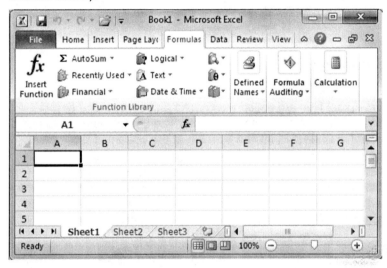

FIGURE 2.4
Windows version Formulas tab.

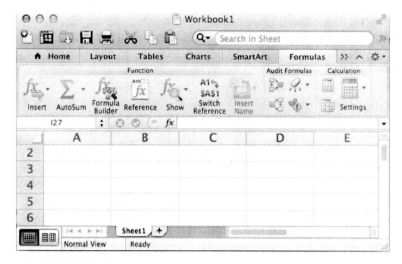

FIGURE 2.5
Macintosh version Formulas tab.

Excel files are called workbooks and contain one or more worksheets or, more simply sheets. The default name of the first sheet is Sheet1 identified by a tab at the bottom of the spreadsheet as shown above. Each sheet represents a rectangular grid of columns, labeled with letters, and rows, labeled with numbers. New sheets can be added by clicking the + tab at the bottom of the spreadsheet. Different sheets can be viewed and made active by clicking the desired sheet tab.

The intersection of a column and row is a cell identified by column and row address, e.g., A1. Multiple cells are identified by a shorthand notation using the colon symbol, e.g., A1:A3 means cells A1, A2, and A3. The above cell references are relative addresses.

However, at times one needs to copy a formula for other cells. One can copy and paste formulas from one cell to another, but they are pasted relative to their original position. For example if reference to cell A1 is copied from cell B1 to B2, the pasted address becomes A2 instead of A1. To paste cell address A1 one needs to use an absolute address for cell A1.

Absolute addresses include the $ symbol before the column portion of the reference and/or the row portion of the reference and indicates to Excel that it should not increment the column and/or row reference as one fills a range with a formula or copies and pastes a range. For example, A1 is a relative address, while $A$1 is an absolute address for both column and row. If one enters =A1 in a cell and pastes the contents of that cell in another cell, the reference changes relative to the original position. If one enters =$A$1 in a cell and pastes the contents of that cell in another cell, the reference remains $A$1.

There is a short cut to pasting the contents of a cell in multiple adjacent cells that is called Fill Down, Up, Left, or Right. To perform this operation:

1. select the cell that has the original formula

2. hold the shift key down and click on the last cell (in the series that needs the formula)

3. under the Excel Edit menu select Fill and select Fill Down, Up, Left, or Right, as appropriate

Individual cells can contain a number, text, a logical value, e.g., TRUE or FALSE, or a formula, e.g., =A1+A2 is a formula that adds the values in cells A1 and A2. Formulas start with an = sign and contain no spaces. Parentheses can be included to specify order of operations. One can view a list and description of all Excel operators by selecting the Excel Formulas tab and clicking the Reference icon. Formulas can include arithmetic, comparison operators, and/or text operators.

Arithmetic operators:

Excel Formula tab
Reference Icon.
formulas

+ for addition, e.g., =A1+A2
− for subtraction, e.g., =A1-A2
* for multiplication, e.g., =A1*A2
/ for division, e.g., =A1/A2

Comparison operators:

> for greater than, e.g., A1>A2
< for less than, e.g., A1<A2
>= for greater than or equal, e.g., A1>=A2
<= for less than or equal, e.g., A1<=A2
<> for not equal to, e.g., A1<>A2

Text operator:

& for connecting two values to produce one text value, e.g., "one"&"-way"

Mathematical functions can also be used in Excel formulas. Functions are pre-defined operations. For example, =SUM(A1:B5) adds the numbers in cells A1 through B5. The IF function adds a decision making capability. It is defined as follows: IF(logical_test,value_if_true,value_if_false). The function returns one value if the condition is TRUE and a different value if the condition is FALSE. For example, =IF(A1>=50,TRUE,FALSE) returns TRUE if the content of A1 has a value greater than or equal to 50 and FALSE if the content of A1 has a value less than 50.

There is an order of operations when Excel evaluates a formula. Formulas are evaluated from left to right, with expressions enclosed in parentheses evaluated first, then multiplication, division, addition, and subtraction. For example, take the formula =A1/(A2+A3). The first operation is the addition of A2 and A3 followed by the division of A1 by that sum.

Independent data is typically organized in a stacked format with the grouping or independent variable contained in one column and the dependent variable contained in another. Variable names are usually contained in the first row above the data as shown below.

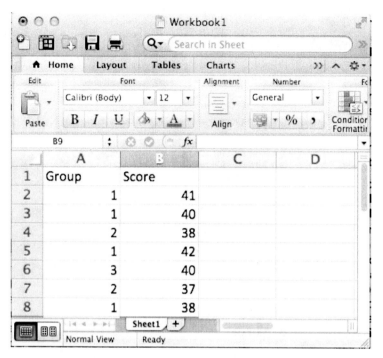

Dependent data is organized in an unstacked format with data for each dependent measure contained in separate columns as shown below.

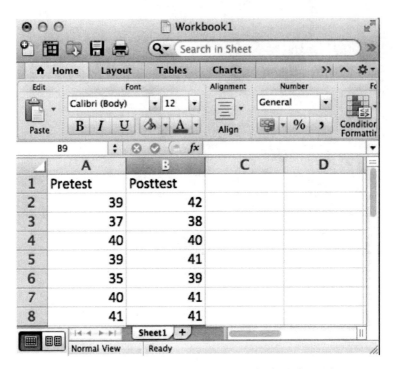

Although Excel is a powerful program, it does have its limitations.

- The process can be time-consuming.

- Formula or data entry errors are possible because of the numerous and sometimes complex entries required resulting in extra time to ensure accuracy.

- Missing values are handled inconsistently requiring one to edit data for missing entries.

- Excel has no template for a histogram, a common chart used in statistical analysis. Consequently, one must manually create a histogram using the column chart template as a starting point, requiring extra steps and time. However, once a histogram is created, it can be saved as a template and applied to future charts.

- Excel versions dated prior to 2010 are not well-suited for sophisticated statistical analysis because of issues regarding precision of results.

- Data organization sometimes differs according to analysis requiring one to reorganize data for different analyses. For example, it is often more convenient to organize independent data in an unstacked format as shown below where data for different groups are contained in different columns.

Tables

A table is a set of values that is organized using vertical columns (variables) and horizontal rows (cases). Typically, the first row consists of column names. Tables allow one to analyze data quickly.

Procedures

Task: Use the Excel file Motivation.xlsx located at http://www.watertreepress.com/stats if you want to create a table using new or existing data. The Table tab contains the data used in the analysis described below.

1. Open the Design tab (if a Windows user) or the Table tab (if a Macintosh user) of the *Motivation.xlsx* file using Excel.

Note the sample data in cells A1:E169 contain no blank rows or columns and reflect the labels and data for variables gender (1 = female, 2 = male), alienation, isolation, powerl (powerlessness), and norml (normlessness).

2. To create a table using this data, select the data by highlighting any single cell inside the dataset, e.g., cell A3.

	A	B	C	D	E
1	gender	alienation	isolation	powerl	norml
2	1	72	26	29	17
3	1	89	33	32	24
4	1	68	26	27	15
5	1	82	30	29	23

3. Go to the Excel Insert tab (if using Windows) or the Excel Insert menu item (if using Macintosh) and select Table. Excel automatically selects the data and creates a table using all the data. Creating the table enables a variety of Excel tools to modify the table.

4. Go to the Excel Design tab (if using Windows) or the Excel Tables tab (if using Macintosh) and, with any cell in the table selected, check Total Row. Excel places a new row (170) at the bottom of the table that adds the last column (norml).

Windows

Macintosh

	Home	Layout	Tables	Charts

Table Options

☑ Header Row   ☐ First Column
☑ Total Row   ☐ Last Column
New   ☑ Banded Rows   ☐ Banded Columns

	A	B	C	D	E
166	2	55	20	22	13
167	2	53	26	19	8
168	2	57	27	18	12
169	2	55	20	23	12
170	Total				2546

5. Selecting other cells in row 170 permits changing the displayed statistic.

	gender	alienation	isolation	powerl	norml
168	2	57	27	18	12
169	2	55	20	23	12
170	Total				2546
171		✓ None			
172		Average			
173		Count			
174		Count Numbers			
175		Max			
176		Min			
177		Sum			
178		StdDev			
179		Var			
		More Functions...			

6. For example, changing each cell in row 170 to Average, results in a display of means for each column (variable).

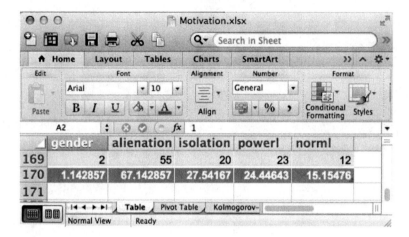

Pivot Tables

A pivot table is an Excel reporting tool that facilitates extracting information from large tables of data without the use of formulas and displaying various statistics using different formats.

Procedures

Task: Use the Excel file Motivation.xlsx located at http://www.watertreepress.com/stats if you want to create a pivot table. The Pivot Table tab contains the data used in the analysis described below.

1.   Open the Pivot Table tab of the *Motivation.xlsx* file using Excel. Note the sample data in cells A1:E169 contain no blank rows or columns and reflect the labels and data for variables gender (1 = female, 2 = male), alienation, isolation, powerl (powerlessness), and norml (normlessness). Moreover, the data contain five columns (three columns or more are required to create a pivot table. Also note the data contains no blank rows or columns. A minimum of three columns of data are required to create a pivot table.

2.   To create a manual pivot table, select the data by highlighting cells A1:E169. Go to the Excel Insert tab (if using Windows) or the Excel Data tab (if using Macintosh). Click the inverted triangle next to the PivotTable icon and select PivotTable (if a Windows user, see Figure 2.6) or Create Manual PivotTable (if a Macintosh user, see Figure

2.7).

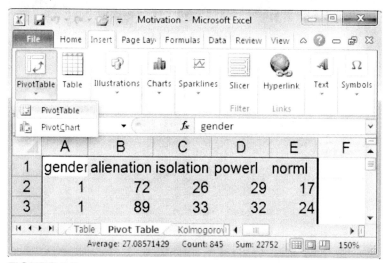

FIGURE 2.6
Creating a Pivot Table using the Windows version of Excel.

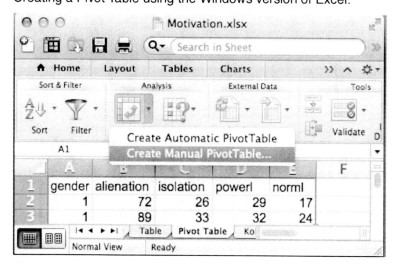

FIGURE 2.7
Creating a Pivot Table using the Macintosh version of Excel.

3. Excel opens the Create PivotTable dialog. Note that the highlighted data in cells A1:E169 are already identified as the data to be analyzed. Choose the location to place the

pivot table. For this example select the location G1 on the existing worksheet. Click the OK button.

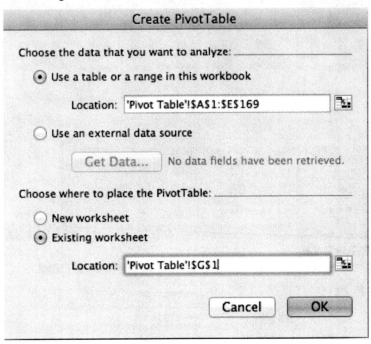

4. Excel reserves the following space for the pivot table.

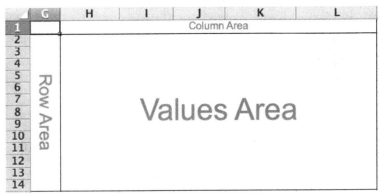

5. Excel also displays the following PivotTable Builder dialog. Note the field names from the selected data are displayed in the dialog. Select each listed field by checking the box to the left of each field name.

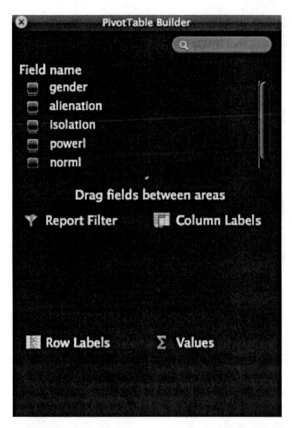

6.   As the field names are checked, Excel places fields in various panels of the dialog and creates a default pivot table with isolation in the Row Labels panel and sum as the default value for each field.

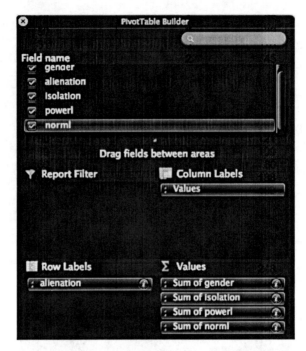

7.   Drag the alienation field from the Row Labels panel to the top field position in the Values panel. Drag the gender field from the Values panel to the Row Labels panel. Click the i symbol to the right of the Sum of alienation field in the Values panel and change Summarize by from Sum to Average in the PivotTable Field dialog.

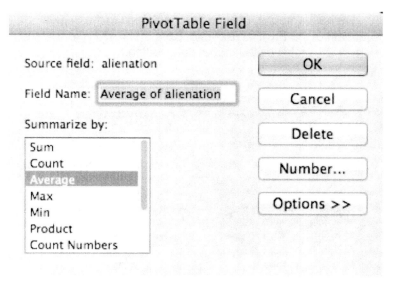

8. Repeat this step for the remaining fields in the Values panel.

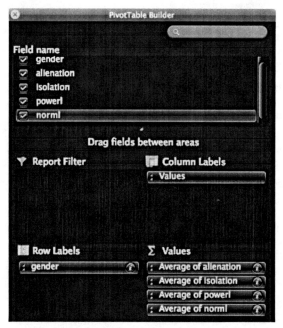

9. Excel produces the following pivot table showing the

averages (means) of each field contained in the Values
panel of the PivotTable dialog. Note that row 1 = females and
row 2 = males based on the data coding.

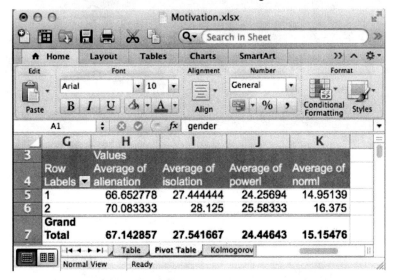

10. Clicking the inverted triangle symbol adjacent to Row
Labels opens the gender dialog permitting changes to the
displayed results.

11. If additional values for each field are required, e.g.,
standard deviation, drag additional instances of fields from
the Field name panel to the Values panel using the
PivotTable Builder dialog and click the i symbol to the right of
the additional fields in the Values panel and change
Summarize by from Sum to StdDev in the PivotTable Field
dialog. Move the Values field from the Column Labels panel
to the Row Labels panel, and move the gender field from the
Row Labels panel to the Column Labels panel using the
PivotTable Builder dialog.

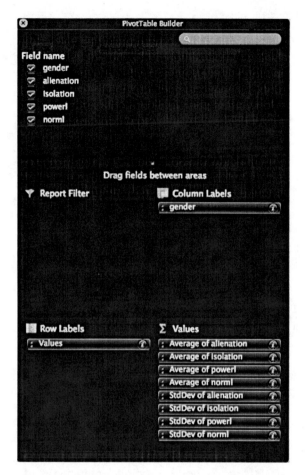

12. Excel produces the following pivot table showing the averages (means) and standard deviations of each field contained in the Values panel of the PivotTable Builder dialog.

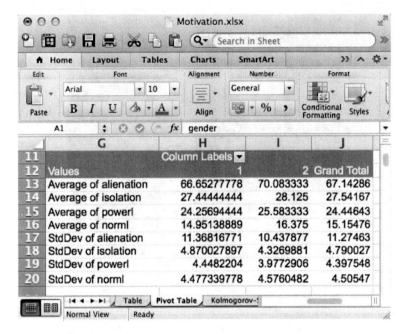

	G	H	I	J
11		Column Labels ▼		
12	Values	1	2	Grand Total
13	Average of alienation	66.65277778	70.083333	67.14286
14	Average of isolation	27.44444444	28.125	27.54167
15	Average of powerl	24.25694444	25.583333	24.44643
16	Average of norml	14.95138889	16.375	15.15476
17	StdDev of alienation	11.36816771	10.437877	11.27463
18	StdDev of isolation	4.870027897	4.3269881	4.790027
19	StdDev of powerl	4.4482204	3.9772906	4.397548
20	StdDev of norml	4.477339778	4.5760482	4.50547

Generating Random Numbers

Random numbers are frequently used by researchers to create random samples. The Excel RAND and RANDBETWEEN functions are used to generate random numbers from the uniform distribution.

Excel Functions Used

RAND(). Returns a random number between 0 and 1.

Note: RAND()*(b-a)+a returns a random number between a and b.

RANDBETWEEN(bottom,top), where bottom = smallest integer and top = largest integer. Returns a random number between bottom and top values.

Procedures

Assume the sampling frame consists of 100 cases and one desires to select a simple random sample of approximately 25 cases from this sampling frame to form an experimental group.

1. Assign each case an identification number, e.g., case #1, case #2, case #3, etc. In this example there are 100 cases.

2. Generate a random number using the formula = RANDBETWEEN(1,4) for each case. The random number generator will produce 100 random integers between 1 and 4. Each integer should appear approximately 25 times (the number of cases desired in the sample). (Note: a new random number is generated each time the sheet is calculated; the random sample is selected based on one instance of the random numbers displayed.)

	A	B
1	Cases	Random Numbers
2	case #1	4
3	case #2	3
4	case #3	1
5	case #4	4
6	case #5	4
7	case #6	2
8	case #7	2
9	case #8	2
10	case #9	1
11	case #10	2

3. Blindly choose a number (1, 2, 3, or 4). Assign cases with this random number to the sample. Reject all other cases. Approximately 25 cases will be selected for the simple random sample.

2.2: Measures of Central Tendency

Measures of central tendency indicate where the middle of a distribution lies. Researchers typically report the best measures of central tendency and dispersion for each variable in research reports. This section describes the most commonly used measures of central tendency used in reporting social science research.

COUNT

The count (N, n) is a statistic that reflects the number of cases selected in the dataset. It is often used to represent sample (N) or sub-sample (n) size. It is an important statistic in any research study.

$$N = n_1 + n_2 + ...n_k$$

Excel Functions Used

COUNT(value1,value2,...). Counts the numbers in the range of numbers.

COUNTA(value1,value2,...). Counts the cells with non-empty values in the range of values.

MEAN

The mean (M) or arithmetic average is based on the sum of the deviation scores raised to the first power, or what is known as the first moment of the distribution.

The sample mean may be thought of as an estimate of the population mean from which the sample was drawn. By convention, the population mean is denoted by the Greek letter μ (mu) and the sample mean is denoted by M or $\bar{x}$.

The formula for the sample mean is given below. It shows that the sum of all scores is divided by the total number of scores (N) in the sample.

$$\overline{X} = \frac{\sum X}{N}$$

The mean is always located more toward the skewed (tail) end of skewed distributions in relation to the median and mode. If the distribution is normally distributed (i.e, symmetrical and unimodal), the mode, median, and mean coincide.

The mean can be thought of as the balance point of the distribution. If one places the observations on an imaginary see-saw with the mean at the center point, then the two sides of the see-saw should be balanced (that is, both sides are off the ground and the see-saw is level).

When reporting sample mean in the results section of a research report, it is customary to use the M symbol and also report the best measure of dispersion, usually the standard deviation (SD). For example, report classroom community ($M = 57.42$, $SD = 12.53$) and perceived cognitive learning ($M = 7.02$, $SD = 1.65$).

It is customary to compute and report a weighted mean (also known as the aggregate mean) when sample sizes are unequal or when some scores are given more weight than others. The weighted mean is similar to the arithmetic average except that each of the data points do not contribute equally to the final mean because of sample size or other differences.

$$\overline{X}_w = \frac{w_1\overline{X}_1 + w_2\overline{X}_2 + w_n\overline{X}_n}{w_1 + w_2 + w_n}$$

where $w_1, w_2, ... w_n$ are non-negative weights, e.g., sample sizes, that are associated with the corresponding sample means.

> **Key Point**
> For interval/ratio variables, the mean is normally the best measure of central tendency. For strongly skewed variables, both mean and median should be reported.

Excel Functions Used

AVERAGE(number1,number2,...). Returns the arithmetic mean, where numbers represent the range of numbers.

Note: Values must be numbers, arrays, or reference that consist of numbers. Additionally, text and logical values are included in the analysis.

AVERAGEA(value1,value2,...). Returns the arithmetic mean of the values, to include text and logical values.

AVERAGEIF(range,criteria,average_range). Returns the arithmetic mean of the values that meet the specified criteria.

Note:

• Range is the group of cells the function is to analyze, e.g., A1:A50.

• Criteria is the value that defines the data in the Range that will be added, e.g., adding ">0" (with quotation marks) will average all non-zero values in the Range.

• Average_range (optional) defines the range of cells that is averaged when matches are found between the Range and Criteria arguments. If the Average_range argument is omitted, the data matched in the Range argument is averaged instead.

AVERAGEIFS(average_range,criteria_range1,criteria1,criteria_range2,criteria2...). Returns the arithmetic mean of the values that meet multiple specified criteria.

MEDIAN

The median (Mdn) is the score that divides the distribution into two equal halves. It is the midpoint of the distribution when the distribution has an odd number of scores. It is the number halfway between the two middle scores when the distribution has an even number of scores. The median is useful to describe a skewed distribution. If the distribution is normally distributed (i.e, symmetrical and unimodal), the mode, median, and mean coincide.

The median of a distribution is the score that, if subtracted from all other scores in the distribution, results in a sum of the absolute values of the deviations that is less than the sum if any other number had been subtracted.

> Key Point
> For ordinal variables, the median is the best measure of central tendency.

Excel Functions Used

MEDIAN(number1,number2,...). Returns the median of a range of numbers.

MODE

The mode (Mo) is the most frequently occurring score in a distribution. A distribution is called unimodal if there is only one major peak in the distribution of scores when displayed as a histogram. If the distribution is normally distributed (i.e, symmetrical and unimodal), the mode, median, and mean coincide.

The mode is useful when describing nominal variables and in describing a bimodal or multimodal distribution (use of the mean or median only can be misleading).

- Major mode = most common value, largest peak
- Minor mode(s) = smaller peak(s)
- Unimodal (i.e., having one peak or mode)
- Bimodal (i.e., having two peaks or modes)
- Multimodal (i.e., having two or more peaks or modes)
- Rectangular (i.e., having no peaks or modes)

> Key Point
> For nominal variables, the mode is the best measure of central tendency.

Excel Functions Used

MODE.SNGL(number1,number2,...). Returns the most frequently occurring value of the range of data.

Note: Numbers must be numbers, arrays, or reference that consist of numbers. Returns the statistical mode of the distribution defined by the arguments.

MODE.MULT(number1,number2,...). Returns a vertical array of the most frequently occurring values.

Note: Must be entered as an array formula, e.g., A2:A10.

Procedures

Task: Use the Excel file Motivation.xlsx located at http://www.watertreepress.com/stats if you want to follow along with the analysis. The Data tab contains the data used in the analysis described below.

1.   Open the *Motivation.xlsx file using Excel.*

2.   Copy the variable c_community (classroom community) from the Excel workbook, Data tab, and paste the variable in column A of an empty sheet. Copy all 169 cases.

3.   Click the Excel Formulas tab and then click the Insert icon from the Function group of icons to insert the proper

function in the appropriate cell or type-in the formula directly. Enter the labels Count, Mean, Median, and Mode in cells C1:C4. Enter formulas =COUNT(A2:A170), =AVERAGE(A2:A170), =MEDIAN(A2:A170), and =MODE.SNGL(A2:A170) in cells D1:D4

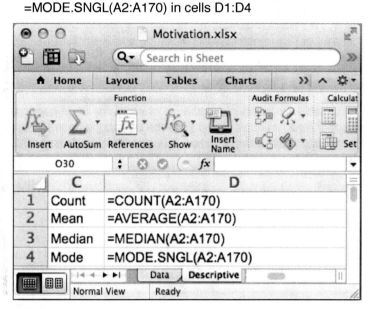

2.3: Measures of Dispersion

Measures of dispersion describe the variability of a distribution. Researchers typically report the best measures of central tendency and dispersion for each variable in research reports. This section describes the most commonly used measures of dispersion used in reporting social science research.

STANDARD DEVIATION

Standard deviation is a measure of variability or dispersion of a set of data. It is calculated from the deviations between each data value and the sample mean. It is also the square root of the variance.

$$\sigma = \sqrt{\frac{\sum(X - \mu)^2}{N}}$$

$$S = \sqrt{\frac{\sum(X - \bar{X})^2}{N}}$$

$$\hat{S} = \sqrt{\frac{\sum(X - \bar{X})^2}{N - 1}}$$

Note that the top formula is for the population standard deviation, σ, where μ is the population mean. The middle formula is for the sample standard deviation, s, and the bottom formula is for the sample estimate of the population standard deviation, s-hat. The sample mean minimizes the sum of squared (SS) deviations. Therefore, $N - 1$ is used in the bottom formula since the SS from the sample will underestimate the population SS.

When reporting sample standard deviation in the results section of a research report, it is customary to use the SD symbol and also report the best measure of central tendency, usually the mean. For example, report classroom community ($M = 57.42$, $SD = 12.53$) and perceived cognitive learning ($M = 7.02$, $SD = 1.65$).

Key Point
Standard deviation is the best measure of dispersion
for interval/ratio scale variables.

Excel Functions Used

STDEV.S(number1,number2,...). Returns the unbiased estimate of population standard deviation, where numbers represent the range of numbers.

STDEV.P (number1,number2,...). Returns the population standard deviation, where numbers represent the range of numbers.

STANDARD ERROR OF THE MEAN

Standard error of the mean (SEM; or mean standard error) is the standard deviation of the sampling distribution of the mean. It is used in the computation of confidence intervals and significance tests for the mean. It is the standard deviation divided by the square root of the sample size (i.e., count).

$$\sigma_M = \frac{\sigma}{\sqrt{N}}$$

The precision of the mean of a sample of data, as an estimate of some unknown or true value of the population mean, is described using the standard error of the mean. Note that as the sample size increases, the sample mean becomes a better estimate of the population mean.

There is a 68.26% probability that the true population mean is ± one standard error of the mean from the sample mean.

Excel Formula Used

=STDEV.P(A2:A170)/SQRT(COUNT(A2:A170))

Note: STDEV.P(number1,number2,...) returns the population standard deviation, SQRT(number) returns the square root of a number, and COUNT((value1,value2,...) counts the numbers in the range of numbers.

VARIANCE

Variance is a measure of variability derived from the average of the sum of the deviation scores from the mean raised to the second power (i.e., the second moment of the distribution). In other words, it is the average of each score's squared difference from the mean. The formulas for the population and sample variances are given below.

$$\sigma^2 = \frac{\sum(X-\mu)^2}{N}$$

$$S^2 = \frac{\sum(X-\overline{X})^2}{N}$$

where σ^2 is the symbol for population variance, s^2 is the symbol for sample variance, and μ is the symbol for population mean.

(Note: dividing by $(N-1)$ rather than N for sample variance results in an unbiased estimate of the population variance; otherwise divide by N for sample variance.)

Adding or subtracting a constant to/from each score just shifts the distribution without changing the variance.

Excel Functions Used

VAR.S(number1,number2,...). Returns the unbiased estimate of population variance, with numbers representing the range of numbers.

VAR.P (number1,number2,...). Returns the population variance, with numbers representing the range of numbers.

SKEWNESS

Skewness is based on the third moment of the distribution, or the sum of cubic deviations from the mean. It measures deviations from perfect symmetry.

$$Skewness = \frac{N}{(N-1)(N-2)}\sum(\frac{X_i - \bar{X}}{S})^3$$

- Positive skewness indicates a distribution with a heavier positive (right-hand) tail than a symmetrical distribution (mode < median < mean) as shown in Figure 2.8 below. A frequency distribution with a positive skew can result from a set of scores from a difficult examination.

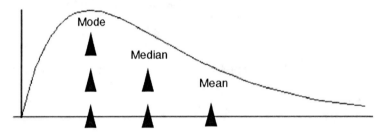

FIGURE 2.8
positive skew distribution.

- Negative skewness indicates a distribution with a heavier negative tail (mean < median < mode) as shown in Figure 2.9 below. A frequency distribution with a negative skew can result from a set of scores from an easy examination.

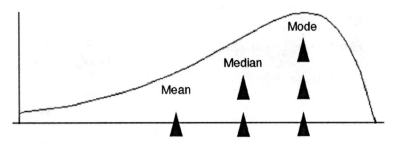

FIGURE 2.9
Negative skew distribution.

- Symmetrical distributions (i.e., zero skewness) have approximately equal numbers of observations above and below the middle with approximately equal tails. Skewness statistic = 0 for a perfectly normal distribution (mean = median = mode). A symmetrical distribution has the appearance of a bell-shaped curve.

Excel Functions Used

SKEW(number1,number2,...). Returns the skewness statistic of a distribution.

STANDARD ERROR OF SKEWNESS

The standard error of skewness is a measure of the accuracy of the skewness coefficient and is equal to the standard deviation of the sampling distribution of the statistic.

Tabachnick and Fidell (2007) provide the following formula for an approximation of the standard error of skewness (SES).

$$SES = \sqrt{\frac{6}{N}}$$

Normal distributions produce a skewness statistic of approximately zero. The skewness coefficient divided by its standard error produces the standard coefficient of skewness that can be used as a test of normality (that is, one can reject normality if this ratio is less than −2 or greater than +2).

Excel Formula Used

=SQRT(6/COUNT(value1,value2,...))

Note: SQRT(number) returns the positive square root of a number and COUNT((value1,value2,...) counts the numbers in the range of numbers.

KURTOSIS

Kurtosis is derived from the fourth moment (i.e., the sum of quartic deviations). It captures the heaviness or weight of the tails relative to the center of the distribution. Kurtosis measures heavy-tailedness or light-tailedness relative to the normal distribution. A heavy-tailed distribution has more values in the tails (away from the center of the distribution) than the normal distribution, and will have a negative kurtosis. A light-tailed distribution has more values in the center (away from the tails of the distribution) than the normal distribution, and will have a positive kurtosis.

Kurtotic shapes of distributions are generally recognized with various labels as depicted in Figure 2.10 below.

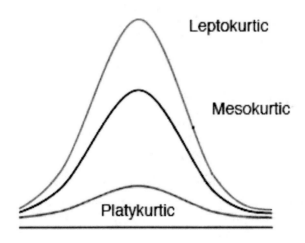

FIGURE 2.10
Examples of leptokurtic, mesokurtic, and platykurtic shapes.

- Leptokurtic – peaked shape, kurtosis statistic above 0, small standard deviation.
- Mesokurtic – between extremes, normal shape. Kurtosis statistic = around 0 for an approximately normal distribution.
- Platykurtic – flat shape, kurtosis statistic below 0, large standard deviation.

Excel Functions Used

KURT(number1,number2,...). Returns the kurtosis statistic of a distribution.

STANDARD ERROR OF KURTOSIS

The standard error of kurtosis is a measure of the accuracy of the kurtosis coefficient and is equal to the standard deviation of the sampling distribution of the statistic.

Tabachnick and Fidell (2007) provide the following formula for an approximation of the standard error of kurtosis (SEK).

$$SEK = \sqrt{\frac{24}{N}}$$

Normal distributions produce a kurtosis statistic of approximately zero. The kurtosis coefficient divided by its standard error produces the standard coefficient of kurtosis that can be used as a test of normality (that is, one can reject normality if this ratio is less than –2 or greater than +2).

Excel Formula Used

=SQRT(24/COUNT(value1,value2,...))

Note: SQRT(number) returns the positive square root of the number and COUNT((value1,value2,...) counts the numbers in the range of numbers.

RANGE

The *range* of a distribution is calculated by subtracting the minimum score from the maximum score.

$$Range = X_{Max} - X_{Min}$$

The range is not very stable (reliable) because it is based on only two scores. Consequently, outliers have a significant effect on the range of variable.

> ## Key Point
> For ordinal and nominal variables, the range is the best measure of dispersion.

Excel Formula Used

=MAX(number1,number2,...)−MIN(number1,number2,...)

Note: MAX(number1,number2,...) returns the maximum value in a set of numbers and MIN(number1,number2,...) returns the minimum value in a set of numbers.

INTERQUARTILE RANGE

The interquartile range (IQR) is the distance between the 75th percentile (P_{75}) and the 25th percentile (P_{25}). In other words, the IQR is the range of the middle 50% of the data and is used to summarize the extent of data spread. It is calculated by subtracting the first quartile (Q1) from the third quartile (Q3).

$$IQR = Q_3 - Q_1$$

The IQR is:
- not affected by a few outliers.
- used with ratio and interval scales.

Excel Formula Used

=QUARTILE.INC(array,3)−QUARTILE.INC(array,1)

Note: QUARTILE.INC(array,3) returns the 3rd quartile in a set of numbers and QUARTILE.INC(array,1) returns the 1st quartile in a set of numbers.

Procedures

Task: Use the Excel file Motivation.xlsx located at http:// www.watertreepress.com/stats if you want to follow along with the analysis. The Data tab contains the data used in the analysis described below.

1. Open the *Motivation.xlsx file using Excel.*

2. Copy the variable c_community (classroom community) from the Excel workbook, Data tab, and paste the variable in column A of an empty sheet. Copy all 169 cases.

3. Click the Excel Formulas tab and then click the Insert icon from the Function group of icons to insert the proper function in the appropriate cell or type-in the formula directly. Enter the labels Standard deviation, Mean,standard error, Variance, Skewness, SE skewness, Kurtosis, SE kurtosis, Range, and Interquartile range in cells C6:C14. Enter formulas =STDEV.P(A2:A170), =STDEV.P(A2:A170)/ SQRT(COUNT(A2:A170)), =VAR.P(A2:A170), =SKEW(A2:A170), =KURT(A2:A170), =MAX(A2:A170)-MIN(A2:A170), and =QUARTILE.INC(A2:A170,3)-QUARTILE.INC(A2:A170,1) in cells D6:D14.

	C	D
6	Standard deviation	=STDEV.P(A2:A170)
7	Mean standard error	=STDEV.P(A2:A170)/SQRT(COUNT(A2:A170))
8	Variance	=VAR.P(A2:A170)
9	Skewness	=SKEW(A2:A170)
10	SE skewness	=SQRT(6/COUNT(A2:A170))
11	Kurtosis	=KURT(A2:A170)
12	SE kurtosis	=SQRT(24/COUNT(A2:A170))
13	Range	=MAX(A2:A170)-MIN(A2:A170)
14	Interquartile range	=QUARTILE.INC(A2:A170,3)-QUARTILE.INC(A2:A170,1)

	C	D	E
6	Standard deviation	6.223018156	
7	Mean standard error	0.478693704	
8	Variance	38.72595497	
9	Skewness	0.073045168	
10	SE skewness	0.188422288	
11	Kurtosis	-1.044172509	
12	SE kurtosis	0.376844576	
13	Range	25	
14	Interquartile range	10	

2.4: Measures of Relative Position

Measures of relative position indicate how high or low a score is in relation to other scores in a distribution. These measures not only include percentile and quartile ranks described in this section, but also standard scores, e.g., z-scores, T-scores, NCE-scores, stanines, etc., that are described in the next section.

PERCENTILES

A percentile (P) is a measure that tells one the percent of the total frequency that scored below that measure. Percentiles divide the data into 100 equal parts based on their statistical rank and position from the bottom. It is the value of a variable below which a given percent of the cases lie. For example, the 50th percentile, P_{50}, which represents the median value, indicates that 50% of scores are below P_{50}. Therefore, a percentile is a cutoff score and not a range of values.

Excel Functions Used

PERCENTILE.INC(array,k). Returns the kth percentile in a range of numbers.

Note: k = the percentile value in the range 0 to 1, inclusive, e.g., when k = 0.30, the argument returns the 30th percentile of the variable defined by the array.

QUARTILES

A quartile (Q) divides the data into four equal parts based on their statistical ranks and position from the bottom. In other words, quartiles are the values that divide a list of numbers into quarters, $Q_1 = P_{25}$, $Q_2 = P_{50} = Mdn$, $Q_3 = P_{75}$. Like the percentile, the quartile is a cutoff score and not a range of values. One may be above or below Q_2, but not in Q_2.

Excel Functions Used

QUARTILE.INC(array,quart). Returns the specified quartile, in a range of numbers.

Note: quart = 0 returns the minimum value, quart = 1 returns Q_1, quart = 2 returns Q_2 (median), quart = 3 returns Q_3, quart = 4 returns the maximum value.

Procedures

Task: Use the Excel file Motivation.xlsx located at http:// www.watertreepress.com/stats if you want to follow along with the analysis. The Data tab contains the data used in the analysis described below.

1.   Open the *Motivation.xlsx file using Excel.*

2.   Copy the variable c_community (classroom community) from the Excel workbook, Data tab, and paste the variable in column A of an empty sheet. Copy all 169 cases.

3.   Click the Excel Formulas tab and then click the Insert icon from the Function group of icons to insert the proper function in the appropriate cell or type-in the formula directly. Enter the labels 90th percentile, 10th percentile, 1st quartile, 2nd quartile, and 3rd quartile in cells C16:C20. Enter formulas =PERCENTILE.INC(A2:A170,0.9), =PERCENTILE.INC(A2:A170,0.1), =QUARTILE.INC(A2:A170,1), =QUARTILE.INC(A2:A170,2), and =QUARTILE.INC(A2:A170,3) in cells D16:D20.

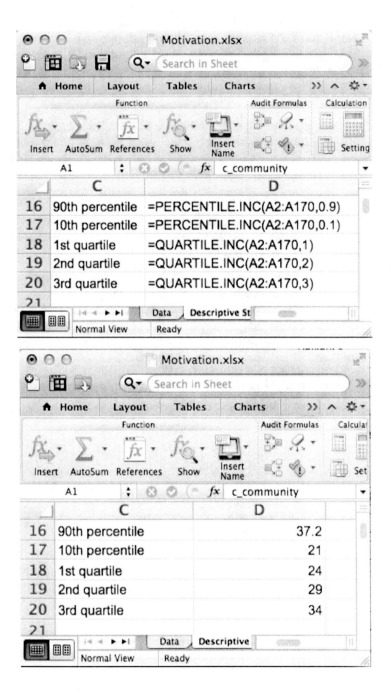

2.5: Normal Curve

THE NORMAL DISTRIBUTION

A smooth curve is referred to as a probability density curve (rather than a frequency curve as one sees in the histogram). The area under any probability density curve is 1 because there is a 100% probability that the curve represents all possible occurrences of the associated event. Since the density curve represents the entire distribution, the area under the curve on any interval represents the probability of those occurrences in that interval.

The normal distribution is an example of a density curve (see Figure 2.11 below).

- 34.1% of the occurrences will fall between μ and 1σ
- 13.6% of the occurrences will fall between 1σ & 2σ
- 2.15% of the occurrences will fall between 2σ & 3σ

Therefore, 49.85% of the occurrences (34.1% + 13.6% + 2.15%) of a normally distributed variable fall between the mean and either $+3\sigma$ or -3σ. In other words, 99.7% of the occurrences fall between -3σ and $+3\sigma$. The concept of "Six Sigma" is found in business quality programs that attempt to reduce error to outside the range of 6σ (i.e., products are 99.99966% free of defects).

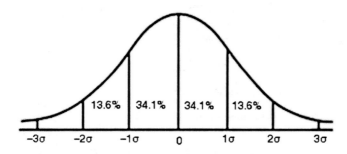

FIGURE 2.11
The normal curve viewed as a density curve.

The normal distribution has the appearance of a bell-shaped curve. Other normal curve characteristics:

- Normal curves are unimodal and symmetric about the mean.

- For a perfectly normal distribution, mean = median = mode = Q_2 (second quartile) = P_{50} (fiftieth percentile). If the mean is not equal to the median, the distribution is skewed, with the mean being closer than the median to the skewed end of the distribution.

- Normal curves are asymptotic to the abscissa (refers to a curve that continually approaches the horizontal x-axis but does not actually reach it until x equals infinity; the axis so approached is the asymptote).

- Normal curves involve a large number of cases.

The normal or Gaussian distribution is the statistical distribution used in parametric statistics. The notation for a normal distribution is $N(\mu, \sigma)$. Its importance flows from the fact that any sums of normally distributed variables are normally distributed. Sums of variables that individually are not normally distributed also tend to be normally distributed.

One reason the normal distribution is important is that many social science variables are distributed approximately normally. Although the distributions are only approximately normal, they are usually quite close. A second reason the normal distribution is so important is that it is easy for statisticians to work with it. Many types of statistical tests can be used for normal distributions. Additionally, if the mean and standard deviation of a normal distribution are known, it is easy to convert back and forth from raw scores to percentiles.

TRANSFORMING RAW SCORES INTO STANDARDIZED SCORES

Transforming raw scores into standardized scores serves two purposes:

- It facilitates interpretation of raw scores.
- It allows comparison of multiple scores on different normally-distributed scales.

A standard score is a general term referring to a score that has been transformed for reasons of convenience, comparability, etc. The basic type of standard score, known as a z-score, is an expression of the deviation of a score from the mean score of the group in relation to the standard deviation of the scores of the group. Most other standard scores are linear transformations of z-scores, with different means and standard deviations.

(Z-Score, N(0,1)

A z-score distribution is the standard normal distribution, N(0,1), with mean = 0 and standard deviation = 1. A z-score is a way of standardizing the scales of two or more distributions.

Z-scores permit one to describe a particular score in terms of where it fits into the overall group of scores in a normal distribution. A positive z-score indicates the number of standard deviations a score is above the mean of its own distribution, whereas a negative z-score indicates the number of standard deviations a score is below the mean of its own distribution.

Examples:

- A z-score of 1.0 is one standard deviation above the mean.
- A z-score of -1.5 is one-and-a-half standard deviations below the mean.
- A z-score of 0 is equal to the mean.

The formulas for calculating z-scores from raw scores and for converting z-scores back to raw scores are given below.

$$Z = \frac{(X - M)}{SD}$$

$$X = (Z)(SD) + M$$

where M and SD pertain to the raw scores.

Excel Functions Used

STANDARDIZE(number,AVERAGE(number1,number2,...),STDEV.S(number1,number2,...)). Returns a standardized value.

Note: number = raw score.

T-Score, N(50,10)

A *T-score* is a normalized standard score with a mean of 50 and a standard deviation of 10. Thus a *T*-score of 60 represents a score one standard deviation above the mean. In a great number of testing situations, especially in education and psychology, scores are reported in terms of *T*-scores. Since *T*-scores do not contain decimal points or negative signs they are used more frequently than *z*-scores.

T-scores are calculated from z-scores as follows

$$T = 10Z + 50$$

Excel Formula Used

=10*z-score+50

Note: To covert raw scores to *T*-scores, first convert raw scores to *z*-scores and then apply the above formula.

Normal Curve Equivalent (NCE) Score, N(50, 21.06)

Another increasingly popular standardized score is the *NCE-score*. NCE-scores are normalized standard scores with a mean of 50 and a standard deviation of 21.06. The standard deviation of 21.06 was chosen so that NCE scores of 1 and 99 are equivalent to the 1st (P_1) and 99th (P_{99}) percentiles.

NCE scores are computed from *z*-scores as follows

$$NCE = 21.06Z + 50$$

Excel Formula Used

Converting *z*-scores to *NCE*-scores:

=21.06*z-score+50

Note: To covert raw scores to *NCE*-scores, first convert raw scores to *z*-scores and then apply the above formula.

STANINE SCORE

Stanine scores are groups of percentile ranks consisting of nine specific bands, with the 5th stanine centered on the mean, the first stanine being the lowest, and the ninth stanine being the highest. Each stanine is one-half standard deviation wide. Stanines are most often used to describe achievement test results as follows:

9th stanine, very superior, top 4% of scores.
8th stanine, superior, next 7% of scores.
7th stanine, considerably above average, next 12% of scores.
6th stanine, slightly above average, next 17% of scores.
5th stanine, average, middle 50% of scores.
4th stanine, slightly below average, next 17% of scores.
3rd stanine, considerably below average, next 12% of scores.
2nd stanine, poor, next 7% of scores.
1st stanine, very poor, bottom 4% of scores.

STANDARDIZED NORM-REFERENCED TESTING

A norm-referenced test defines the performance of test-takers in relation to one another. In contrast, a criterion-referenced test defines the performance of each test taker without regard to the performance of others. The success is being able to perform a specific task or set of competencies at a certain predetermined level or criterion.

A standardized norm-referenced test is a norm-referenced test that assumes human traits and characteristics, such as academic achievement and intelligence, are normally distributed. The test compares a student's test performance with that of a sample of similar students. The normal curve represents the norm or average performance of a population and the scores that are above and below the mean within that population. Common standardized norm-referenced tests include the following:

ACT (formerly American College Testing Program or American College Test), $N(20,5)$
Graduate Record Examination (GRE), $N(500,100)$

SAT (formerly Scholastic Aptitude Test, Scholastic
   Assessment Test), $N(500,100)$
Law School Admission Test (LSAT), $N(500,100)$
Graduate Management Admission Test (GMAT), $N(500,100)$
Minnesota Multiphasic Personality Inventory (MMPI), uses T-
   scores, $N(50,10)$
Wechsler Adult Intelligence Scale, $N(100,15)$
Stanford–Binet Intelligence Scales, $N(100,16)$
Otis–Lennon School Ability Test (OLSAT), $N(100,16)$

Procedures

*Task: Use the Excel file Motivation.xlsx located at http://
www.watertreepress.com/stats if you want to follow along with
the analysis. The Data tab contains the data used in the analysis
described below.*

1.   Open the *Motivation.xlsx file using Excel.*

2.   Copy the variable c_community (classroom community)
from the Excel workbook, Data tab, and paste the variable in
column A of an empty sheet. Copy all 169 cases.

3.   Enter the label z-scores in cell F1 and the formula and
formula =STANDARDIZE(A2,AVERAGE(A$2:A
$170),STDEV.P(A$2:A$170)) in cell F2. Fill Down to row 170
to create *z*-scores. Note the use of the $ sign to ensure the
raw score array is fixed during the Fill Down process.

4.   Enter the label T-scores in cell G1 and the formula and
formula =10*F2+50 in cell G2. Fill Down to row 170 to create
T-scores.

5.   Enter the label NCE scores in cell H1 and the formula
and formula =21.06*F2+50 in cell H2. Fill Down to row 170
to create NCE-scores.

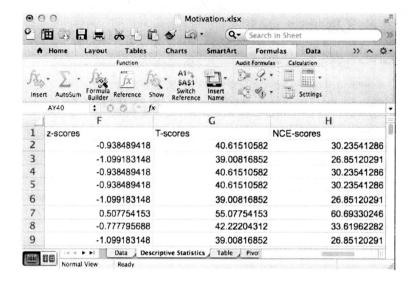

	F	G	H
1	z-scores	T-scores	NCE-scores
2	-0.938489418	40.61510582	30.23541286
3	-1.099183148	39.00816852	26.85120291
4	-0.938489418	40.61510582	30.23541286
5	-0.938489418	40.61510582	30.23541286
6	-1.099183148	39.00816852	26.85120291
7	0.507754153	55.07754153	60.69330246
8	-0.777795688	42.22204312	33.61962282
9	-1.099183148	39.00816852	26.85120291

Data · **Descriptive Statistics** · Table · Pivot

Normal View   Ready

2.6: Charts

CREATING CHARTS

Imagery is the key to understanding statistics. One can create and edit a variety of charts using Excel that provide consumers of statistics with the imagery that promotes meaning and understanding of statistical results. The most common types of charts are summarized in this section. To create a chart, start by entering the numeric data for the chart on a sheet in an Excel workbook. Once the data is available one can highlight the data to be charted and use the Insert tab (Windows users, see Figure 2.12) or the Charts tab (Macintosh users, see Figure 2.13) to select the desired chart type.

FIGURE 2.12
Windows version Insert tab.

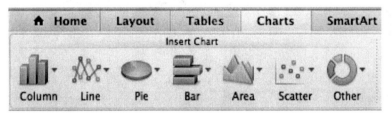

FIGURE 2.13
Macintosh version Charts tab.

Once the chart type is identified, Excel generates a preview of the selected chart, which can now be modified using Chart Layouts (Windows users, see Figure 2.14) or Chart Quick Layouts (Macintosh users, see Figure 2.15) and Chart Styles.

Chart Layouts

FIGURE 2.14
Windows version Chart Layouts.

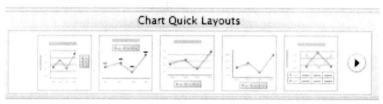

Chart Quick Layouts

FIGURE 2.15
Macintosh version Chart Quick Layouts.

A chart has many elements. One can change the display of chart elements by moving, resizing, or by changing the format. One can also remove chart elements by highlighting the element and selecting Cut from the Edit menu. One can also double-click an element of the chart, which will open a Format Data Series dialog, where one can make changes to the highlighted element such as adjusting line color, adding gradients and arrows to lines, adjusting line weight, adding titles and data labels, and various other properties unique to the chart being edited. One can apply special effects, such as shadow, reflection, glow, soft edges, bevel, and 3-D rotation to chart elements.

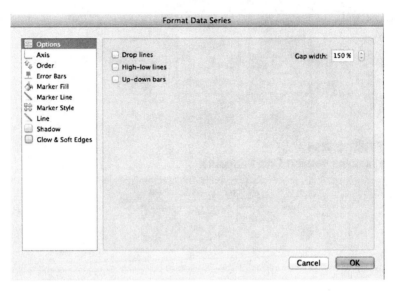

Switching to the the Design and Layout tabs (Windows users) or the Chart Layout tab (Macintosh users) reveals additional tools one can use to modify a chart. Depending on the chart type used and chart element selected, different tools and options will be available.

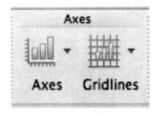

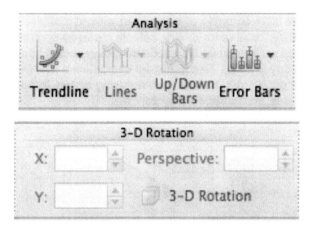

One can reuse a customized chart by saving it as a chart template (.crtx) in the Excel chart templates folder using the Save as Template option under the Chart menu. When one creates a new chart, one can apply the saved chart template.

Below is a description of various charts that one is most likely to require for social science research reporting.

Line Chart

A line chart allows one to visually examine the mean (or other statistic) of a continuous variable as a series of data points connected by straight lines. Line charts, often called profile plots, are ideally suited to show trends for data over time in longitudinal studies or time-series designs. For example, the x-axis can be observation, e.g., observation 1, observation 2, observation 3, etc., or a series of years or months.

Excel produces four types of line charts:

• Line Chart With or Without Markers — displays trends over time.

• Stacked Line Chart With or Without Markers — displays trends of the contribution of each value.

• 100% Stacked Line Chart Displayed With or Without Markers — displays the trend of the percentage each value contributes over time.

• 3D Line Chart — displays each row or column of data as a 3-D ribbon.

Below is an example of a line chart without markers produced by Excel representing sample mean computer confidence among university students (*y*-axis) across three observations (*x*-axis). This particular chart shows how the computer confidence means are increasing across three observations, disaggregated by gender.

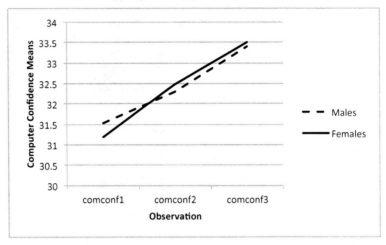

A single line chart can include multiple lines (variables) in a factorial design consisting of multiple factors. For example, one line can display the trend over time of male students and a second line could show the trend for female students in a model that includes observation as the within subjects factor and gender as the between subjects factor, as shown above. Parallel lines suggest no interaction between factors while intersecting lines suggest an interaction between factors.

Additionally, one can add error bars to indicate the estimated error in a measurement. An error bar can indicate the amount of uncertainty in a value with error amounts expressed as a fixed value, percentage, standard deviation(s), or standard error. Below is an example of a line chart with error bars showing the standard error for computer confidence means among males across three observations.

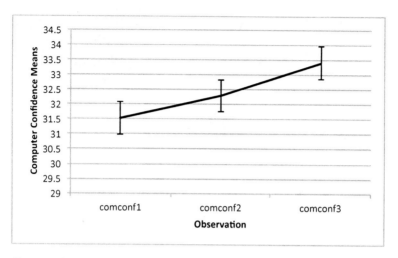

Procedures

Use the Excel file Computer Anxiety.xlsx located at http://www.watertreepress.com/stats if you want to follow along. Requires a copy of Microsoft Excel.

1. Open the *Computer Anxiety.xlsx* file using Excel.

2. Copy variables gender, comconf1 (computer confidence pretest), comconf2 (computer confidence posttest), and comconf3 (computer confidence delayed test) from the Excel workbook Data tab to columns A, B, and C on an empty sheet. Copy all 75 cases with no missing values.

3. Sort cases in ascending order by gender. (Note: male = 1, female = 2.)

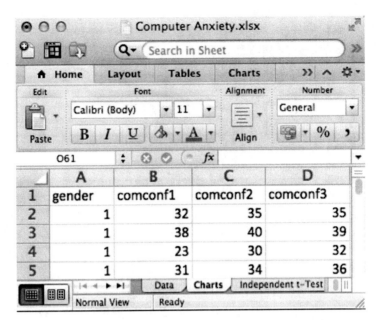

4. Enter labels comconf1, comconf2, and comconf3 in cells E2:E4 and Males and Females in cells F1:G1. Enter formulas =AVERAGE(B2:B18), =AVERAGE(C2:C18), and =AVERAGE(D2:D18) in cells F2:F4 and =AVERAGE(B19:B76), =AVERAGE(C19:C76), and =AVERAGE(D19:D76) in cells G2:G4.

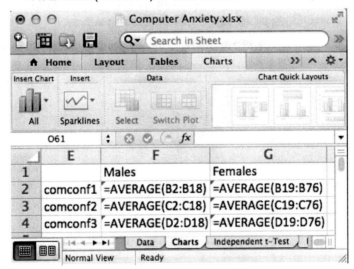

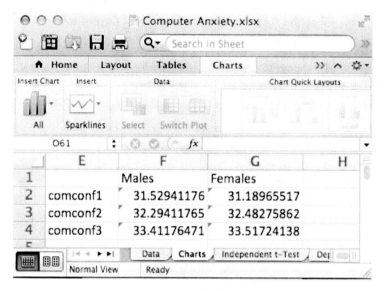

5. Highlight the range of values to plot, E1:G4 in the above example.

6. Select the Charts tab. Click Line on the Insert Chart group of icons.

7. Select Line (the drop-down menu allows selection of a variety of line charts). The selected chart type appears on the workbook active sheet.

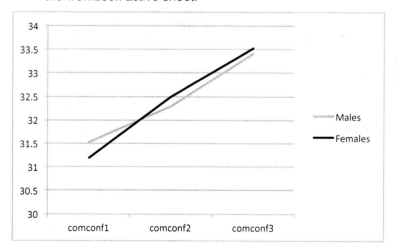

8.   Click the Axis Titles icon in the Chart Layout tab and enter titles for the x-axis and y-axis.

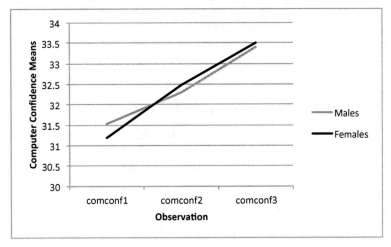

9.   Double-click each line in the legend, in turn, to expose the Format Legend dialog. One can make a variety of changes to the chart to each line via this dialog, to include changing line colors and weights. Change default colors to black (under the Solid tab for both males and females) and dashed (under the Weights and Arrows tab for males).

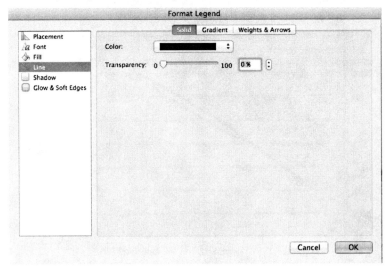

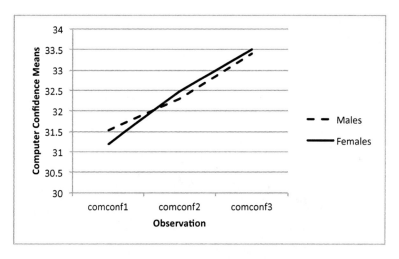

10. Double-click any chart element to edit the selected element.

11. Move or resize any element as desired.

Area Chart

An area chart allows one to visually examine the mean (or other statistic) of a continuous variable as a series of data points connected by straight lines. It is very similar to the line chart with one major exception: the area between the line and the x-axis are depicted in colors or patterns. Area charts are ideally suited to show trends for data over time in longitudinal or time-series studies. For example, the x-axis can be observation, e.g., observation 1, observation 2, observation 3, etc., or a series of years or months.

Excel produces six types of area charts:

- 2-D Area.
- 2-D Stacked Area.
- 2-D 100% Stacked Area.
- 3-D Area.
- 3-D Stacked Area.
- 3-D 100% Stacked Area.

Below is an example of a 2D area chart produced by Excel representing sample mean computer confidence among university students (y-axis) across three observations (x-axis).

This particular chart shows how the estimated marginal means are increasing across three observations for a within subjects factor. The charted data is the same as used for the line chart above.

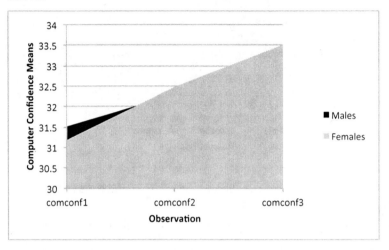

A single area chart can include multiple areas (variables) in a factorial design consisting of multiple factors. For example, one area can display the trend over time of male students and a second area could show the trend for female students in a model that includes observation as the within subjects factor and gender as the between subjects factor, as shown above. Note how the female plot obscures the male plot for posttest and delayed test observations where females scored higher, on average, than males. A common business application is to use an area chart to plot company performance over time, with trend lines representing sales and/or expenses.

Procedures

Use the Excel file Computer Anxiety.xlsx located at http:// www.watertreepress.com/stats if you want to follow along. Requires a copy of Microsoft Excel.

1. Open the *Computer Anxiety.xlsx file using Excel.*

2. Use the same data that is used to create the line chart example.

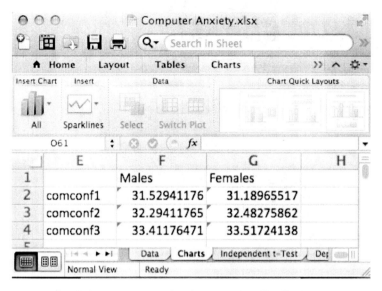

3. Highlight the range of values to plot, E1:G4 in the above example.

4. Select the Charts tab. Click Area on the Insert Chart group of icons.

5. Select 2-D Area (the drop-down menu allows selection of a variety of line charts). The selected chart type appears on the workbook active sheet.

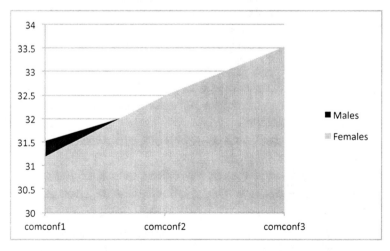

6. Click the Axis Titles icon in the Chart Layout tab and enter titles for the x-axis and y-axis.

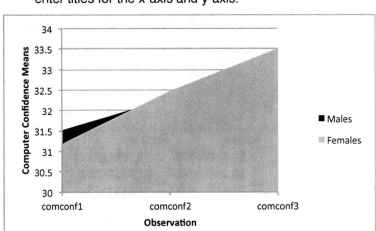

7. Double-click any chart element to edit the selected element.

8. Move or resize any element as desired.

Column Chart

A column chart (also called a vertical bar chart) is made up of columns positioned over the x-axis that represents a categorical variable. It is essentially a vertical bar chart. The height of the column represents the size of the group defined by the y-axis variable. Excel produces five types of column charts:

• 2-D Column – displays a 2-D column chart with columns depicted as rectangles (see example below).
• 3-D Column – displays a 3-D column char with columns depicted as rectangles.
• Cylinder – displays a chart with columns depicted as cylinders.
• Cone – displays a chart with columns depicted as cones.
• Pyramid – displays a chart with columns depicted as pyramids.

Below is an example of a 2-D column chart produced by Excel representing mean computer confidence score across three observations disaggregated by gender. It uses the same data used in the line and area chart examples above.

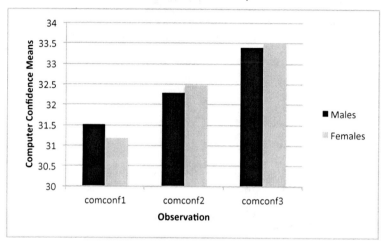

Procedures

Use the Excel file Computer Anxiety.xlsx located at http:// www.watertreepress.com/stats if you want to follow along. Requires a copy of Microsoft Excel.

1. Open the *Computer Anxiety.xlsx file using Excel.*

2. Use the same data that is used to create the above charts.

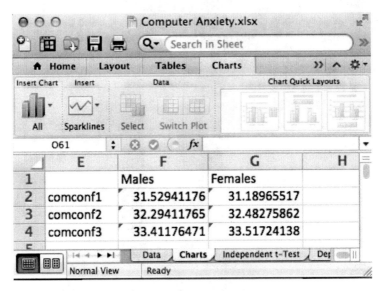

3. Highlight the range of values to plot, E1:G4 in the above example.

4. Select the Charts tab. Click Column on the Insert Chart group of icons.

5. Select 2-D Clustered Column (the drop-down menu allows selection of a variety of column charts). The selected chart type appears on the workbook active sheet.

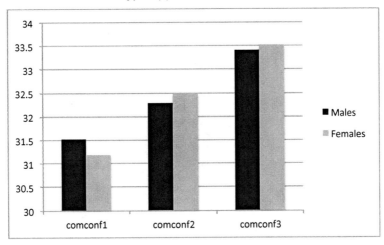

6. Click the Axis Titles icon in the Chart Layout tab and enter titles for the x-axis and y-axis.

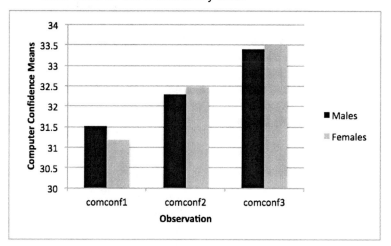

7. Alternative layouts are available under the Chart Quick Layouts group of icons. For example, Layout 5 produces the following chart that includes title and statistical values.

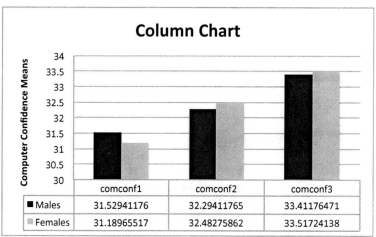

8. Double-click any chart element to edit the selected element.

9. Move or resize any element as desired.

Bar Chart

A bar chart is made up of bars positioned along side the y-axis that represents a categorical variable. It is essentially a horizontal column chart. The length of the bar represents the size of the group defined by a second variable plotted on the x-axis. A bar chart switches the axes used in the column chart so that the categorical variable is plotted on the y-axis instead of the x-axis. Excel produces five major types of bar charts with three subtypes available for each:

- 2-D Bar
- 3-D Bar
- Cylinder
- Cone
- Pyramid

Below is an example of a 2-D clustered bar chart produced by Excel representing mean computer confidence score across three observations disaggregated by gender.

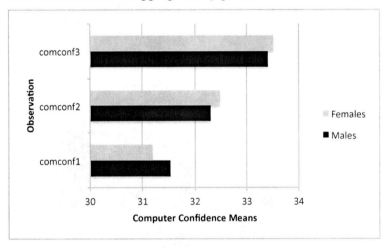

Procedures

Use the Excel file Computer Anxiety.xlsx located at http://www.watertreepress.com/stats if you want to follow along. Requires a copy of Microsoft Excel.

1. Open the *Computer Anxiety.xlsx* file using Excel.

2. Use the same data that is used to create the above charts.

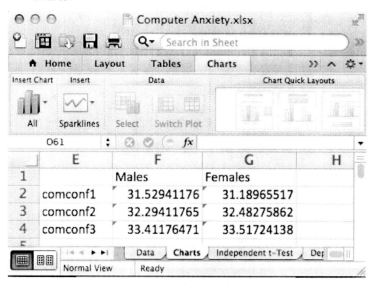

3. Highlight the range of values to plot, E1:G4 in the above example.

4. Select the Charts tab. Click Bar on the Insert Chart group of icons.

5. Select 2-D Clustered Bar chart (the drop-down menu allows selection of a variety of bar charts). The selected chart type appears on the workbook active sheet.

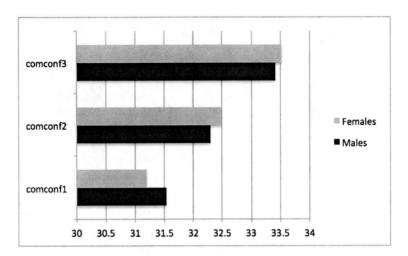

6. Click the Axis Titles icon in the Chart Layout tab and enter titles for the x-axis and y-axis.

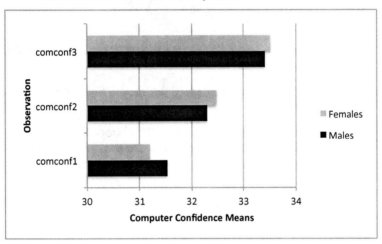

7. Alternative layouts are available under the Chart Quick Layouts group of icons. For example, Layout 4 produces the following chart.

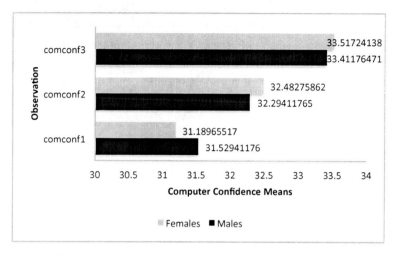

8. Double-click any chart element to edit the selected element.

9. Move or resize any element as desired.

Scatterplot

Scatterplots (also called scattergrams and XY charts) show the relationship between two continuous variables. They are frequently used to evaluate the assumption of linearity between variables. Each dot on a scatterplot is a case. The dot is placed at the intersection of each case's scores on x and y.

Excel produces several types of scatterplots:

• Marked Scatter (this is the typical type of scatterplot one encounters in social science research reports).
• Smooth Marked Scatter
• Smooth Lined Scatter
• Straight Marked Scatter
• Straight Lined Scatter

Below is an example of a marked scatterplot produced by Excel representing computer confidence pretest (x-axis) and computer confidence posttest (y-axis). The plot suggests a linear relationship between the two variables.

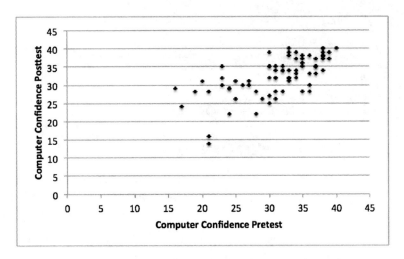

One can also add a linear trendline using the Trendline icon in the Chart Layout tab.

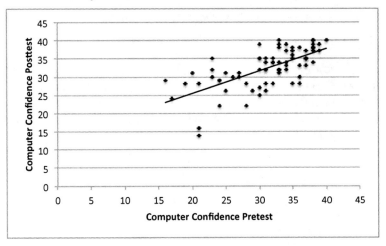

Procedures

Use the Excel file Computer Anxiety.xlsx located at http://www.watertreepress.com/stats if you want to follow along. Requires a copy of Microsoft Excel.

1. Open the *Computer Anxiety.xlsx* file using Excel.

2. Copy the variable comconf1 (computer confidence pretest) and comconf2 (computer confidence posttest)

from the Excel workbook, Data tab, and paste the variables in columns B and C of an empty sheet. Copy 75 cases.

	B	C
1	comconf1	comconf2
2	32	35
3	38	40
4	23	30
5	31	34

3. Highlight the range of values to plot, B2:C76.

4. Select the Charts tab. Click Scatter on the Insert Chart group of icons.

5. Select Marked Scatter under the Scatter icon (the drop-down menu allows a choice of scatterplots). The selected chart type appears on the workbook active sheet. (Note: Excel will create a scatterplot with the variable in the first column (computer confidence pretest) plotted on the x-axis and the variable in the second column (computer confidence posttest) plotted on the y-axis.)

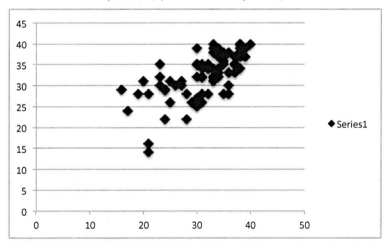

6. Delete the legend by highlighting it and hitting the Delete key.

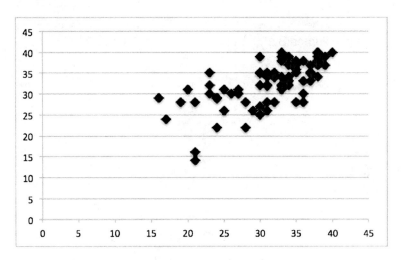

7. Click the Axis Titles icon in the Chart Layout tab and enter titles for the x-axis and y-axis.

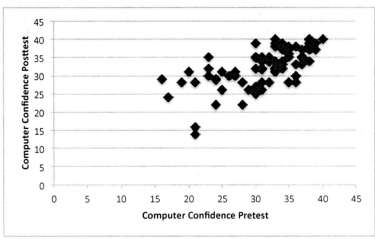

8. If desired, add a linear trendline using the Trendline icon. This is helpful if the scatterplot is used to assess linearity.

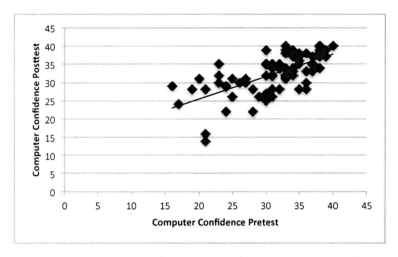

9. Additionally, if desired, change the marker style to circles and reduce size from 9 (default) to 2 by double-clicking a marker and making changes in the Format Data Series dialog.

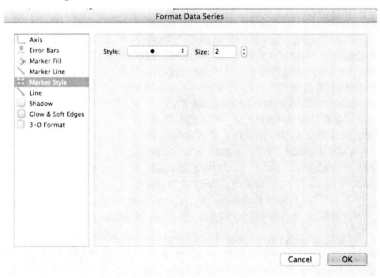

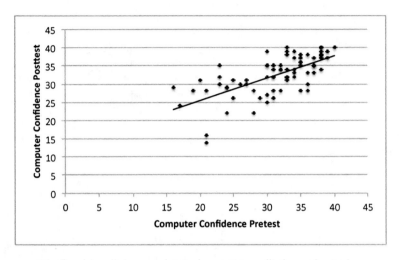

10. Double-click any chart element to edit the selected element.

11. Move or resize any element as desired.

Histogram

A histogram is an example of a frequency curve that displays a univariate dataset. It is constructed by dividing the range of continuous data into equal-sized adjacent bins (classes or groups). It is helpful to view these bins as fixed-interval containers that accumulate data that causes the bins to increase in height. For each bin, a rectangle is constructed with an area proportional to the number of observations falling into that bin. Bins are plotted on the x-axis and frequencies (the number of cases accumulated in each bin) are plotted on the y-axis. The y-axis ranges from 0 to the greatest number of cases deposited in any bin. The x-axis includes the entire data range. The total area of the histogram is equal to the number of data points.

Histograms are similar to column charts. However, with column charts, each column represents a group defined by a categorical variable. In contrast, with histograms, each column or bin represents a group defined by a continuous variable. Typically, there are no spaces between columns in a histogram while column charts include spaces.

Unfortunately, Excel has no histogram chart template. Consequently, one must manually construct a histogram using a column chart template.

There is no single rule regarding the number of bins displayed by a histogram. Different size bins often reveal different characteristics of a distribution, so experimentation with the number of bins is often useful. A popular formula for determining the minimum number of bins (k) in a distribution is given below (must be 6 or higher).

$$k = \sqrt{N}$$

Bin width is determined by subtracting the minimum value from the maximum value, dividing by the k (number of bins), and rounding up. Next, one identifies the bins by starting with a bin that includes the minimum data value and use bin width to produce subsequent bins, stopping when the bin that includes the maximum data value is reached. Finally, one creates a frequency table that encompasses each bin and uses this table to produce a histogram.

Below is an example of a histogram produced by Excel without use of plug-ins representing computer confidence posttest of university students enrolled in a distance education program. This histogram shows that the shape of the distribution is unimodal and not symmetrical with a negative skew.

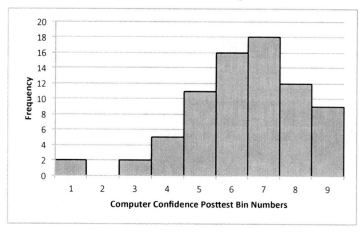

Histograms are useful for evaluating:

- The shape of a distribution
- Symmetry, skewness, and kurtosis
- Modality
- Presence of outliers

Procedures

Use the Excel file Computer Anxiety.xlsx located at http:// www.watertreepress.com/stats if you want to follow along. Requires a copy of Microsoft Excel.

1. Open the *Computer Anxiety.xlsx* file using Excel.

2. Copy the variable comconf2 (computer confidence posttest) from the Excel workbook, Data tab, and paste the variable in column C of an empty sheet. Copy 75 cases.

3. One must now determine the number of bins. Bins must have a constant interval and should encompass all the data. Additionally, discrete numbers should represent bin boundaries. Enter the labels N, SquareRoot N, Minimum, Maximum, Range, and Interval in cells S2:S7 and comconf2 in cell T1. Enter formulas =COUNT(C2:C76), =SQRT(T2), =MIN(C2:C76), =MAX(C2:C76), =T5-T4, and =T6/T3 in cells T2:T7 to assist in determining number of bins.

	S	T
1		comconf2
2	N	=COUNT(C2:C76)
3	SquareRoot N	=SQRT(T2)
4	Minimum	=MIN(C2:C76)
5	Maximum	=MAX(C2:C76)
6	Range	=T5-T4
7	Interval	=T6/T3

	S	T
1		comconf2
2	N	75
3	SquareRoot N	8.660254038
4	Minimum	14
5	Maximum	40
6	Range	26
7	Interval	3.0022214

4. Round up the square root of N to identify the minimum number of bins. Round down the interval to identify maximum bin width. In the above example, the histogram will include 9 bins with a bin width of 3.

5. Create a label and set of bin upper boundary values for the histogram in cells S9:S18. Identify the first bin by adding the bin width to the minimum value (rounded). Then identify the upper boundary of subsequent bins by adding the bin width to the previous upper bin boundary as shown below.

	S
9	Bins
10	17
11	20
12	23
13	26
14	29
15	32
16	35
17	38
18	41

6. Next, enter "Frequency" as a label in cell T9. Then highlight cells T10:T18 and enter the array formula

"=FREQUENCY(C2:C76,S10:S18)" and hit the CTRL-
SHIFT-ENTER (or RETURN) buttons at the same time.

	S	T
9	Bins	
10	17	=FREQUENCY(C2:C76,S10:S18)
11	20	=FREQUENCY(C2:C76,S10:S18)
12	23	=FREQUENCY(C2:C76,S10:S18)
13	26	=FREQUENCY(C2:C76,S10:S18)

	S	T
9	Bins	
10	17	2
11	20	0
12	23	2
13	26	5
14	29	11
15	32	16
16	35	18
17	38	12
18	41	9

7. Highlight the range of values to plot, T10:T18 in the
    above example.

8. Select the Charts tab. Click Column on the Insert Chart
    group of icons.

9. Select 2-D Clustered Column (the drop-down menu
    allows selection of a variety of column charts). The
    selected chart type appears on the workbook active sheet.

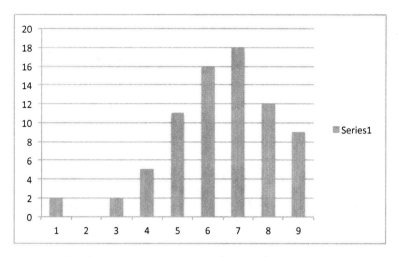

10. Highlight the legend and hit Delete. Double-click a column to open the Format Data Series dialog. Select Options and change gap width from 150% (default) to 0%. Also, select Line and select black as the color so that columns are outlined in black. Click OK to close the dialog and make the change.

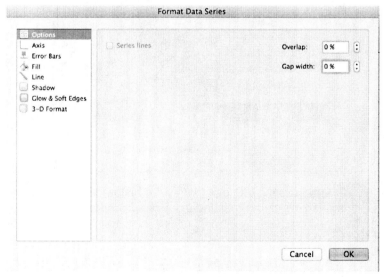

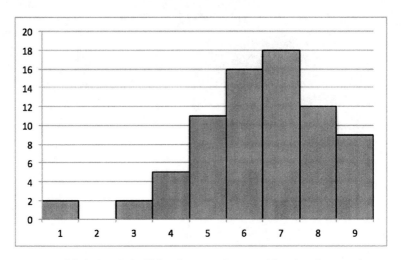

11. Click the Axis Titles icon and enter titles for the x-axis and y-axis.

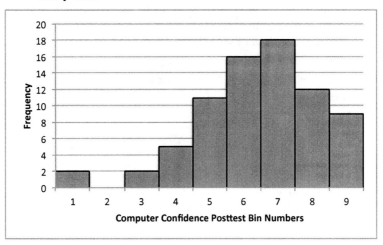

12. If necessary, one can modify the histogram by reducing the bin width and creating more bins to increase resolution.

Pie Chart

A pie chart (also called a circle chart) is a circular chart that is divided into sectors or slices to show proportions, i.e., relative size of data. They are useful for comparing proportions. For example, one may use a pie chart to show the makeup of a sample by displaying the proportions of respondents who answer yes and no to whether or not they own a personal computer.

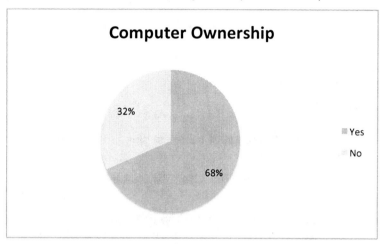

Pie charts are not commonly found in the research literature because they are regarded by many statisticians as a less accurate way of displaying information since comparison of proportions by slice is less accurate than comparison by length. Consequently, column charts tend to be preferred over pie charts, although pie charts are very common in marketing brochures and other non-scientific literature.

Procedures

Use the Excel file Computer Anxiety.xlsx located at http:// www.watertreepress.com/stats if you want to follow along. Requires a copy of Microsoft Excel.

1. Open the *Computer Anxiety.xlsx file using Excel.*

2. Copy variable comown (computer ownership) from the Excel workbook Data tab to column K on an empty sheet. (Note: Yes = 1, No = 2).

3. Enter labels Yes and No in cells L1:L2. Enter formulas =COUNTIF(K2:K93,1) and =COUNTIF(K2:K93,2) in cells M1:M2.

	L	M
1	Yes	=COUNTIF(K2:K93,1)
2	No	=COUNTIF(K2:K93,2)

	L	M
1	Yes	63
2	No	29

4. Highlight the range of values to plot, L1:M2 in the above example.

5. Select the Charts tab. Click Pie on the Insert Chart group of icons.

6. Select 2-D Pie chart (the drop-down menu allows selection of a variety of pie charts). The selected chart type appears on the workbook active sheet. Alternative layouts are available under the Chart Quick Layouts group of icons. For example, Layout 6 produces the following chart.

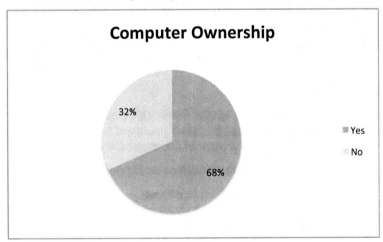

7. Double-click any chart element to edit the selected element.

8. Move or resize any element as desired.

2.7: Automated Procedures

One can automate the task of generating descriptive statistics with the use of Analysis ToolPak for Windows or StatPlus LE for Windows and Mac.

Use the following procedures for Analysis ToolPak.

1. Launch Microsoft Excel for Windows and open the Motivation.xlsx file.

2. Select the Data tab and click the Data Analysis icon to open the Data Analysis dialog. Select Descriptive Statistics and click OK to open the Descriptive Statistics dialog.

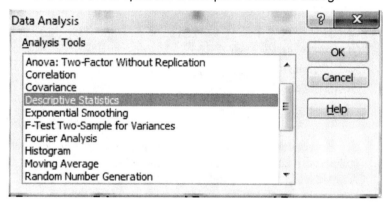

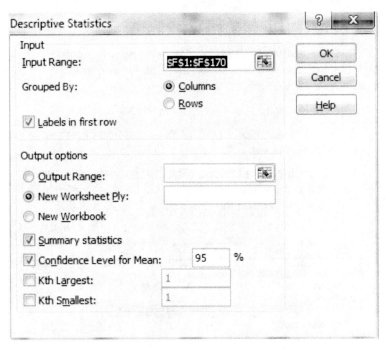

3. Select the Input Range by highlighting the c_community (classroom community) data, to include label in first row. Alternatively, enter the following input range $F$1:$F$170. Complete the dialog as shown above and click the OK button to execute the procedure. Excel places the following output in a new sheet.

	A	B
1	c_community	
2		
3	Mean	28.84023669
4	Standard Error	0.480116274
5	Median	29
6	Mode	22
7	Standard Deviation	6.241511565
8	Sample Variance	38.95646661
9	Kurtosis	-1.044172509
10	Skewness	0.073045168
11	Range	25
12	Minimum	15
13	Maximum	40
14	Sum	4874
15	Count	169
16	Confidence Level(95.0%)	0.947838439

Use the following procedures for StatPlus LE.

1. Launch Microsoft Excel and open the Motivation.xlsx file. Highlight the variable c_community (classroom community), i.e., highlight cells F1:F170.

2. Launch StatPlus LE and select Statistics > Basic Statistics and Tables > Descriptive Statistics from the StatPlus menu bar. Note: not all sub-menu items are enabled in StatPlus LE.

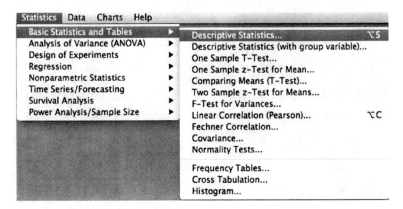

3.   StatPlus automatically fills in the "Variables" box of the Descriptive Statistics dialog based on the highlighted variable. Retain the check in the "Labels in first row" box.

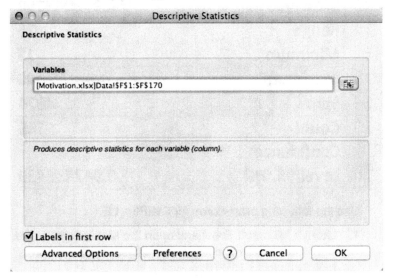

4.   Click the Advanced Options button on the Descriptive Statistics dialog to open the following dialog. Make selections as shown below and click the OK button.

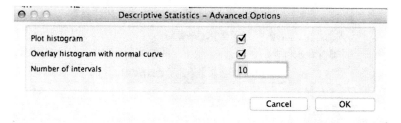

5. Click the Preferences button on the Descriptive Statistics dialog to open the following dialog. Make changes to the defaults shown, if desired, and click the OK button.

6. Click the OK button on the Descriptive Statistics dialog to execute the procedure. StatPlus places the following output in Excel.

	A	B
1	Alpha value (for confidence interval)	0.05
2	Variable #1 (c_community)	
3	Count	169
4	Mean	28.84024
5	Mean LCL	27.8924
6	Mean UCL	29.78808
7	Variance	38.95647
8	Standard Deviation	6.24151
9	Mean Standard Error	0.48012
10	Minimum	15.
11	Maximum	40.
12	Range	25.
13	Sum	4,874.
14	Sum Standard Error	81.13965
15	Total Sum Squares	147,112.
16	Adjusted Sum Squares	6,544.68639
17	Geometric Mean	28.15169
18	Harmonic Mean	27.45319
19	Mode	22.

The Mean LCL and the Mean UCL represent the lower and upper bounds of the confidence interval of the mean based on the t-distribution with $N-1$ degrees of freedom. Normality is assumed.

	C	D
1		
2	**Variable #1 (c_community)**	
3	Skewness	0.0724
4	Skewness Standard Error	0.18567
5	Kurtosis	1.95117
6	Kurtosis Standard Error	0.36485
7	Alternative Skewness (Fisher's)	0.07305
8	Alternative Kurtosis (Fisher's)	-1.04417
9	Coefficient of Variation	0.21642
10	Mean Deviation	5.34792
11	Second Moment	38.72595
12	Third Moment	17.4467
13	Fourth Moment	2,926.17066
14	Median	29.
15	Median Error	0.04629
16	Percentile 25% (Q1)	24.
17	Percentile 75% (Q2)	34.
18	IQR	10.
19	MAD (Median Absolute Deviation)	5.

Note that the Alternative Skewness (Fisher's) and Alternative Kurtosis (Fisher's) are the coefficients generated by Excel's SKEW and KURT functions. Also, the 75th Percentile should be labelled Q_3, not Q_2. MAD is simply the median of the absolute deviations from the variable's median.

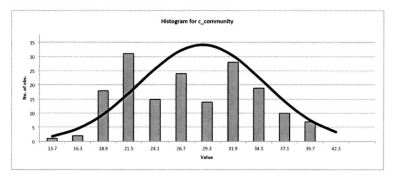

One can modify the above histogram in Excel. For example, one can eliminate the space between bins by double-clicking the bins to open the Format Data Series Dialog and under Options reduce the Gap Width from 150% (default) to 0%. The result is a traditional histogram shown below.

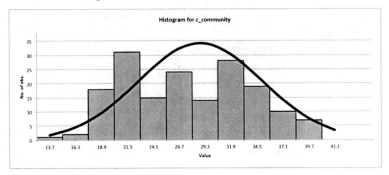

2.8: Chapter 2 Review

Move selected variable(s) to the *Variables* box. Specify theoretical distribution (usually normal). Click *OK*.

The answer key is at the end of this section.

1. What measure of central tendency is most appropriate for ordinal data?

    A. Mean

    B. Median

    C. Mode

    D. Count

2. What measure of dispersion is most appropriate for interval data?

    A. Standard deviation

    B. Range

    C. Mode

    D. Standard error of the mean

3. How would adding 5 to every observation affect the mean of a variable?

    A. No effect

    B. Increase mean by 5

    C. Increase mean by 25

    D. Decrease mean by 5

4. How would adding 5 to every observation affect the variance of a variable?

    A. No effect

    B. Increase variance by 5

    C. Increase variance by 25

    D. Decrease variance by 5

5. How would multiplying every observation by 5 affect the variance of a variable?

   A. No effect

   B. Increase variance by 5

   C. Increase variance by 25

   D. Decrease variance by 5

6. Which of the following symbols is used to represent the population variance?

   A. σ

   B. σ^2

   C. s

   D. s^2

7. Which of the following charts is most useful in examining the relationship between two variables?

   A. Line chart

   B. Pie chart

   C. Column chart

   D. Scatterplot

8. What chart is most useful for comparing proportions?

   A. Line chart

   B. Pie chart

   C. Column chart

   D. Scatterplot

9. The median is the value that...

   A. occurs most often

   B. divides an ordered dataset into two equal halves

   C. is the arithmetic average

   D. none of the above

10. What is the interquartile range for a distribution with the following percentiles: $P_{25} = 25$, $P_{50} = 50$, $P_{75} = 75$?

    A. 50

    B. 25

    C. 75

    D. 100

11. The interquartile range allows one to make a statement about...

    A. the top 50% of observations

    B. the middle 75% of observations

    C. the middle 50% of observations

    D. the middle 25% of observations

12. The mode is...

    A. the typical way of measuring central tendency for ordinal data

    B. the typical way of measuring central tendency for nominal data

    C. the middle value in a group of scores

    D. affected by outliers

13. What statement is correct regarding variance?

    A. The average amount that scores differ from the mean

    B. Point at which half the scores are above and half are below

    C. Unaffected by the extremity of individual scores

    D. The average of the squared deviations from the mean

14. Which of the following is not a measure of dispersion?

    A. Median

    B. Range

    C. Standard deviation

    D. Standard error of the mean

15. A distribution with a kurtosis statistic = 0 is best described using what term?

    A. Leptokurtic

    B. Platykurtic

    C. Mesokurtic

    D. None of the above

16. Which statement about skewness is correct?

    A. Skewness is a measure of modality

    B. Skewness measures deviations from perfect symmetry

    C. Skewness is a measure of whether the data are peaked or flat relative to a perfectly normal distribution

    D. Negative skewness reflects a heavy positive tail

17. Z-scores of 0 to 1 define approximately what % of a population?

    A. 68%

    B. 34%

    C. 95%

    D. 14%

18. Z-scores of 0 to 2 define approximately what % of a population?

    A. 68%

    B. 34%

    C. 14%

    D. 48%

Chapter 2 Answers

1B, 2A, 3B, 4A, 5C, 6B, 7D, 8B, 9B, 10A, 11C, 12B, 13D, 14A, 15C, 16B, 17B, 18D

Chapter 3: Inferential Statistics

Inferential statistics goes beyond the sample and draws conclusions about the population from which the sample was drawn. This chapter describes point and interval estimation, hypothesis testing, and the evaluation of test assumptions.

Chapter 3 Learning Objectives

- Explain inferential statistics.

- Estimate a population mean and a population proportion from a sample.

- Evaluate the accuracy of sample estimates using standard errors.

- Differentiate between parametric and nonparametric tests.

- Describe the different types of variables.

- Explain the pros and cons of using gain and loss scores in statistical analyses.

- Construct an interval estimate for a population parameter.

- Compose research and null hypotheses.

- Explain Type I error, Type II error, significance level, one- and two-tailed tests, degrees of freedom, statistical power, and effect size.

- Differentiate between statistical significance and practical significance.

- Apply different methods for controlling familywise Type I error.

- Evaluate independence of observations, univariate and bivariate normality, linearity, homogeneity of variance, and homoscedasticity using a dataset and Microsoft Excel.

- Describe the steps used in hypothesis testing.

3.1: Basic Concepts

INTRODUCTION

The purpose of inferential statistics is to reach conclusions that extend beyond the sample measured to a target population. It is divided into estimation and hypothesis testing as depicted in Figure 3.1 below.

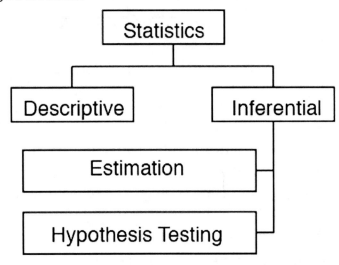

FIGURE 3.1
Divisions of statistics and inferential statistics.

Inferential statistics are used to address the following issues:

- How confident can one be that statistical results are not due to chance? One looks at the statistical test's significance level. If p ≤ the *à priori* significance level (usually .05 for social science research), the results are statistically significant.

- Is a statistically significant effect of any practical significance? One calculates and reports the effect size statistic as a proxy measure to assess practical significance. Effect size is a measure of the magnitude of a research result.

- What is the direction of the effect? For a difference research question, one compares each group's best measure of central tendency (usually mean for interval or ratio data). For a relationship question, one examines the sign of the correlation coefficient. A plus sign indicates a positive (direct) relationship in which both variables covary in the same direction. A negative sign indicates an inverse relationship in which both variables covary in opposite directions.

> **Key Point**
> Findings are statistically significant only when they are unlikely to be explained by chance.

There are two types of inferential tests:

- parametric tests
- nonparametric tests

A parametric test is a statistical procedure that assumes data come from a probability distribution and makes inferences about the parameters of the distribution. All such tests make the following assumptions, as a minimum:

- The data are normally distributed and the DV(s) are interval or ratio scale. Robustness studies have established that mild to moderate violations of normality have little effect on substantive conclusions in many instances (e.g., Cohen, 1988).

- Variances are equal throughout all groups (i.e. homogeneity of variance).

- Measurements are independent in the sense that one case or outside influence does not influence another case (i.e., independence of observations).

Since all common parametric statistics are relational, the range of procedures used to analyze one continuous DV and one or more IVs (continuous or categorical) are mathematically similar. The underlying model is called the general linear model (GLM).

A nonparametric test does not make assumptions regarding the distribution. Consequently, a nonparametric test is considered a distribution-free method because it does not rely on any underlying mathematical distribution. Nonparametric tests do, however, have various assumptions that must be met.

A nonparametric test is limited in its ability to provide the researcher with grounds for drawing conclusions – parametric tests provide more detailed information. Consequently, researchers prefer parametric to nonparametric tests because they are more powerful when parametric assumptions have been met.

Nonparametric tests have the following advantages:

• They are useful when parametric test assumptions cannot be met, although not all parametric tests have a nonparametric counterpart.

• If the sample is very small, distributional assumptions linked to parametric tests are not likely to be met. Therefore, an advantage is that no distributional assumptions are required for nonparametric tests.

• Nonparametric tests can be applied to variables at any scale of measurement.

• Interpretations are often less complex than parametric results.

Types of Variables

There are several important types of variables used in inferential statistics. Independent variables (IVs) make up one type. These are the predictor variables that one expects to influence other variables. In an experiment, the researcher manipulates the IV(s), which typically involve an intervention of some type. For example, if a researcher sets up two classes using two different teaching methods for the purpose of comparing the effectiveness of these methods, the IV is teaching method (method A, method B).

Dependent variables (DVs) make up a second type of variable. These are outcome variables, or those that one expects to be affected by IVs. For example, if different teaching methods (the IV) result in different student achievement as measured by test scores, then student achievement (or, operationally, test score) is the DV.

IVs are variables that are manipulated whereas DVs are variables that are measured. The terms IV and DV apply especially to experimental research where some variables are manipulated or to regression studies where one addresses prediction. In this case the IV is the predictor variable and the DV is the criterion variable. IV's and DV's can be summarized by the following example:

IV > DV

Cause > Effect (Outcome)

Level of Education > Income Level

Moderating variables are introduced to account for situations where the relationship between the IV and the DV is presumed to depend on some third variable.

In general terms, a moderator is a qualitative (e.g., sex, race, class) or quantitative (e.g., level of reward) variable that affects the direction and/or strength of the relation between an independent or predictor variable and a dependent or criterion variable. Specifically within a correlational analysis framework, a moderator is a third variable that affects the zero-order correlation between two other variables. ... In the more familiar analysis of variance (ANOVA) terms, a basic moderator effect can be represented as an interaction between a focal independent variable and a factor that specifies the appropriate conditions for its operation. (Baron & Kenny, 1986, p. 1174)

For example, gender can act as a moderator variable in the following relationship as it influences both level of education and income level.

Level of Education > Income Level

Mediating variables (also called intervening variables) may be introduced to explain why an antecedent variable affects a consequent variable.

> In general, a given variable may be said to function as a mediator to the extent that it accounts for the relation between the predictor and the criterion. Mediators explain how external physical events take on internal psychological significance. Whereas moderator variables specify when certain effects will hold, mediators speak to how or why such effects occur. (Baron & Kenny, 1986, p. 1176)

Cause > Mediating Variable(s) > Effect

Level of Education > Occupation > Income Level

An extraneous variable is one that unintentionally interferes with the effect of the independent variable. "Researchers usually try to control for extraneous variables by experimental isolation, by randomization, or by some statistical technique such as analysis of covariance" (Vogt, 1993, p. 88). Extraneous variables are related, in a statistical sense, with both the DV and the IV. An extraneous variable becomes a confounding variable when the researcher cannot or does not control its effects, thereby adversely affecting the internal validity of a study by increasing error. Confounding variables are sometimes called lurking variables. For example, confounding can occur when a researcher does not randomly assign participants to groups and a type of difference between groups, which is not controlled, affects research results (e.g., motivation, ability, etc.).

Gain and Loss Scores

Gain and loss scores are sometimes used as DVs by researchers in pretest-posttest designs. It makes intuitive sense to subtract the pretest from the posttest measures (or vice versa) and then determine whether the gain (or loss) is statistically significant between groups. However, this can be a controversial procedure; e.g., Cronbach and Furby (1970) and Nunnally (1975).

Cronbach and Furby (1970) wrote that when the pretest and post scores are highly correlated, the gain scores have a dramatic loss in reliability. Cronbach and Furby argued that: "gain scores are rarely useful, no matter how they may be adjusted or refined" (p. 68) and "investigators who ask questions regarding gain scores should ordinarily be better advised to frame their questions in other ways" (p. 80).

However, other researchers, e.g., Williams and Zimmerman (1996), argue that the validity and reliability of difference scores can be higher than formerly believed. The arguments presented do not suggest that simple difference scores are always or even usually valid and reliable. The arguments suggest that validity and reliability cannot be ruled out solely by virtue of statistical properties and depends on other factors, such as the measuring instrument.

CENTRAL LIMIT THEOREM

A sampling distribution is a distribution of a sample of N cases, such as a sample of all possible means for samples of size N created by various random samples drawn from the same population. According to the Central Limit Theorem, a sampling distribution of means possesses the following characteristics:

- It has a mean equal to the population mean μ.

$$\mu_{\bar{X}} = \mu$$

- It has a standard deviation (standard error or mean standard error) equal to the population standard deviation divided by the square root of the sample size.

$$\sigma_M = \frac{\sigma}{\sqrt{N}}$$

- The shape of the sampling distribution of the mean approaches normal as N increases.

According to the Central Limit Theorem, the sampling distribution of sample means is approximated by a normal distribution when the sample is a simple random sample and the sample size is large.

> **Key Point**
> The sampling distribution of any statistic will be normal or nearly normal if the sample size is large enough.

The Central Limit Theorem is the basis for inferential statistics. Assuming a large sample, it allows one to use hypothesis tests that assume normality, even if the data appear non-normal. This is because the inferential tests use the sample mean, which the Central Limit Theorem posits is approximately normally distributed.

A sample size of 100 or more units is generally considered sufficient to permit applying the Central Limit Theorem. If the population from which the sample is drawn is symmetrically distributed, $N > 30$ may be sufficient. However, if the population distribution is far from normal, it may be necessary to draw a very large sample (e.g., 500 or more) to produce a sampling distribution of the mean that is approximately normal.

ESTIMATION

Estimation is a way to estimate a population parameter based on measuring a sample. It can be expressed in two ways:

- A point estimate of a population parameter is a single value of a statistic. For example, the sample mean of a random sample of n observations is the best estimate of the population mean μ and the sample proportion p (x/n) of x successes out of n trials is the best point estimate of the population proportion p.

- An interval estimate is defined by two numbers, between which a population parameter is said to lie. A confidence interval is a type of interval estimate with a specified confidence level, e.g., 95% confidence interval of the mean.

An unbiased estimator is one that produces the right answer, on average, over a set of replications. Bias occurs when there is a systematic error in the measure that shifts the estimate more in one direction than another, on average. One should randomly sample from the target population to avoid bias.

In addition to being on target, one also wants the distribution of an estimator to have a small variance; i.e., to be efficient, precise. More efficient statistics have smaller sampling variances, smaller standard error, and are preferred because if both are unbiased, one is closer to the parameter, on average. Larger sample sizes tend to be more efficient.

Additionally, one wants the estimator to be consistent (i.e., reliable) so that as the number of observations gets large, the variability around the estimate approaches zero and the estimate approaches more closely the parameter that one is trying to estimate. The estimator is consistent if its bias and variance both approach zero. In other words, we expect the mean square error (MSE) to approach zero.

Drawing from probability theory, a probability distribution is a function that describes the probability of a random variable taking certain values. Probability distributions are a fundamental concept in statistics as they serve several useful purposes including:

- The calculation of point estimates and confidence intervals for parameters and to calculate critical regions for hypothesis tests.

- Determining a model for the distribution; e.g., normal distribution or binomial distribution. Inferential tests assume certain distribution models that require evaluation before using the specific test.

If one draws all possible samples of size N from a given population and computes a statistic – e.g., mean, for each sample – the resultant probability distribution of this statistic is called a sampling distribution.

Confidence Intervals

A confidence interval (or margin of error) gives an estimated range of values that is likely to include an unknown population parameter. For example, the 95% confidence interval for the mean provides the estimated range of values that is 95% likely to include the population mean. In other words, a survey may have a margin of error of plus or minus a specified number of units at a 95 percent level of confidence.

The following steps are necessary to construct an interval estimate for an unknown population parameter.

- Obtain the point estimate of the parameter, e.g., μ or p.

- Select a confidence level, e.g., 95%.

- Calculate the confidence interval for the unknown population parameter.

Use the following formula to calculate a confidence interval for an unknown population mean when σ Is known

$$CI\_for\_\mu = \bar{X} \pm C\sigma_M$$

where x-bar is the point estimate of the population mean (i.e., the sample mean), C is the critical value for the required confidence interval in standard deviation units (z-values), and σ_M is the mean standard error.

Use the following formula to calculate a confidence interval for an unknown population proportion

$$CI\_for\_p = \hat{p} \pm C\sqrt{\frac{\hat{p}(1-\hat{p})}{n}}$$

where p-hat is the point estimate of the population proportion (i.e., the sample proportion), C is the critical value for the required confidence interval in standard deviation units, and n is the size of the random sample.

The critical value C for a 95% confidence interval is 1.96 (the value of 1.96 is based on the fact that 95% of the area of a normal distribution is within 1.96 standard deviations of the mean). Figure 3.2 that displays the 95% confidence interval using a density curve.

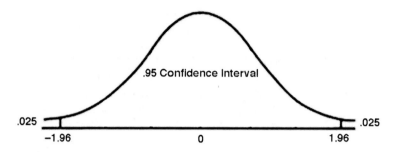

FIGURE 3.2
Density curve showing a 95% confidence interval.

In the above figure, the 95% confidence interval in the standard normal distribution is displayed for a two-tailed test at the .05 significance level. Thus, the significance level is the sum of probabilities that a sample statistic goes beyond the critical value (larger than 1.96 and less than −1.96).

- The critical value for a 90% confidence interval is 1.645 (the value of 1.645 is based on the fact that 90% of the area of a normal distribution is within 1.645 standard deviations of the mean).

- The critical value for a 99% confidence interval is 2.58 (the value of 2.58 is based on the fact that 99% of the area of a normal distribution is within 2.58 standard deviations of the mean).

When the population standard deviation is not known but must be estimated from sample data one should use the *t*-distribution rather than the normal distribution to obtain critical values. When the sample size is large – e.g. > 100 – the *t*-distribution is similar to the standard normal distribution and the critical values provided above are adequate. The critical values of *t* to be used in a confidence interval can be looked up in a table of the *t*-distribution based on degrees of freedom and confidence level.

HYPOTHESIS TESTING

Hypothesis testing is a method for making decisions about the target population based on the characteristics of a random sample drawn from that population. The overall goal of a hypothesis test is to rule out chance (sampling error) as a plausible explanation for the research results. In other words, hypothesis testing is the use of statistics to determine the probability that a given hypothesis is true. All hypothesis tests are based on probability theory and have risks of reaching a wrong conclusion.

> Key Point
> No amount of statistical skill will overcome research design flaws.

Probability

Probability is the chance that something random will occur in order to predict the behavior of defined systems. The basic rules of probability are (Gall, Gall, & Borg, 2007):

- Any probability of any event, $p(E)$, is a number between 0 and 1.

- The probability that all possible outcomes can occur is 1.

- If there are k possible outcomes for a phenomenon and each is equally likely, then each individual outcome has probability of $1/k$.

- The chance of any (one or more) of two or more events occurring is the union of the events. The probability of the union of events is the sum of their individual probabilities.

- The probability that any event E does not occur is $1 - p(E)$.

- If two events E_1 and E_2 are independent, then the probability of both events is the product of the probabilities for each event, $p(E1 \text{ and } E2) = p(E_1)p(E_2)$.

For example, in a population with 50 males and 40 females, the probability of randomly selecting a male is $p(M) = 50/90 = .56$ and the probability of not selecting a male (i.e., selecting a female) is $p(F) = 1 - p(M) = .44$. The probability of selecting two males $= p(M)p(M) = .31$.

Significance Level

The significance level is the probability of making a Type I error (α), that is, falsely rejecting a true null hypothesis. It is also referred to as a p-value (probability value). A researcher needs to assign a value to the significance level before he or she conducts any statistical analysis (*à priori* significance level) in hypothesis testing. Assigning a significance level after data are analyzed results in loss of objectivity in classical hypothesis testing. However, the Bayesian approach to hypothesis testing is to base rejection of the hypothesis on the the *posterior* probability.

For social science research the *à priori* significance level is typically set at .05 or .01 (.10 is sometimes used for exploratory research). A significance level of .05 means that if one rejects H_0, one is willing to accept no more than a 5% chance that one is wrong (if the significance level were set at .01, one is willing to accept no more than a 1% chance that one is wrong). In other words, with a .05 significance level, one wants to be at least 95% confident that if one rejects H_0 the correct decision was made. The confidence level in this situation is .95 ($1 - \alpha$).

Hypotheses

The first step in hypothesis testing is to identify the null and research (or alternate) hypotheses and deciding upon an appropriate significance level as discussed above. The procedure will determine whether or not there is sufficient evident to reject the null hypothesis at the designated *à priori* significance level.

- The research hypothesis, denoted by H_1 or H_a or H_A, is the hypothesis that sample observations are influenced by a nonrandom cause (i.e., the intervention).

- The null hypothesis, denoted by H_0, is the hypothesis of no difference or no relationship.

Bartos (1992) identifies the following characteristics of a usable hypothesis:

- Possesses explanatory power
- States the expected relationship between variables
- Must be testable
- Is linked to the professional literature
- Is stated simply and concisely

Hypothesis tests have four possible outcomes. Probabilities for each statistical outcome are depicted in Table 3.1 below.

TABLE 3.1

Hypothesis test outcomes.

	H_0 is True	H_0 is False
Reject H_0	Type I Error (α)	No Error ($1 - \beta$)
Fail to Reject H_0	No Error ($1 - \alpha$)	Type II Error (β)

Statistical tests involve Type I (α) and Type II (β) risks or errors. Type I error is the probability of deciding that a significant effect is present when it is not. Type II error is the probability of not detecting a significant effect when one exists. In other words, Type I error is committed when one rejects the null hypothesis (H_0) when it is true. The probability of the Type I error is denoted by the Greek letter alpha (α). Type II error is committed when one fails to reject the null hypothesis when the alternative hypothesis (i.e., the research hypothesis) is true. The probability of the Type II error is shown by the Greek letter beta (β).

Researchers usually begin by formulating H_0 and assuming it is true. This is analogous to the presumption of innocence if one is a defendant at a trial. If the H_0 is true, what is the biggest difference between the sample means that can occur by chance at a reasonable level of probability? In other words, how different can we expect the means to become simply as a result of chance?

The next step is to determine if the data support rejecting or not rejecting H_0 as true. If the statistical analysis suggests that the differences or relationships one sees are unlikely to be due to chance, then one rejects H_0 and accepts H_1. Since hypothesis testing deals with probabilities, there is a chance that the statistical conclusion will be wrong.

Suppose that a researcher believes that teachers are more likely to adopt technology in their teaching if they possess greater knowledge of computers. The researcher could conduct a study that compares the level of teacher technology adoption in one group (e.g., teachers who have a high level of computer knowledge) to those in another group (e.g., teachers with a lower level of computer knowledge). Accordingly, the IV is group (high computer knowledge, low computer knowledge) and the DV is a measure of classroom technology use. H_0 would be there is no difference in the mean technology adoption scores of teachers in the two groups. The research hypothesis could be that teachers in the high computer knowledge group will have a higher mean technology adoption score than teachers in the low computer knowledge group (implying a one-tailed test), or more simply, that there will be a difference between the mean scores of the two groups (implying a two-tailed test).

If one has a correlation study (i.e., a study that seeks to determine if there is a relationship between variables), the process of developing hypotheses is similar. For example, if the research question is:

Is there a relationship between intelligence and GPA?

then the null hypothesis is:

H_0: There is no relationship between intelligence and GPA.

The purpose of the hypothesis test is to decide between the following two conclusions:

- Failure to reject H_0

    - When the calculated significance level (p-value) is larger than the à priori significance level, one concludes any observed results (e.g., differences in means) are not statistically significant and are therefore probably due to sampling error or chance.

- Failure to reject H_0 does not necessarily mean that H_0 is true. It simply means that there is not sufficient evidence to reject H_0. A H_0 is not accepted just because it is not rejected. Data not sufficient to show convincingly that a difference between means is not zero do not prove that the difference is zero. Such data may even suggest that H_0 is false but not be strong enough to make a convincing case that it is false. In this situation one had insufficient statistical power to reject a false H_0. Consider ways of increasing statistical power.

- Rejection of H_0

  - One concludes that the observed results are statistically significant and are probably due to some determining factor or condition other than chance.

  - Rejection of H_0 does not necessarily mean that the alternative hypothesis is true. There is always the probability of a Type I error.

The ability to reject H_0 depends upon:

- Significance level (α) – usually set to be .05, although this is somewhat arbitrary. This is the probability of rejecting H_0 given that H_0 is true.

- Sample size (N) – a larger sample size leads to more accurate parameter estimates and more statistical power.

- Effect size – the bigger the size of the effect in the population, the easier it will be to find and reject a false H_0.

When H_0 is rejected, the outcome is said to be "statistically significant;" when H_0 is not rejected then the outcome is said be "not statistically significant." However, keep in mind that an event that has a 5% chance of occurring should occur, on average, 1 in 20 times. Therefore, one may have falsely rejected H_0 because an event with a 5% probability has occurred. One's response to this problem may be to set α to some lower value such as .01 to lower the risk of rejecting a true H_0. This may be needed if an important decision, such as expenditure of resources, is to be made based on the results of the study. For example, in medical research where life may be placed in jeopardy based on a wrong decision, significance levels are normally set at a very low level; e.g., .0001.

> ### Key Point
> The p-value cannot be zero. A p-value of zero represents certainty that no Type I error took place.

One- and Two-Tailed Hypotheses

Hypotheses can be one- or two-tailed, based on how the research question is worded:

- Two tailed – this hypothesis is non-directional (i.e., the direction of difference or association is not predicted), e.g., $H_0: \mu_1 = \mu_2$, $Ha: \mu_1 \neq \mu_2$. The test determines whether or not the mean of the sample group is either less than or greater than the mean of the control group.

- One-tailed – this hypothesis is directional (i.e., the direction of difference or association is predicted); e.g., $H_0: \mu_1 \gtrless \mu_2$, $Ha: \mu_1 > \mu_2$. For example, sense of classroom community in graduate students is higher in face-to-face courses than online courses. Here the DV is sense of classroom community and the IV is type course (face-to-face, online).

Figure 3.3 below depicts a one-tailed test with a .95 confidence interval and a .05 significance level using the standard normal distribution. The significance level is the probability that a sample statistic goes beyond the critical value (larger than 1.645 in this situation). A one-tailed test tests either if the sample mean is significantly greater than x or if the mean is significantly less than x, but not both as in a two-tailed test. Then, depending on the chosen tail, the mean is significantly greater than or less than x if the test statistic is in the top 5% of its probability distribution or bottom 5% of its probability distribution, depending on the direction specified in the hypothesis.

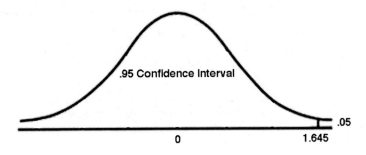

FIGURE 3.3
Density curve showing a one-tailed test with a .95 confidence interval and a .05 significance level.

The issue of two- versus one-tailed hypotheses becomes important when performing the statistical test and determining the p-value. For example, in a two-tailed test when α is set at .05, the .05 is actually divided equally between the left and right tails of the sample distribution curve. The condition being tested is that the group A mean is different from the group B mean. In the case of a one-tailed test with $\alpha = .05$, the entire .05 appears in the right or high tail of the curve if the directional hypothesis were $H_a: \mu_1 > \mu_2$ or in the left tail if the directional hypothesis were $H_a: \mu_1 < \mu_2$. The result is that the calculated p-value will be lower and it will be easier to reject the H_0 if a one-tailed test is used instead of a two-tailed test, all else being equal.

> **Key Point**
> Convert a two-tailed significance level to a one-tailed significance level by taking half of the two-tailed value, provided the underlying distribution is symmetric.

Degrees of Freedom

Statistical analysis can be based upon different amounts of information. The number of independent pieces of information that go into the estimate of a parameter is called the degrees of freedom (df). In general, the degrees of freedom of an estimate is equal to the number of independent scores that go into the estimate minus the number of parameters estimated as intermediate steps in the estimation of the parameter itself. The higher the degrees of freedom, the more representative the sample will be of the population.

Statistical Power

The statistical power (or observed power or sensitivity) of a statistical test is the probability of rejecting a false H_0. It is equal to 1 minus the probability of accepting a false H_0 $(1 - \beta)$. It represents the degree one is willing to make a Type II error. The desired standard is 80 percent or higher, leaving a 20 percent chance, or less, of error.

> Key Point
> One should interpret nonsignificant results with statistical power < .80 as inconclusive results as the outcome could be statistically significant with increased power.

The following factors affect statistical power.

- Level of significance (i.e., probability of a Type I error), normally .05 – smaller alpha levels (e.g., .01) produce lower power levels (that is, the greater the likelihood of Type II error) for a given sample size.

- Sample size – the smaller the sample, the greater the likelihood of a Type II error and the lower the power.

- Effect size – the smaller the effect size, the more likely a Type II error and thus the lower the power for a given sample size.

- Statistical test used – typically, parametric tests have greater statistical power than nonparametric tests; one-tailed tests have more statistical power than two-tailed tests.

- Variability in each sample.

One can increase statistical power by:

- Increasing the sample size.

- Increasing the significance level.

- Using all the information provided by the data (e.g., do not transform interval scale variables to ordinal scale variables prior to the analysis).

- Using a one-tailed (versus a two-tailed) test.

- Using a parametric (versus nonparametric) test.

> Key Point
> Large samples can be statistically significant because of increased statistical power, but have little practical significance.

Effect Size

In very large samples, small differences are likely to be statistically significant. This sensitivity to sample size is a weakness of hypothesis testing and has led to the use of an effect size statistic to complement interpretation of a significant hypothesis test.

> # Key Point
> Statistical significance does not imply an effect is meaningful or important

Effect size is a measure of the magnitude of a treatment effect. Researchers frequently refer to effect size as practical significance in contrast to statistical significance. While statistical significance is concerned with whether a statistical result is due to chance, practical significance is concerned with whether the result is useful in the real world.

> # Key Point
> There is no practical significance without statistical significance.

The effect size helps policymakers and educators decide whether a statistically significant difference between programs translates into enough of a difference to justify adoption of a program. It is the degree to which H_0 is false. In general, effect size can be measured in one of the following ways (Kline, 2004):

1. the standardized difference between two means; e.g., Cohen's *d*.

2. the correlation between the independent variable and the individual scores on the dependent variable; e.g., Pearson *r*, Spearman rank order correlation coefficient, phi coefficient, Cramér's *V*, and eta squared (η^2).

3. estimates corrected for error; e.g., adjusted R^2.

4. risk estimates; e.g., odds ratio.

5. omega squared (ω^2), an estimate of the dependent variable variance accounted for by the independent variable.

The *Publication Manual of the American Psychological Association* (APA, 2010) notes that

> For the reader to appreciate the magnitude or importance of a study's findings, it is almost always necessary to include some measure of effect size in the results section. Whenever possible, provide a confidence interval for each effect size reported to indicate the precision of estimation of the effect size. Effect sizes may be expressed in the original units (e.g., the mean number of questions answered correctly; kg/month for a regression slope) and are most easily understood when reported in original units. It can often be valuable to report an effect size not only in original units but also in some standardized or units-free unit (e.g., as a Cohen's *d* value) or a standardized regression weight. (p. 34)

The guidelines for interpreting various effect size statistics are meant to be flexible. Cohen's caution regarding the assignment of standardized interpretations to effect size values is relevant:

> The terms 'small,' 'medium,' and 'large' are relative, not only to each other, but to the area of behavioral science or even more particularly to the specific content and research method being employed in any given investigation....In the face of this relativity, there is a certain risk inherent in offering conventional operational definitions for these terms for use in power analysis in as diverse a field of inquiry as behavioral science. This risk is nevertheless accepted in the belief that more is to be gained than lost by supplying a common conventional frame of reference which is recommended for use only when no better basis for estimating the *ES* index is available. (p. 25)

A generic formula for calculating effect size using standard deviation units follows

$$ES = \frac{(M_E - M_C)}{SD_C}$$

where ES = effect size, M_E = mean of the experimental group, M_C = mean of the control group, and SD_C = standard deviation of the control group (or pooled standard deviation). This measure of effect size is equivalent to a z-score. For example, an effect size of .50 indicates that the score of the average person in the experimental group is .50 standard deviations above the average person in the control group. A small effect size is between .2 and .5 standard deviation units, a medium effect size is one that is between .5 and .8 standard deviation units, and a large effect size is one that is .8 or more standard deviation units (Rosenthal & Rosnow, 1991).

Cohen's d is frequently used in conjunction with t-tests and represents standard deviation units. Consequently, it can be quite large (i.e., -3.0 to 3.0). Cohen (1988) defined the magnitude of d as small, $d = .20$; medium, $d = .50$; and large, $d = .80$. The formula for Cohen's d for one-sample and dependent t-tests follows

$$d = \frac{t}{\sqrt{N}}$$

where t = t-statistic and N = sample size.

The formula for Cohen's d for the independent t-test is

$$d = t \sqrt{\frac{N_1 + N_2}{N_1 N_2}}$$

where N represents the size of each group.

The correlation coefficient (r) is also suitable for estimating effect size when analyzing continuous, normally distributed variables. According to Cohen (1988, 1992), the effect size as measured by r can be interpreted as follows:

Low effect if r varies around 0.1
Medium effect if r varies around 0.3
Large effect if r varies more than 0.5

The coefficient of multiple determination (R^2) is also commonly used as effect size statistics for regression analyses. R^2 can be interpreted as follows (Cohen, 1988):

Small effect = .0196
Medium Effect = .1300
Large effect = .2600

Cohen's d and Pearson r can be converted one from another using the following formulas

$$r = \sqrt{d^2 / (d^2 + 4)}$$

$$d = 2r / \sqrt{(1 - r^2)}$$

Effect size can also be measured by eta squared (η^2) and partial eta squared (η_p^2) statistics, where .01 = small effect size, .06 = medium effect size, and .14 = large effect size (Tabachnick & Fidell, 2007). These statistics are very frequently used in conjunction with ANOVA,. Eta squared represents the effect size of the model and partial eta squared is the effect size of a specific effect; e.g., a main effect or interaction effect. However, it should be noted that η_p^2 statistics are non-additive and can add to over 100% of total variance explained.

The formula for eta squared follows

$$\eta^2 = \frac{SS_{effect}}{SS_{total}}$$

where SS_{effect} is sum of squares for a specific effect and SS_{total} is the total sum of squares for all effects (main, interaction, and error).

The formula for partial eta squared is

$$\eta_p^2 = \frac{SS_{effect}}{SS_{effect} + SS_{error}}$$

Leech and Onwuegbuzie (2002) write:

Reporting effect sizes is no less important for statistically significant nonparametric findings than it is for statistically significant parametric results... However, it should be noted that just as parametric tests are adversely affected by departures from [general linear model] assumptions, so too are parametric effect sizes... Therefore, researchers should consider following up statistically significant nonparametric p-values with nonparametric effect sizes. Nonparametric effect sizes include Cramér's V, the phi coefficient, and the odds ratio. (pp. 14-15)

Phi can be used as an effect size statistic for 2 x 2 contingency tables. Cramér's V can be used for larger tables and corrects for table size. For 2 x 2 tables, Cramér's V equals phi. Cohen (1988) proposed the following standards for interpreting Cramér's V as effect size for chi-square analysis:

For $df = 1$, small effect = 0.10, medium effect = 0.30, large effect = 0.50

For $df = 2$, small effect = 0.07, medium effect = 0.21, large effect = 0.35

For $df = 3$, small effect = 0.06, medium effect = 0.17, large effect = 0.29

The Spearman rank order correlation coefficient can be used to estimate effect size of ordinal data.

Steps in Hypothesis Testing

1. Preliminary steps:

   - Identify a problem or issue and form a research question and a research hypothesis based on a theoretical rationale.

   - Select a suitable research design.

   - Identify the target population and select a sample from that population to measure. Probability sampling methods are superior to non-probability sampling methods with regard to the ability to make generalizations based on research findings.

   - Operationalize the variables by determining how each will be measured. Measuring instruments should be valid and reliable. Typically, reliability coefficients should be no less than .70.

2. Develop a null hypothesis; e.g., H_0: $\mu_1 = \mu_2$ or $r = 0$. The null hypothesis is the one tested. This is the hypothesis that one hopes to reject by the statistical test, assuming the research hypothesis is correct.

3. Decide on the appropriate statistical test to use in order to evaluate the null hypothesis. When selecting an appropriate test keep the following issues in mind:

   - What type of hypothesis is being tested: (a) hypothesis of difference or (b) hypothesis of association?

   - How many variables are there?

   - What is the scale of measurement for each variable? For categorical variables, how many categories (i.e., levels or groups) are there?

   - Are the data related (e.g., pretest-posttest or a matching procedure was used) or independent (e.g., independent groups)?

   - Evaluate test assumptions for the selected test. If one or more assumptions are not tenable, estimate whether the violation is mild, moderate, or severe. Check the robustness of the selected test to violations (robustness means that the test provides p-values close to the true ones in the presence of departures from its assumptions). The following options are available:

- If the test is sufficiently robust, conduct the test and note the issue(s) in the results section of the research report.

- If the test is not sufficiently robust, apply a transformation or use an alternate method, if available and appropriate. For example, if the homogeneity of variance assumption of the independent t-test is not tenable, use the t-test results that utilize the Welch-Satterthwaite method, which does not use the pooled estimate for the error term for the t-statistic and makes adjustments to the degrees of freedom.

- If assumptions are not tenable for the test and other alternatives are not available or feasible, select a different test if one is available. In the case of parametric tests, select an equivalent nonparametric test. For example, if the normality assumption of the independent t-test is not tenable, select the Mann-Whitney U test. Whenever conducting a nonparametric test because normality was not tenable, include this piece of information in the results section of the research report or journal article. Whenever possible conduct both the parametric test and the equivalent nonparametric test to determine if the results of the two tests are the same regarding the null hypothesis. If the conclusions are different use the conclusion associated with the nonparametric test.

• Use the most statistically powerful test available that evaluates the null hypothesis. Usually this means selecting a parametric test over a nonparametric test, provided parametric test assumptions are tenable. For example, parametric tests involve interval or ratio scale variables that are approximately normal in distribution (data are sampled from a Gaussian distribution). If this assumption cannot be met, then a suitable nonparametric test is selected. If ordinal scale data are to be analyzed, then one would select the most statistically powerful nonparametric test that evaluates the null hypothesis. This usually means selecting a suitable nonparametric test that analyzes ranked data versus frequency counts (i.e., nominal data).

- The Central Limit Theorem ensures that parametric tests work well with large samples even if the population is non-Gaussian. In other words, parametric tests are robust to deviations from Gaussian distributions, provided the samples are large. The problem the statistician faces is that it is impossible to say how large is large enough, as it depends on the nature of the particular non-Gaussian distribution.

- Nonparametric tests are suitable to use with large samples from Gaussian populations. The p-values tend to be a bit larger, thereby increasing the probability of a Type II error.

- Small samples present problems. The nonparametric tests are not very statistically powerful and the parametric tests are not robust since one cannot rely on the Central Limit Theorem, so p-levels may be inaccurate.

4. Determine the number of participants required and collect an appropriate sample from the target population.

5. Decide on the à priori significance level. If potentially serious consequences could occur if a wrong decision is made, a researcher may choose to decrease the significance level; e.g., from .05 to .01 or to .001.

6. Decide whether to use a one-tailed test or two-tailed test. This decision is based on the wording of the research and null hypotheses to be tested. Normally, one selects a two-tailed test.

7. Conduct the statistical test and make a decision. If the calculated p-value is less than or equal to the à priori significance level, one has sufficient evidence to reject the null hypothesis. If the calculated p-value is greater than the significance level, one has insufficient evidence to reject the null hypothesis and can conclude the effect was not significant. However, if the statistical power (i.e., observed power) < .80 one should interpret nonsignificant results as

inconclusive as the outcome could be statistically significant with increased power.

> **Key Point**
> Failure to reject the null hypothesis does not constitute proof that the research hypothesis is false. It only indicates that the data were not sufficient to reject the null hypothesis.

7. Report the statistical results in accordance with an appropriate style manual or author guidelines, if preparing a manuscript for publication. Consider reporting the following information, as a minimum, in order to provide a measure of uniformity across studies:

   • The null hypothesis associated with the research question (the purpose of the results section of a research report is to provide an evaluation of this null hypothesis).

   • Appropriate descriptive statistics to include the best measures of central tendency and dispersion as well as sample and group sizes.

   • Identification of the omnibus test and the results of evaluation of test assumptions.

   • Statistical results of the omnibus test and any post hoc tests.

   • The statistical decision regarding the null hypothesis.

   • Effect size if the results are significant.

   • Other statistics that are appropriate for the test that was conducted. For example, identify the unstandardized prediction equation for significant regression tests.

Controlling Type I Error

Type I error is the probability of deciding that a significant effect is present when it isn't. That is, it is the probability of rejecting a true null hypothesis. Type I error is controlled by the researcher by specifying an *à priori* significance level for a single hypothesis test. This is known as the experimentwise Type I error rate.

When several tests are conducted simultaneously using the same dataset, they constitute a family of tests. Familywise Type I error rate is the probability for a family of tests that at least one null hypothesis will be rejected assuming that all of the null hypotheses are true. However, unless the researcher takes steps to control for familywise error, the Type I error rate becomes inflated. This happens because the more statistical tests one performs the more likely one is to reject the null hypothesis when it is true (i.e., commit a Type I error).

Bonferroni Correction

The Bonferroni correction is a simple procedure for controlling familywise Type I error for multiple pairwise comparisons. It requires the following steps (Green & Salkind, 2008):

- Identify familywise Type I error rate; e.g., $p = .05$.

- Determine the number of pairwise comparisons (n).

- Compute p-values for each individual test, $p_1, p_2, ... p_n$.

- Reject the null hypothesis for each test if

$$p < \frac{p*}{n}$$

where $p* =$ familywise Type I error rate and $n =$ number of pairwise comparisons.

However, the Bonferroni method is often considered too conservative.

Holm's Sequential Bonferroni Correction

A variant of the Bonferroni correction that is less conservative is the Holm's sequential Bonferroni correction. Holm (1979) observes:

> Except in trivial non-interesting cases the sequentially rejective Bonferroni test has strictly larger probability of rejecting false hypotheses and thus it ought to replace the classical Bonferroni test at all instants where the latter usually is applied (p. 65).

This procedure involves the following steps (Green & Salkind, 2008; Holm, 1979):

- Identify familywise Type I error rate; e.g., $p = .05$.

- Determine the number of pairwise comparisons (n).

- Conduct the pairwise comparisons.

- Rank-order the comparisons on the basis of their p-values from smallest to highest.

- Evaluate the comparison with the smallest p-value. Compare the p-value to the à priori modified familywise Type I error rate as calculated using the Bonferroni method. Reject the null hypothesis for the test if

$$p < \frac{p^*}{n}$$

where p^* = familywise Type I error rate and n = number of pairwise comparisons.

- Evaluate the comparison with the next smallest p-value. Reject the null hypothesis for the test if

$$p < \frac{p^*}{n-1}$$

where p^* = familywise Type I error rate and n = number of pairwise comparisons.

- Continue as above by rejecting the next smallest p-value if

$$p < \frac{p*}{n-2}$$

where $p*$ = familywise Type I error rate and n = number of pairwise comparisons.

- Continue this procedure until all comparisons have been evaluated, making sure to evaluate each p-value based on the number of completed comparisons.

3.2: Evaluating Test Assumptions

INTRODUCTION

Various hypothesis tests make different assumptions about the distribution of the variable(s) being analyzed. These assumptions must be addressed when choosing a test and when interpreting the results. Parametric tests have more assumptions and tend to be more powerful than nonparametric tests (i.e., they are more likely to reject a false null hypothesis).

Below is a list of the more common test assumptions that require evaluation as well as a description of how they can be evaluated. Generally, all parametric tests assume independence of observations, homogeneity of variance, and normality. Specific parametric tests may have additional assumptions. Nonparametric tests do not assume normality and have fewer assumptions than parametric tests. Check the specific test to determine its assumptions.

INDEPENDENCE OF OBSERVATIONS

Observations are independent if the sampling of one observation does not affect the choice of the second observation. Independence of observations (i.e., absence of autocorrelation) means that multiple observations are not acted on by an outside influence. A small violation of this assumption produces a substantial effect on both the level of significance and statistical power of a test (e.g., Stevens, 2002, Scariano & Davenport, 1987).

Independence of observations is achieved by careful sampling techniques and is best evaluated by reviewing the sampling protocols used in the research. It is an important aspect of the research design and internal validity of the research study. For example, if the research protocols employ random selection of cases and random assignment of treatments to cases, then one has evidence to support independence of observations. However, if cases are influenced by each other or some common outside influence during the measurement process, independence of observations is likely not tenable.

The assumption of independence of observations means different things for different statistical procedures. For example, for between subjects designs, it means as described above, i.e., the measurement of one case is not influenced by another case or other outside influence. For within subjects (i.e., repeated measures) designs, independence of observations still refers to the measurement of one case not being influenced by another case or other outside influence, but it also recognizes the non-independence within each case of the repeated measurements.

MEASUREMENT WITHOUT ERROR

The assumption of measurement without error refers to the need for error-free measurement when using the general linear model. Measurement without error in social science research is difficult to achieve because of the reliability characteristics of most instruments that are used to measure social phenomena. Pedhazur (1997) writes "the presence of measurement errors in behavioral research is the rule rather than the exception" and "reliabilities of many measures used in the behavioral sciences are, at best, moderate" (p. 172). Unreliable measurements can create problems, especially in correlation and regression analyses. When IVs are measured with error in regression analysis, both the least squares estimators and the variance estimators are biased.

It is therefore important that researchers pay attention to the reliability characteristics of all instruments used in their research and select instruments with high reliability – e.g., .70 or higher – and confirm instrument reliability as part of their research. Whenever this is not possible, errors in measurement should be identified as a study limitation.

NORMALITY

Normality refers to the shape of a variable's distribution. The variable of interest is a continuous probability distribution modeled after the normal or Gaussian distribution, which means it is symmetrical and shaped like a bell-curve. Parametric tests assume normality (i.e., the variable or variables of interest are approximately normally distributed). There are three types of normality: univariate, bivariate, and multivariate normality.

Univariate Normality

The perfectly normal univariate distribution has standardized kurtosis and skewness statistics equal to zero. That is, the shape of the distribution is neither flat nor peaked and is symmetrical and shaped like a bell, where $M = Mo = Mdn$. However, the assumption of normality does not require a perfectly normal shape. There can be some variation. For example, the standard coefficients of kurtosis and skewness can each vary, as long as they are > -2 or and $< +2$. Also, the mean, mode, and median do not need to be equal. Research suggests that many parametric procedures – e.g., one-way ANOVA – are robust in the face of light to moderate departures from normality (e.g, Tiku, 1971). Finally, the Central Limit Theorem holds that the sampling distribution of any statistic will be normal or nearly normal if the sample size is large enough. Consequently, sample means are normally distributed as long as the sample size is sufficiently large.

> Key Point
> The assumption of normality is satisfied if the relevant distribution is approximately normal and sufficiently large.

The assumption of normality, like the assumption of independence of observations, means different things for different statistical procedures. For example, for the independent t-test, the assumption means that the dependent variable in each group must be normally distributed, while for the dependent t-test, the differences between paired measures must be normally distributed. In other procedures, normality refers to the distribution of residuals.

Univariate normality is evaluated by statistical and/or graphical methods. For example, normality can be assessed visually using the histogram in order to discern the overall shape of the distribution. The histogram in Figure 3.4 below created using Excel shows a non-symmetrical, negatively-skewed shape.

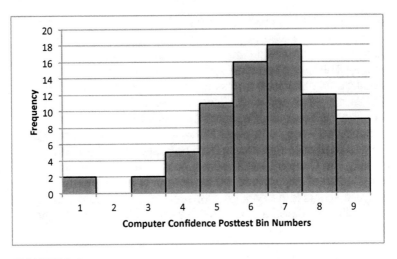

FIGURE 3.4
Histogram showing a non-symmetrical, negatively-skewed distribution.

Kurtosis measures heavy-tailedness or light-tailedness relative to the normal distribution. A heavy-tailed distribution has more values in the tails (away from the center of the distribution) than the normal distribution. A light-tailed distribution has more values in the center (away from the tails of the distribution) than the normal distribution. The ratio of kurtosis to its standard error is used as a test of normality. If this ratio is < –2 or > +2, normality is not tenable. (Note: some researchers use a more stringent range of +1 to –1 as a standard for normality.)

The standard coefficient of kurtosis for the computer confidence posttest data displayed in the above histogram is 2.66, indicating a non-normal distribution.

If the data are not distributed symmetrically, the distribution is said to be skewed. One way of determining skewness is by looking at histogram. Another way of determining skewness is by comparing the values of the mean, median and mode. If the three are equal, then the data are symmetrical. The ratio of skewness to its standard error is used as a test of normality. If this ratio is < –2 or > +2, normality is not tenable. (Note: some researchers use a more stringent range of +1 to –1 as a standard for normality.)

The standard coefficient of skewness for the computer confidence posttest data displayed in the above histogram is -3.52, indicating a non-normal, negatively-skewed distribution.

Standard errors are directly related to sample size. Consequently, very large samples may fail the standards for standardized coefficients of kurtosis and skewness even though the variables may not differ enough from normality to make a real difference. On the other hand, one may conclude that very small samples are normally distributed despite substantial deviations from normality. Consequently, one should take sample size into consideration when assessing kurtosis and skewness.

The Kolmogorov-Smirnov (K-S) test (Chakravarti, Laha, & Roy, 1967) is an inferential test tool available to evaluate normality. This test has several important limitations:

- It only applies to continuous distributions.

- It tends to be more sensitive near the center of the distribution than it is at the tails.

- It is a conservative test (i.e., there is an increased likelihood of a finding of non-normality, especially for very large sample sizes when the statistical power of the test is high).

The K-S test is defined by:

H_0: The data follow a specified distribution (typically, this is specified as the normal distribution).

H_a: The data do not follow the specified distribution.

It is a good practice not to rely on a single tool to evaluate the normality assumption of a parametric test. Additionally, one will want to estimate the severity of the issue and determine if the parametric test is sufficiently robust to the violation. If not, one may want to conduct an alternative test that does not assume normality.

> **Key Point**
> There is no clear consensus regarding normality and how much deviation from normality is a problem for specific parametric tests (i.e., each test's robustness to violations of normality).

Bivariate Normality

Bivariate normality indicates that scores on one variable are normally distributed for each value of the other variable, and vice versa. Univariate normality of both variables does not guarantee bivariate normality, but is a necessary requirement for bivariate normality. A circular or symmetric elliptical pattern in a scatterplot with a heavier concentration of points in the middle is evidence of a bivariate normal distribution.

Figure 3.5 displays a scatterplot of locus of control and trait anxiety from the Computer Anxiety.xlsx file. The approximately elliptical pattern suggests bivariate normality is tenable. However, both variables need to be evaluated for univariate normality before a bivariate normality conclusion is reached.

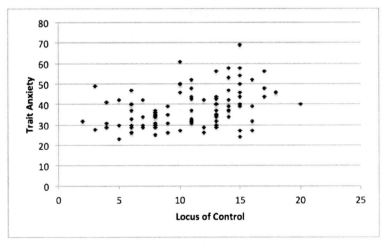

FIGURE 3.5
Scatterplot showing bivariate normality.

Figure 3.6 is a scatterplot of classroom social community and classroom learning community from the Motivation.xlsx file. The non-elliptical pattern suggests bivariate normality is not tenable.

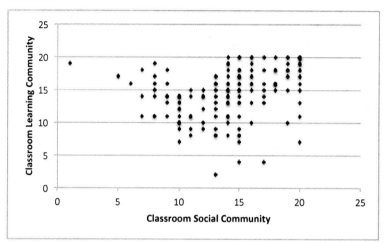

FIGURE 3.6
Scatterplot showing bivariate normality is not tenable.

ABSENCE OF EXTREME OUTLIERS

Outliers are anomalous observations that have extreme values with respect to a single variable. Chatterjee and Hadi (1988) define an outlier as an observation with a large residual. Reasons for outliers vary from data collection or data entry errors to valid but unusual measurements. Other possibilities include using a case outside the target population (Glenberg, 1996) or including a research subject who does not understand or is inattentive to a self-report survey (Cohen, 2001).

It is common to define extreme univariate outliers as cases that are more than three standard deviations above the mean of the variable or less than three standard deviations from the mean. Normal distributions do not include extreme outliers. OLS procedures used in regression analysis, in particular, are strongly influenced by outliers, especially extreme outliers. This means that a single extreme observation can have an excessive influence on the regression solution and make the results very misleading.

Univariate outliers can be identified by converting raw scores to standardized scores (i.e., z-scores with $M = 0$ and $SD = 1$). Z-scores < −3 and > +3 are extreme outliers. For example, take the variable amotivation from the Motivation.xlsx file. Converting raw scores (A column) to z-scores (B column) and then sorting z-scores in descending order results in the identification of six high extreme outliers as shown in Figure 3.7 below.

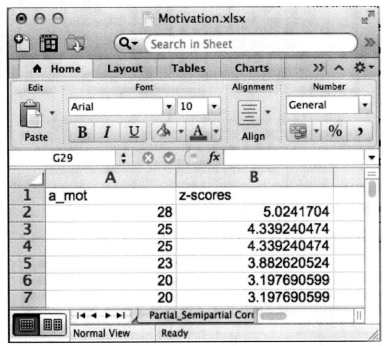

FIGURE 3.7

Identifying extreme outlier based on z-scores.

Procedures

1. Convert raw scores to z-scores using either of the the following following two formulas:

=STANDARDIZE(X,mean,standard_deviation)

=(X−mean)/standard_deviation

(Note: substitute the mean and standard deviation of the raw scores in these formulas.)

2. Sort the resultant z-scores. Z-scores < −3 and > +3 are extreme outliers as are their equivalent raw scores.

Key Point
Outliers represent a very serious threat to normality. Extreme scores can have dramatic effects on the accuracy of correlations and regressions.

Examining standard residuals and studentized residuals is another method of detecting outliers. In a normal distribution one expects about 5% of values to be < −2 or > +2 and less than 1% to be < −3 or > +3. Residuals in this 1% category are problematic.

LINEARITY

The assumption of linearity is that there is an approximate straight line relationship between two continuous variables. That is, the amount of change, or rate of change, between scores on two variables are constant for the entire range of scores for the variables. It is a common assumption in many bivariate and multivariate tests, such as correlation and regression analysis, because solutions are based on the general linear model (GLM). If a relationship is nonlinear, the statistics that assume it is linear will either underestimate the strength of the relationship or fail to detect the existence of a relationship.

There are relationships that are best characterized as curvilinear rather than linear. For example, the relationship between learning and time is not linear. Learning a new subject shows rapid gains at first but then the pace slows down over time. This is often referred to as the learning curve.

Pedhazur (1997) recommends two ways of detecting nonlinearity. The first is the use of theory or prior research. However, this method has drawbacks in so far as other researchers may not have adequately evaluated the assumption of linearity.

A second method is the use of graphical methods that include the examination of residual plots and scatterplots, often overlaid with a trend line. However, this strategy is sometimes difficult to interpret. Outliers may fool the observer into believing a linear model may not fit. Alternatively, true changes in slope are often difficult to discern from only a scatter of data. The key is to determine central patterns without being strongly influenced by outliers. Figure 3.8 below, including a linear trendline, depicts a linear relationship between powerlessness and normlessness since the amount of change between values on the two variables are close to constant for the entire range of scores for the variables. That is, the plot resembles a cigar-shaped band with no curves, suggesting linearity.

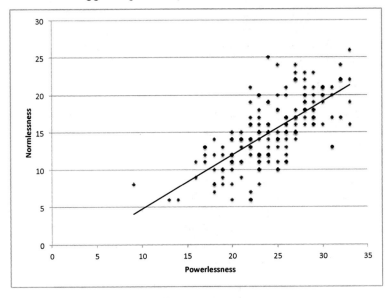

FIGURE 3.8
Scatterplot showing a linear relationship.

Figure 3.9 below is a scatterplot of two hypothetical variables with a curvilinear component. There is a distinct bend in the pattern of dots where the x-axis variable = 34.

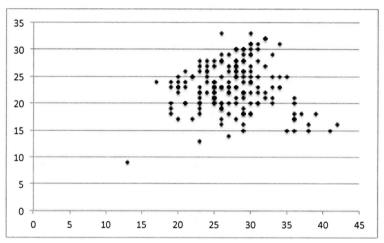

FIGURE 3.9
Scatterplot showing a curvilinear relationship.

A less stringent assumption is one of monotonicity. A monotonic relationship is one where the value of one variable increases as the value of the other variable increases or the value of one variable increases as the value of the other variable decreases, but not necessarily in a linear fashion. Consequently, a monotonic relationship can be either linear or curvilinear.

HOMOGENEITY OF VARIANCE

Homogeneity of variance is the univariate version of the bivariate assumption of homoscedasticity and the multivariate assumption of homogeneity of variance-covariance matrices. Homogeneity of variance (or error variance) is the assumption that two or more groups have equal or similar variances. The assumption is that the variability in the DV is expected to be about the same at all levels of the IV. In other words, it is assumed that equal variances of the DV exist across levels of the IVs.

This is a common assumption for many univariate parametric tests such as the independent *t*-test (but not the dependent *t*-test) and the ANOVA with one DV and one or more IVs. This assumption legitimizes the use of a single variance estimate from the aggregate of the sum of squares from groups and the associated pooled degrees of freedom (Glass & Hopkins, 1996, p. 293).

One can get a feel for whether this assumption is tenable by comparing the standard deviations or variances of each group. However, this is not a reliable procedure. The problem one will encounter is the determination of how much the variances can differ before the assumption is no longer tenable.

The *F*-test of Equality of Variance, which tests the null hypothesis that the variance of the DV is equal across groups determined by the IV, is robust in the face of departures from normality. If the data satisfy the assumption of homogeneity of variance, the significance level of the *F*-test should not be significant. If the significance level equals .05 or lower, the results are significant and one has evidence to reject the null hypothesis. Under these circumstances one can conclude that the assumption of homogeneity of variance is not tenable.

HOMOSCEDASTICITY

In univariate analyses, such as one-way analysis of variance (ANOVA), homoscedasticity goes by the name homogeneity of variance. In this context, it is assumed that equal variances of one variable exist across levels of other variables. In bivariate analyses, homoscedasticity (also spelled homoskedasticity) means all pairwise combinations of variables have equal variances and are normally distributed. In other words, homoscedasticity refers to the assumption that one variable exhibits similar amounts of variance across the range of values for a second variable. The assumption of homoscedasticity in regression analysis requires residuals of each level of predictor variable(s) to have approximately equal variances. In other words, the variance of one variable is the same for all values of a second variable.

Homoscedasticity is evaluated for pairs of variables with scatterplots. Figure 3.10 below is an example of a scatterplot that displays a relationship where homoscedasticity is not tenable (i.e., the relationship reflects heteroscedasticity). This is because classroom learning community scores do not exhibit a similar range of values for classroom social community across its entire range of values.

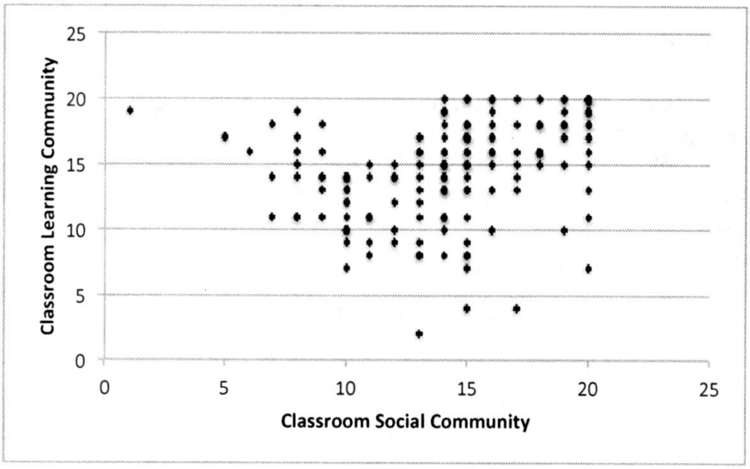

FIGURE 3.10
Scatterplot showing a heteroscedastic relationship.

In regression analysis this assumption can be evaluated by creating a residuals scatterplot of the standardized residuals against the standardized predicted values. If homoscedasticity is satisfied, residuals should vary randomly around zero and the spread of the residuals should be about the same throughout the plot, with no systematic patterns.

SPHERICITY

Sphericity is an assumption of within subjects ANOVA. In a repeated measures design, the univariate ANOVA tables will not be interpreted properly unless the variance/covariance matrix of the DVs is circular in form. In other words, the variance of the difference between all pairs of means is constant across all combinations of related groups. The sphericity assumption is always met for designs with only two levels of a repeated measures factor but must be evaluated for designs with three or more levels.

ABSENCE OF RESTRICTED RANGE

Absence of restricted range is an assumption of correlation and regression analysis. It means that the data range is not truncated in any variable). Range restriction occurs when one or or more variables are restricted in their values. For example, suppose one wants to know the strength of relationship between Graduate Record Examination (GRE) scores and graduate grade point average (GPA). The result will likely be an artificially low correlation coefficient due to restriction of range in GRE – only higher scoring students are accepted for graduate enrollment – and restriction of range in GPA – graduate students with low GPA will drop out of the graduate program so there will be a disproportionate number of low GPA students (if any) in the sample.

DEALING WITH DEVIATIONS

Each inferential test has a set of assumptions and requirements that need to be met in order for the test to produce valid results. Parametric tests, as a rule, possess more assumptions (most notably the assumption of normality) than do nonparametric tests. However, each test has varying degrees of robustness to violations of assumptions that need to be addressed for the specific test in question and the seriousness of the violation.

Independence of Observations

This is a sampling issue and is controlled during measurement. Generally, implementation of a survey questionnaire minimizes possibilities of dependence among the observations provided the researcher implements controls to prevent respondents from discussing their responses prior to completing the survey.

Homogeneity of Variance

One can use a test that is robust to violations of equal variances if the assumption of homogeneity of variance is not supported. For the independent t-test, if Levene's test for equality of variances is statistically significant, indicating unequal variances, one can correct for this violation by not using the pooled estimate for the error term for the t-statistic and making adjustments to the degrees of freedom. Excel output for the independent t-test includes statistics for both "equal variances assumed" and "equal variances not assumed."

Normality

When data is not normally distributed, the cause for non-normality should be determined and appropriate remedial actions should be taken as appropriate. Typically non-normality will be first detected by examining a histogram and obtaining significant results from a Kolmogorov-Smirnov test. Non-normality is frequently the result of severe skewness, severe kurtosis, and/or the presence of outliers, especially extreme outliers.

One should ensure that a non-normal distribution has not occurred due to a data coding or entry error. If such errors are not detected, a decision must be made in terms of how to deal with a non-normal distribution. Several options are available (Tabachnick & Fidell, 2007). Whatever option is selected, the researcher must report the procedure used.

- Option 1 – use an equivalent nonparametric statistical test since such tests do not assume normality. However, these tests are less powerful than parametric tests.

- Option 2 – delete the extreme outliers that create the problem. However, outliers should only be deleted as a last resort and then only if they are found to be errors that cannot be corrected. The major limitation associated with this option is that it involves removing participants from the research. Outliers that should not be in the dataset, e.g., typos and invalid responses, should be removed. Outliers as the result of rare but legitimate reasons should remain in the dataset.

- Option 3 – replace the extreme score(s) with more normal score(s); e.g., replace extreme outliers with mild outliers. Once again, the major limitation associated with this option is that it involves altering scores generated by research participants.

> **Key Point**
> Always report and justify removal or modification of cases.

- Option 4 – analyze data with and without extreme score(s) and compare results. Many of the parametric statistical tests are considered to be robust to violations of normality. If results from the two analyses are similar, the extreme scores are retained. However if the two outputs differ, another option should be considered, e.g., use an equivalent nonparametric test.

- Option 5 – increase sample size and/or re-sample using a more accurate instrument. Distributions tend to more closely reflect the characteristics of a normal distribution as the sample size increases. Additionally, instruments with poor resolution can make otherwise continuous data appear discrete and not normal.

- Option 6 – transform data. Data transformation is a process designed to change the shape of a distribution so that it more closely approximates a normal curve. A new variable is created by altering the original scores in a consistent manner. After data transformation is conducted on a variable, the distribution is reexamined to determine how well it approximates a normal distribution. Although transformed variables may satisfy the assumption of normality of distribution, they tend to complicate the interpretation of findings as scores no longer convey the same meaning as the original values. Tabachnick and Fidell (2007) suggest the guidelines shown in Table 3.2 below for transforming variables:

TABLE 3.2
Data transformation guidelines.

Data Transformations		
Problem	*Severity*	*Transformation*
Positive skew	Moderate	Square root
	Substantial	Logarithm
	Severe	Inverse
Negative skew	Moderate	Square root*
	Substantial	Logarithm*
	Severe	Inverse*

Note: *reflect first. To reflect a variable: (a) find the largest score in the distribution, (b) add one to it to form a constant that is larger than any score in distribution, (c) create a new variable by subtracting each score from this constant.

Linearity

When a relationship is not linear, one can transform one or both variables to achieve a linear relationship. Four common transformations to induce linearity are the square root transformation, the logarithmic transformation, the inverse transformation, and the square transformation. These transformations produce a new variable that is mathematically equivalent to the original variable, but expressed in different measurement units; i.e. logarithmic units instead of decimal units.

Homoscedasticity

If homoscedasticity is not tenable, one can transform the variables and test again for homoscedasticity. The three most common transformations used are the logarithmic transformation, the square root transformation, and the inverse transformation.

Sphericity

Violations of sphericity can be adjusted based on corrections developed by Greenhouse and Geisser and Huynh and Feldt. They adjust the degrees of freedom in order to produce a more accurate p-value based on the amount of departure from the sphericity assumption. This is accomplished by way of the epsilon (ε) statistic. When $\varepsilon = 1$ there is no violation of sphericity and no correction is required. However, the departure from sphericity becomes more pronounced the more epsilon drops in value from 1. For less severe departures from sphericity ($\varepsilon > .75$), the Huynh-Feldt ε is used, while Greenhouse-Geisser ε is used for more severe violations of the sphericity assumption.

3.3: Chapter 3 Review

The answer key is at the end of this section.

1. If one rejects the null hypothesis, one is proving that...

    A. the research hypothesis is true

    B. the null hypothesis is false

    C. the IV has an impact on the DV

    D. none of the above

2. What is a variable called that is presumed to cause a change in another variable?

    A. Dependent variable

    B. Independent variable

    C. Criterion variable

    D. Categorical variable

3. In hypothesis testing, one...

    A. attempts to prove the research hypothesis

    B. attempts to prove the null hypothesis

    C. attempts to obtain evidence to reject the null hypothesis

    D. attempts to obtain evidence to accept the research hypothesis

4. What does a significance level of .01 mean?

    A. If the null hypothesis is true, one will reject it 1% of the time

    B. If the null hypothesis is true, one will not reject it 1% of the time

    C. If the null hypothesis is false, one will reject it 1% of the time

    D. If the null hypothesis is false, one will not reject it 1% of the time

5. For a given hypothesis test, the *p*-value of the test statistic equals 0.04. This implies a 0.04 probability of making a...

A. Type I error

B. Type II error

C. correct decision in rejecting the null hypothesis

D. choices B and C are correct

6. What confidence interval do social science researchers tend to use in their hypothesis testing?

A. 5%

B. 90%

C. 95%

D. 10%

7. In a population with 50 males and 40 females, what is the probability of randomly selecting a female?

A. $p(F) = 0.56$

B. $p(F) = 0.44$

C. $p(F) = 0.40$

D. $p(F) = 0.35$

8. If there is a 40% chance of rain, what are the odds for rain?

A. .40

B. .54

C. .67

D. .73

9. What is a Type I error?

A. The probability of deciding that a significant effect is not present when it is present

B. The probability of deciding that a significant effect is present when it is not present

C. The probability that a true null hypothesis (H_0) is not rejected

D. The probability that a false H_0 is rejected

10. What is a Type II error?

    A. The probability that a true null hypothesis (H_0) is not rejected

    B. The probability of deciding that a significant effect is present when it is not present

    C. The probability of deciding that a significant effect is not present when it is present

    D. The probability that a false H_0 is rejected

11. What is a confidence level?

    A. The probability of deciding that a significant effect is not present when it is present

    B. The probability of deciding that a significant effect is present when it is not present

    C. The probability that a true null hypothesis (H_0) is not rejected

    D. The probability that a false H_0 is rejected

12. What is statistical power?

    A. The probability of deciding that a significant effect is not present when it is present

    B. The probability of deciding that a significant effect is present when it is not present

    C. The probability that a true null hypothesis (H_0) is not rejected

    D. The probability that a false H_0 is rejected

13. What is the cutoff called that a researcher uses to decide whether or not to reject the null hypothesis?

    A. Alpha

    B. Significance level

    C. Confidence level

    D. choices A and B are correct

14. You are researching the following research question: Is sense of classroom community higher in on-campus rather than online courses? What kind of test would you use?

   A. Two-tailed test

   B. One-tailed test

   C. Either choice A or B

   D. None of the above

15. What is the best graphical technique to use in order to evaluate linearity?

   A. Line chart

   B. Histogram

   C. Column chart

   D. Scatterplot

16. What is the best graphical technique to use in order to evaluate homoscedasticity?

   A. Line chart

   B. Histogram

   C. Scatterplot

   D. Bar chart

17. Which symbol represents a population parameter?

   A. Σ

   B. M

   C. s^2

   D. μ

18. What measure does NOT increase statistical power?

   A. Increase sample size

   B. Increase significance level

   C. Use a two-tailed rather than one-tailed test

   D. Use a parametric rather than non-parametric test

19. What value is at the center of a confidence interval?

    A. Point estimate

    B. Population parameter

    C. Margin of error

    D. Standard error

20. The 95% confidence interval for μ, calculated from sample data, produces an interval estimate that ranges from 115 to 131. What does this NOT suggest?

    A. The margin of error is 8

    B. The sample mean is 123

    C. There is a 95% chance that the population mean ranges between 115 and 131

    D. One should reject the null hypothesis for any value between 115 and 131

21. When will a confidence interval widen?

    A. The confidence level is increased from 95% to 99%

    B. Sample standard deviation is higher

    C. Sample size is decreased

    D. All of the above

22. Effect size is used to determine...

    A. Statistical significance

    B. Practical significance

    C. Reliability

    D. Validity

23. If H_0 is false and you fail to reject it, you make...

    A. A Type I error

    B. A Type II error

    C. Both a Type I and Type II error

    D. No error

24. If H_0 is true and you reject it, you make a...

    A. Type I error

    B. Type II error

    C. Both a Type I and Type II error

    D. No error

25. If H_0 is true and you fail to reject it, you make a...

    A. Type I error

    B. Type II error

    C. Both a Type I and Type II error

    D. No error

26. In which situation is the Central Limit Theorem not applicable?

    A. The sample is small and the population is not normal.

    B. The sample is large and the population is not normal.

    C. The sample is small and the population is normal.

    D. The sample is large and the population is normal.

27. Changing a 95% confidence interval to a 99% confidence interval will result in what change to the interval?

    A. The confidence interval becomes narrower.

    B. The confidence interval becomes wider.

    C. There is no change to the confidence interval.

Chapter 3 Answers

1D, 2B, 3C, 4A, 5A, 6C, 7B, 8C, 9B, 10C, 11C, 12D, 13D, 14B, 15D, 16C, 17D, 18C, 19C, 20D, 21D, 22D, 23B, 24A, 25D, 26A, 27B

Chapter 4: Hypothesis Tests

Hypothesis tests provide evidence regarding whether or not observed data are sufficiently different from the null hypothesis to justify rejecting it at a predetermined probability level, p-level, usually set at .05 for social science research. This chapter describes common inferential test procedures that can be conducting using Microsoft Excel.

Chapter 4 Learning Objectives

• Identify the most appropriate hypothesis test to evaluate a null hypothesis.

• Conduct univariate and bivariate hypothesis tests given a null hypothesis to evaluate, a dataset, and Microsoft Excel.

• Conduct internal consistency reliability analysis of a measurement instrument using Microsoft Excel.

• Draw appropriate conclusions from data analyses.

• Identify what to report for each statistical procedure.

4.1: Hypothesis Test Overview

The following outline will assist one in identifying an appropriate inferential test to conduct to analyze one's data. Keep in mind that research questions flow from the problem statement and specify relations or differences between identified constructs that the research addresses. Also, the research question implies a research hypothesis, research design, and inferential test.

The words "difference" or "different" can sometimes appear in research questions that imply tests other than hypothesis of group difference tests, e.g., a goodness of fit research question might be phrased in terms of whether a given distribution is different from a theoretical distribution. Conversely, a hypothesis of group difference research question may not contain the words "difference" or "different" but, nonetheless, imply a difference test, e.g., did the treatment group perform better on the DV than the control group?

Goodness-of-Fit Tests

One-Sample t-Test – parametric, compares a calculated sample mean to a known population mean or a previously reported value, interval or ratio DV.

Binomial Test – nonparametric, compares the proportion in one of two categories to a hypothesized test proportion.

Chi-Square (χ^2) Goodness-of-Fit Test – nonparametric, determines if a sample of data for one categorical variable comes from a population with a specific distribution, nominal data.

Kolmogorov-Smirnov Test – nonparametric, determines if a sample of continuous data comes from a population with a normal distribution.

Comparing Two Independent Samples

F-Test of Equality of Variance – parametric, compares the variance (σ^2) of two groups, interval or ratio DV.

Independent t-Test – parametric, compares two independent samples, interval or ratio DV.

Mann-Whitney U Test – nonparametric, compares two independent samples, ordinal DV.

Pearson Chi-Square (χ^2) Contingency Table Analysis – nonparametric, determines if frequencies produced by cross-classifying observations simultaneously across two categorical variables are independent, nominal data.

Comparing Multiple Independent Samples

One-Way Between Subjects ANOVA – parametric, compares three or more independent samples, interval or ratio DV.

Kruskal-Wallis H Test – nonparametric, compares multiple independent samples, ordinal DV.

Comparing Two Dependent Samples

Dependent t-Test – parametric, compares two dependent samples, interval or ratio DV.

Wilcoxon Matched-Pair Signed Ranks Test – nonparametric, compares two dependent samples, ordinal DV.

Related Samples Sign Test – nonparametric; compares two dependent samples, nominal or ordinal DV.

McNemar Test – nonparametric, compares two dependent samples, dichotomous DV.

Comparing Multiple Dependent Samples

One-Way Within Subjects ANOVA – parametric, compares three or more dependent samples, interval or ratio DV.

Friedman Test – nonparametric, compares three or more dependent samples, ordinal DV.

Correlations

Pearson Product-Moment Correlation Test – parametric, determines symmetric linear relationship between two variables, interval or ratio.

Partial Correlation – parametric, determines the relationship between two interval/ratio variables while holding the third interval/ratio variable constant for both variables.

Semipartial correlation – parametric, determines the relationship between two interval/ratio variables while holding the third interval/ratio variable constant for just one of the two variables.

Reliability Analysis

Split-Half Internal Consistency Reliability Analysis – parametric, splits a scale into two parts and examines the correlation between the two parts.

Cronbach's Alpha Internal Consistency Reliability Analysis – parametric, determines average inter-item correlation.

Spearman Rank Order Correlation Test (Spearman rho) – nonparametric, determines monotonic symmetric relationship between two ranked variables.

Phi (Φ) – nonparametric, determines symmetric relationship between two nominal variables, used for 2x2 tables, chi-square based.

Cramér's V – nonparametric, determines symmetric relationship between two nominal variables, used for tables larger than 2x2, chi-square based.

Linear Regression

Bivariate Regression – parametric, predicts one interval/ratio DV using one interval/ratio IV.

HYPOTHESIS TEST PROCEDURES

Each hypothesis test listed above has its own section in this chapter divided into the following subsections.

Test Identification

This subsection identifies and describes the hypothesis test, provides relevant computational formulas, and identifies supplementary information such as degrees of freedom and appropriate effect size measures.

Key Assumptions and Requirements

This subsection lists and describes each major test assumption and test requirement. Procedures used to evaluate assumptions are presented in Chapter 3.

Excel Functions Used

The Excel functions used in the test procedures are listed and described in this subsection to include identification of arguments and the statistic generated by the function.

Test Procedures

The procedures described in this subsection consists of a step-by-step approach of analyzing authentic data by creating formulas using Excel's mathematical and logical operators and functions.

Workbooks with authentic research data used in the examples presented in this book and other learning resources are available online at *http://www.watertreepress.com/stats*.

Automated Procedures

Once the user learns the procedure, he or she may want to automate the process. However, automation has its advantages and disadvantages. The biggest advantage is that it is a time save. The biggest disadvantage is that the user loses a measure of flexibility, such as changing significance levels and switching from a two-tailed to a one-tailed test.

There are two Excel add-in programs that automate statistical tasks. Microsoft Excel for Windows 2010 and Microsoft Excel for Windows 2013 includes an Analysis ToolPak add-in that must be activated to use. To activate, go to the Excel Options menu, click Add-Ins and select Manage: Add-Ins. In the Add-Ins dialog select Analysis ToolPak and click OK. The Data Analysis icon is now available under the Excel Data tab that provides a variety of analysis tools to automate many statistical procedures. This add-in is not available for Microsoft® Excel® for Mac 2011. However StatPlus LE is available as a free download at http://www.analystsoft.com/en/products/statplus/ for

Macintosh and Windows users that automates many of the procedures described in this book.

StatPlus, once downloaded and installed, works as a separate application in parallel with Microsoft Excel. It provides a graphic user interface in which the desired statistical procedure and data in an active Excel workbook are identified. The software then executes the procedure and displays all output in the Excel workbook.

Reporting Test Results

Once data has been analyzed and results obtained, one will want to share results. How one accomplishes this task is greatly influenced by one's audience. The final topic identifies what and how to report hypothesis test results in the results section of a research report or article intended for audiences who are interested in details. Other audiences may be more interested in an overview of the results.

The format used in this book is based on the Style Manual of the American Psychological Association. This style manual is widely used across many social science disciplines. One should check with one's organization or publisher to obtain a style guide if one intends to report research findings in writing or submit findings for publication.

4.2: Goodness-of-Fit Tests

ONE-SAMPLE *T*-TEST

The One-Sample *t*-Test is a parametric procedure that compares a calculated sample mean to a known population mean or a previously reported value in order to determine if the difference is statistically significant.

One can compute the *t*-value using the following formula:

$$t = \frac{(\overline{X} - X_0)}{\dfrac{s_X}{\sqrt{N}}}$$

where x̄ is the mean of the DV, X_0 is the comparison value, s_X is the standard deviation of the DV, and *N* is the sample size.

Degrees of freedom. The degrees of freedom for this test are $N - 1$.

Effect size. Cohen's *d* is used to report effect size using the following equation (Green & Salkind, 2008):

$$d = \frac{t}{\sqrt{N}}$$

where $t = $ *t*-statistic reported by Excel and $N = $ sample size. By convention, Cohen's *d* values are interpreted as follows:

Small effect size = .20
Medium effect size = .50
Large effect size = .80

Alternatively, *r* can be used as a measure of effect size using the following equation (Rosenthal, 1991; Rosnow & Rosenthal, 2005):

$$r = \sqrt{\frac{t^2}{t^2 + df}}$$

where

Small effect size = .10
Medium effect size = .30
Large effect size = .50

Key Assumptions & Requirements

Random selection of samples (probability samples) to allow for generalization of results to a target population.

Variables. One continuous DV measured on the interval or ratio scale.

Independence of observations. Independence of observations means that observations (i.e., measurements) are not acted on by an outside influence common to two or more measurements, e.g., other research participants or previous measurements. Evaluation of this assumption is a procedural issue involving research design, sampling, and measurement. and consists more of a procedural review of the research than it is of statistical analysis. Violation of the independence assumption adversely affects probability statements leading to inaccurate *p*-values and reduced statistical power (Scariano & Davenport, 1987).

Normality. One DV, normally distributed. The one sample *t*-test is robust to minor violations of the assumption of normally distributed data with sample sizes > 50 (Diekhoff, 1992).

Excel Functions Used

ABS(number). Returns the absolute value of the specified number.

AVERAGE(number1,number2,...). Returns the arithmetic mean, where numbers represent the range of numbers.

COUNT(value1,value2,...). Counts the numbers in the range of numbers.

SQRT(number). Returns the square root of a number.

STDEV.S(number1,number2,...). Returns the unbiased estimate of population standard deviation, where numbers represent the range of numbers.

T.DIST.2T(x,deg_freedom). Returns the 2-tailed *t*-distribution probability, where x is the value to be evaluated and deg_freedom is a number representing the degrees of freedom.

One-Sample t-Test Procedures

Research question and null hypothesis:

Is there a difference in the mean sense of classroom community score among university students enrolled in fully online programs and the norm of 30, $\mu \neq 30$?

Note: there is no IV and the DV is classroom community score.

H_0: There is no difference in the mean sense of classroom community score of university students enrolled in fully online programs and the norm of 30, $\mu = 30$.

Task: Use the Excel file Motivation.xlsx located at http://www.watertreepress.com/stats if you want to follow along with the analysis. The Data tab contains the data and the One-Sample t-Test tab contains the One-Sample t-Test analysis described below.

1. Open the *Motivation.xlsx file using Excel.*

2. Copy variable c_community (sense of classroom community) from the Excel workbook Data tab to column A on an empty sheet. Copy all 169 cases.

	A	B
1	c_community	
2	23	
3	22	
4	23	
5	23	

3. Enter the labels N, M, SD, Test value, t, DF, p-level (2-tailed), Mean difference, Cohen's d) in cells B1:B9. Enter formulas =COUNT(A2:A170), =AVERAGE(A2:A170), =STDEV.S(A2:A170), 30, =(C2-C4)/(C3/SQRT(C1)), =C1-1, =T.DIST.2T(ABS(C5,C6), =C2-C4, =C5/SQRT(C1) in cells C1:C9.

	B	C
1	N	=COUNT(A2:A170)
2	M	=AVERAGE(A2:A170)
3	SD	=STDEV.S(A2:A170)
4	Test value	30
5	t	=(C2-C4)/(C3/SQRT(C1))
6	DF	=C1-1
7	p-level (2-tailed)	=T.DIST.2T(ABS(C5),C6)
8	Mean difference	=C2-C4
9	Cohen's d	=C5/SQRT(C1)

	B	C
1	N	169
2	M	28.84023669
3	SD	6.241511565
4	Test value	30
5	t	-2.415588423
6	DF	168
7	p-level (2-tailed)	0.016782061
8	Mean difference	-1.159763314
9	Cohen's d	-0.185814494

The One-Sample t-Test compares the sample mean to test value. The mean difference is the difference between the mean and the test value. Cohen's d is a measure of effect size.

Formatted One-Sample t-Test output summarizing test results:

	B	C	D	E	F	G
11	One-Sample t-Test (Test Value = 30)					
12		t	df	p-level (2-tailed)	Mean Difference	Cohen's d
13	Classroom Community	-2.416	168	0.0168	-1.15976	-0.1858

These results show that the difference between classroom community mean and a test value of 30 is significant because the *p*-level is below the criterion of the researcher's assumed *à priori* significance level of .05.

Automated Procedures

Use the following procedures for StatPlus Pro.

1. Launch Microsoft Excel and open the Motivation.xlsx file.

2. Launch StatPlus Pro and select Statistics > Basic Statistics and Tables > One Sample T-Test from the StatPlus menu bar. Note: this procedure is not enabled in StatPlus LE.

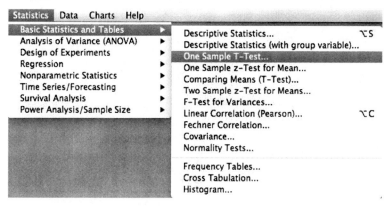

3. Enter the c_community variable in the "Variables" box and the test value of 30 in the "hypothesized value" box. Check Labels in first row.

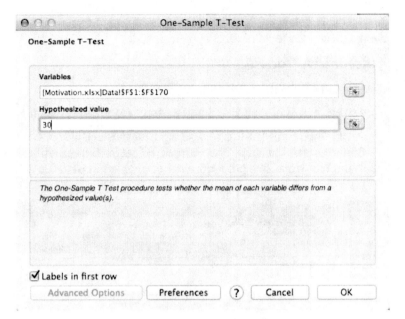

4. Click the OK button to run the procedure.

	A	B	C	D
2		**Mean**	**Mean LCL**	**Mean UCL**
3	*Variable #1 (c_community)*	28.84024	28.04616	29.63431

The Mean LCL and the Mean UCL represent the lower and upper bounds of the confidence interval of the mean based on the *t*-distribution with $N-1$ degrees of freedom. Normality is assumed.

	E	F	G	H
2	**Standard Error**	**Sample size**	**Hypothesized value**	**Difference**
3	0.48012	169	30.	-1.15976

	I	J	K
2	**Test Statistics**	**d.f.**	**p-level - 2-tailed**
3	-2.41559	168	0.01678

The results show $t(168) = -2.42$, $p = .02$.

One-Sample t-Test Reporting

As a minimum, the following information should be reported in the results section of any report: null hypothesis that is being evaluated to include test value, descriptive statistics (e.g., *M, SD, N*), statistical test used (i.e., One-Sample *t*-Test), results of evaluation of test assumptions, and test results. For example, one might report test results as follows.

A One-Sample *t*-Test was conducted to evaluate the null hypothesis that there is no difference in the mean sense of classroom community score of university students enrolled in fully online programs and the norm of 30 ($N = 169$). The test showed that the sample mean ($M = 28.84$, $SD = 6.24$) was significantly less than the test value of 30, $t(168) = -2.42$, $p = .02$, $d = .19$. Consequently, there was sufficient evidence to reject the null hypothesis.

(Note: Assumptions require evaluation and reporting before test results can be relied upon.)

BINOMIAL TEST

The Binomial Test is a nonparametric procedure that determines if the proportion of cases in one of two categories is different from a hypothesized test proportion; e.g., different from .50.

Below is the formula for the test statistic

$$\chi^2 = \sum \left(\frac{(O-E)^2}{E} \right)$$

where O = observed frequency and E = expected frequency.

Degrees of freedom. This test has ($k - c$) degrees of freedom where k = number of non-empty cells and c = number of estimated parameters.

Effect size. Green and Salkind (2008) recommend reporting an effect size as the difference between the observed and hypothesized proportions

$$Effect\_size = P_{Observed} - P_{Hypothesized}$$

Key Assumptions & Requirements

Random selection of samples (probability samples) to allow for generalization of results to a target population.

Variables. One dichotomous DV whose values are mutually exclusive and exhaustive for all cases.

Independence of observations. Independence of observations means that observations (i.e., measurements) are not acted on by an outside influence common to two or more measurements, e.g., other research participants or previous measurements.

Probability of any observation is constant across all measurements.

Sample size. A relatively large sample size ($N > 30$).

Excel Functions Used

BINOM.DIST(number_s,trials,probability_s,cumulative). Returns the binomial distribution probability, where number_s is the number of successful trials, trials is the number of independent trials, probability_s is the probability of success for each trial, and cumulative is a logical value where TRUE returns the cumulative distribution function and FALSE returns the probability density function.

COUNT(value1,value2,...). Counts the numbers in the range of numbers.

COUNTIFS(range1, criteria1, range2, criteria2,...). Counts the number of cells in a range that meet specific criteria, where range is the reference to cells with the data and criteria identifies the criteria for the data to be included in the count.

Binomial Test Procedures

Research question and null hypothesis:

Are the proportions of college students enrolled in distance online courses and traditional on-campus courses different, $P \neq .50$?

H_0: There are no differences in the proportions of college students enrolled in distance online courses and traditional on-campus courses, $P = .50$, in a sample of university students.

Alternatively, H_0: The categories of college enrollment (distance, traditional) occur with probabilities of .50 and .50.

Task: Use the Excel file Community.xlsx located at http://www.watertreepress.com/stats if you want to follow along with the analysis. The Data tab contains the data and the Binomial Test tab contains the Binomial Test analysis described below.

1. Open the *Community.xlsx* file using Excel.

2. Copy the variable mode (type course) from the Excel workbook, Data tab, and paste the variable in column A of an empty sheet. (Note: mode = 0 represents enrollment in traditional courses and mode = 1 represents enrollment in distance courses.)

	A	B
1	mode	
2	1	
3	1	
4	1	
5	1	

3. Enter the labels N, n (distance), n (traditional), Observed proportion (distance), Observed proportion (traditional), Test proportion, p-level) in cells B1:B7. Enter formulas =COUNT(A2:A118), =COUNTIFS(A2:A118,1), =COUNTIFS(A2:A118,0), =C2/C1, =C3/C1, 0.5, and =BINOM.DIST(C2,C1,0.5,FALSE) in cells C1:C7.

	B	C
1	N	=COUNT(A2:A118)
2	n (distance)	=COUNTIFS(A2:A118,1)
3	n (traditional)	=COUNTIFS(A2:A118,0)
4	Observed proportion (distance)	=C2/C1
5	Observed proportion (traditional)	=C3/C1
6	Test proportion	0.5
7	p-level	=BINOM.DIST(C2,C1,0.5,FALSE)

	B	C
1	N	117
2	n (distance)	98
3	n (traditional)	19
4	Observed proportion (distance)	0.837606838
5	Observed proportion (traditional)	0.16239316239316
6	Test proportion	0.5
7	p-level	0.00000000000002

Formatted Binomial Test output summarizing test results:

	B	C	D	E	F	G
9	Binomial Test					
10		Category	N	Observed Prop.	Test Prop.	p-level
11	Group 1	Distance	98	0.8376	0.50	0.00000000000002
12	Group 2	Traditional	19	0.1624		
13	Total		117	1.0000		

The above Excel output shows the observed proportions differed significantly from the hypothesized proportion of .50 since the significance level <= .05 (the assumed *à priori* significance level).

Binomial Test Reporting

As a minimum, the following information should be reported in the results section of any report: null hypothesis that is being evaluated, descriptive statistics (e.g., number of independent trials or sample size, observed proportions, the hypothesized probability of success for each trial or hypothesized proportions), statistical test used (i.e., binomial test test), results of evaluation of test assumptions if violations are present, and binomial test results. For example, one might report results as follows.

The Binomial Test was used to evaluate the null hypothesis that there are no differences in the proportions of college students enrolled distance online courses and traditional on-campus courses (i.e., hypothesized proportions are .50). Out of a sample (N = 117) of surveyed college students, 98 were enrolled in distance courses and 19 were enrolled in traditional courses. Observed proportions were .84 and .16, respectively.

The Binomial Test results were significant, $p < .001$. Consequently, there was sufficient evidence to reject the null hypothesis and conclude that a significantly greater proportion of college students are enrolled in distance courses in the target population. The test proportion was .50. Effect size as a measure of the difference between observed and hypothesized proportions was .34.

CHI-SQUARE (X^2) GOODNESS-OF-FIT TEST

The χ^2 Goodness-of-Fit Test (also known as Pearson's χ^2 Goodness-of-Fit Test) is a nonparametric procedure that determines if a sample of data for one categorical variable comes from a population with a specific distribution (Snedecor & Cochran, 1989). The researcher compares observed values with expected values or outcomes. In other words, the Chi-Square Goodness-of-Fit Test is specifically designed for discrete distributions. It can be applied to continuous distributions only by binning them, that is, transforming them into discrete distributions. If there are only two categories, one should consider using the binomial test.

Below is the formula for the test statistic:

$$\chi^2 = \sum \left(\frac{(O-E)^2}{E} \right)$$

where O = observed frequency and E = expected frequency.

Degrees of freedom. This test has $k - 1$ degrees of freedom where k = number of levels of the categorical variable.

Effect size.

$$Effect\_size = \frac{\chi^2}{N(Categories - 1)}$$

where χ^2 is the chi-square statistic and N = total sample size across all categories.

Key Assumptions & Requirements

Random selection of samples (probability samples) to allow for generalization of results to a target population.

Variables. One categorical variable with two or more categories where categories are reported in raw frequencies. Values/categories of the variable must be mutually exclusive and exhaustive.

Independence of observations. Independence of observations means that observations (i.e., measurements) are not acted on by an outside influence common to two or more measurements, e.g., other research participants or previous measurements.

Sample size. Observed frequencies must be sufficiently large ($N > 30$). Applying chi-square to smaller samples results in a higher Type II error rates. No more than 20% of expected frequencies are less than 5 (no expected frequency is equal to 1 or less).

Excel Functions Used

CHISQ.TEST(actual-range,expected_range). Returns the chi-square distribution probability, where actual-range is the data consisting of actual observations and expected_range is the data consisting of expected frequencies.

COUNT(value1,value2,...). Counts the numbers in the range of numbers.

COUNTA(value1,value2,...). Counts the cells with non-empty values in the range of values.

POWER(number,power). Raises a number to the specified power, e.g., 2 = squared.

Chi-Square Goodness-of-Fit Test Procedures

Research question and null hypothesis:

Is there a difference in the ethnicity of online college students?

Note: ethnicity is measured as frequency counts across two categories (white, other).

H_0: There is no difference in the ethnicity of online college students (i.e., categories are equal).

Task: Use the Excel file Motivation.xlsx located at http:// www.watertreepress.com/stats if you want to follow along with the analysis. The Data tab contains the data and the Chi-Square Goodness-of-Fit Test tab contains the Chi-Square Goodness-of-Fit Test analysis described below.

1. Open the Motivation.xlsx file using Excel.

2. Copy the variable ethnicity from the Excel workbook, Data tab, and paste the variable in column A of an empty sheet.

	A	B
1	ethnicity	
2	2	
3	2	
4	2	
5	2	

3. Sort ethnicity in ascending order. Note that there are only two values: 2 = other, 4 = white.

4. Enter labels Other, White, and Total in cells B2:B4 and labels Observed N, Expected N, and Residual in cells C1:E1. Enter formulas =COUNT(A1:A63), =COUNT(A64:A169), =C2+C3, =C4/2, =C4/2, =C2-D2, and =C3-D3 in cells C2:E4 in order to generate a frequencies table.

	B	C	D	E
1		Observed N	Expected N	Residual
2	Other	=COUNT(A1:A63)	=C4/2	=C2-D2
3	White	=COUNT(A64:A169)	=C4/2	=C3-D3
4	Total	=C2+C3		

5. Enter labels Chi-square, df, p-level, and Effect size in cells B6:B9. Enter formulas =(POWER(D2-C2,2)/D2)+ (POWER(C3-D3,2)/D3), =COUNT(C2:C3)-1, =CHISQ.TEST(C2:D2,C3:D3), and =C6/ C4*(COUNTA(B2:B3)-1) in cells C6:C9.

	B	C
6	Chi-square	=(POWER(D2-C2,2)/D2)+(POWER(C3-D3,2)/D3)
7	df	=COUNT(C2:C3)-1
8	p-level	=CHISQ.TEST(C2:D2,C3:D3)
9	Effect size	=C6/C4*(COUNTA(B2:B3)-1)

	B	C	D	E
1		Observed N	Expected N	Residual
2	Other	63	84.5	-21.5
3	White	106	84.5	21.5
4	Total	169		
5				
6	Chi-square	10.940828		
7	df	1		
8	p-level	0.000030		
9	Effect size	0.0647386		

6. Construct a a clustered column chart showing observed and expected frequency counts (cells B1:D3).

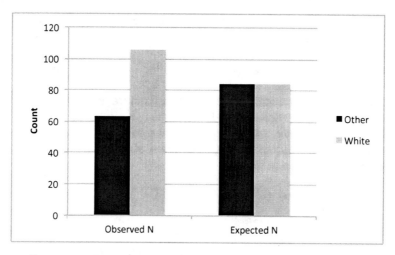

Formatted Chi-Square Goodness-of-Fit Test output summarizing test results:

	B	C
11	Chi-Square Goodness-of-Fit Test	
12		Ethnicity
13	Chi-Square	10.9408284
14	df	1
15	p-level	0.000030

The above Excel output shows the observed proportions differed significantly from the hypothesized proportion of .50 since the significance level <= .05 (the assumed *à priori* significance level).

Chi-Square Goodness-of-Fit Test Reporting

As a minimum, the following information should be reported in the results section of any report: null hypothesis that is being evaluated, descriptive statistics (e.g., observed frequency counts by category, expected frequency counts by category, N), statistical test used (i.e., χ^2 Goodness-of-Fit Test), results of evaluation of test assumptions, and χ^2 goodness-of-fit test results. For example, one might report test results as follows.

The Chi-Square Goodness-of-Fit Test was used to evaluate the null hypothesis that there is no difference in the ethnicity of online college students (i.e., the categories of other and white are equal). The sample (N = 169) reported ethnicity as follows: other = 63 (expected = 84.5) and white = 106 (expected = 84.5). The test showed a statistically significant difference in the ethnicity of online college students, $\chi^2(1, N = 169) = 10.94$, $p < .001$. Consequently, there was sufficient evidence to reject the null hypothesis. Effect size as a measure of chi-square divided by $N *$(categories − 1) was .06.

KOLMOGOROV-SMIRNOV TEST

The Kolmogorov-Smirnov Test (also known as the K-S Test) is a nonparametric procedure that determines whether a sample of data comes from a specific distribution. More specifically, it assesses the significance of the maximum divergence between two cumulative frequency curves. This test is mostly used for evaluating the assumption of univariate normality by taking the observed cumulative distribution of scores and comparing them to the theoretical cumulative distribution for a normally distributed variable. The K-S Test is sometimes criticized and avoided by statisticians because of its low power with small sample sizes and high power with large sample sizes. Consequently, it should not be relied upon as the only tool for evaluating normality.

$$D = \max \left| F(x) - S(x) \right|$$

where D = Kolmogorov-Smirnov test statistic, $F(x)$ = the normal distribution, and $S(x)$ = the cumulative frequency distribution divided by N.

If the K-S Test results are not statistically significant, there is insufficient evidence to reject the null-hypothesis that there is no difference between the tested distribution and a theoretical normal distribution. However, if the test results are statistically significant (i.e., $D >$ the critical value), the test provides no information regarding the reasons for the departure from normality. Consequently, following a significant K-S Test, the researcher should determine the reasons why the tested variable is not normally distributed by examining the shape of the distribution using a histogram, identifying the presence of extreme outliers, and examining the standard kurtosis and skewness coefficients. It is possible, for example, that the researcher will discover data collection or entry errors that, if corrected, will change test results.

Key Assumptions & Requirements

Random selection of samples (probability samples) to allow for generalization of results to a target population.

Variables. One DV.

Sample size. Use caution in interpreting results with unusually small or large sample sizes.

Excel Functions Used

ABS(number). Returns the absolute value of the specified number.

AVERAGE(number1,number2,...). Returns the arithmetic mean, where numbers represent the range of numbers.

COUNT(value1,value2,...). Counts the numbers in the range of numbers.

MAX(number1,number2,...). Returns the maximum value in a set of numbers.

NORM.DIST(x, mean,standard_dev,cumulative). returns the normal distribution for the specified mean and standard deviation.

SQRT(number). Returns the square root of a number.

STANDARDIZE(x,mean,standard_dev). Returns a normalized value from the distribution with the given mean and standard deviation.

STDEV.S(number1,number2,...). Returns the unbiased estimate of population standard deviation, where numbers represent the range of numbers.

Kolmogorov-Smirnov Test Procedures

Research question and null hypothesis:

Is sense of classroom community data normally distributed?

H_0: There is no difference between the distribution of sense of classroom community data and a normal distribution.

Alternatively, H_0: Sense of classroom community data are normally distributed.

Task: Use the Excel file Motivation.xlsx located at http://www.watertreepress.com/stats if you want to follow along with the analysis. The Data tab contains the data and the Kolmogorov-Smirnov Test tab contains the Kolmogorov-Smirnov Test analysis described below.

1. Open the *Motivation.xlsx* file using *Excel*.

2. Copy the variable c_community (classroom community) from the Excel workbook, Data tab, and paste the variable in column A of an empty sheet.

3. Sort cases in ascending order.

	A	B
1	c_community	
2	15	
3	17	
4	18	
5	19	

4. Enter label x in cell B1. Create a list, from lowest to highest, of each discrete value of c_community in cells B2:B26.

	A	B
1	c_community	x
2	15	15
3	17	17
4	18	18
5	19	19
6	19	20
7	19	21
8	19	22
9	19	23
10	20	24

5. Next, enter the label Observed Frequency in cell C1. Highlight cells C2:C26 and enter the array formula =FREQUENCY(A2:A170,B2:B26) and hit the CTRL-SHIFT-ENTER (or RETURN) buttons at the same time.

	A	B	C
1	c_community	x	Observed Frequency
2	15	15	1
3	17	17	1
4	18	18	1
5	19	19	5

6. Enter the label Cumulative Frequency in cell D1. Enter formulas =C2 and =D2+C3 in cells D2:D3. Fill Down from cell D3 through D26.

	D
1	Cumulative Frequency
2	=C2
3	=D2+C3
4	=D3+C4
5	=D4+C5

7. Enter label c_community in cell E2 and labels N, Mean,
Standard Deviation in cells F1:H1. Enter formulas
=COUNT(A2:A170), =AVERAGE(A2:A170), and
=STDEV.S(A2:A170) in cells F2:H2.

	E	F
1		N
2	c_community	=COUNT(A2:A170)

	G	H
1	Mean	Standard Deviation
2	=AVERAGE(A2:A170)	=STDEV.S(A2:A170)

	E	F	G	H
1		N	Mean	Deviation
2	c_community	169	28.840237	6.2415116

8. Enter labels S(x) and z-score in cells I1:J1 Enter
formulas =D2/$F$2 and =STANDARDIZE(B2, $G$2,$H$2) in
cells I2:J2. Fill Down from cell I2 through I26 and from J2
through J26.

	I	J
1	S(x)	z-score
2	=D2/$F$2	=STANDARDIZE(B2,$G$2,$H$2)
3	=D3/$F$2	=STANDARDIZE(B3,$G$2,$H$2)
4	=D4/$F$2	=STANDARDIZE(B4,$G$2,$H$2)
5	=D5/$F$2	=STANDARDIZE(B5,$G$2,$H$2)

	I	J
1	S(x)	z-score
2	0.00591716	-2.217449498
3	0.01183432	-1.897014299
4	0.017751479	-1.7367967
5	0.047337278	-1.5765791

S(x) is the relative frequency of a class and z-score is the

standard score that reflects the number of standard
deviations a raw score deviates from the mean.

9. Enter labels F(x) and Absolute Difference in cells K1:L1.
Enter formulas =NORM.DIST(J2,0,1,TRUE) and =ABS(K2-
J2) in cells K2:L2. Fill Down from cell K2 through K26 and
from L2 through L26.

	K	L
1	F(x)	Absolute Difference
2	=NORM.DIST(J2,0,1,TRUE)	=ABS(K2-J2)
3	=NORM.DIST(J3,0,1,TRUE)	=ABS(K3-J3)
4	=NORM.DIST(J4,0,1,TRUE)	=ABS(K4-J4)
5	=NORM.DIST(J5,0,1,TRUE)	=ABS(K5-J5)

	K	L
1	F(x)	Absolute Difference
2	0.013296195	2.230745693
3	0.028913025	1.925927325
4	0.041211531	1.778008231
5	0.057446202	1.634025303

F(x) is the normal distribution of the standardized scores and
absolute difference is the absolute value of the difference
between F(x) and the z-score.

10. Finally, enter labels D and D critical in cells E4:E5. Enter
formulas =MAX(L2:L170) and =1.36/SQRT(F2) in cells
F4:F5.

	E	F
4	D	=MAX(L2:L170)
5	D critical	=1.36/SQRT(F2)

	E	F
4	D	2.230745693
5	D critical	0.104615385

Note: For samples > 35, the critical value at the .05 significance level is approximately 1.36/SQRT(N).

Formatted Kolmogorov-Smirnov Test output summarizing test results:

	E	F	G	H
7	Kolmogorov-Smirnov Test			
8		N	Value	Critical Value
9	D	169	2.23075	0.10462

The above Excel output shows that the the results of the Kolmogorov-Smirnov Test are significant since $D >$ the critical value at the .05 significance level. Therefore, there is sufficient evidence to reject the null hypothesis and assume normality is not tenable for classroom community.

Automated Procedures

Use the following procedures for StatPlus Pro.

1. Launch Microsoft Excel and open the Motivation.xlsx file. Go to the Kolomogorov-Smirnov sheet.

2. Launch StatPlus Pro and select Statistics > Basic Statistics and Tables > Normality Tests from the StatPlus menu bar. Note: this procedure is not enabled in StatPlus LE.

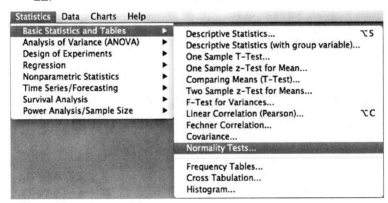

3. Enter the c_community (classroom community) variable in cells A1:A170 in the "Variables" box. Check Labels in first row.

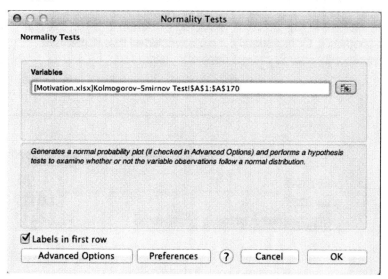

4. Click the OK button to run the procedure.

	A	B
1	**Normality Tests**	
2		
3	*Variable #1 (Var1)*	
4	*Sample size*	169
5	*Standard Deviation*	6.24151
6	*Skewness*	0.0724
7	*Alternative Skewness (Fisher's)*	0.07305

Kolmogorov-Smirnov Test Reporting

As a minimum, the following information should be reported in the results section of any report in which the Kolmogorov-Smirnov Test is used to evaluate the assumption of normality: mean, standard deviation, *N*, and statistical test results. For example, one might report results as follows.

The Kolmogorov-Smirnov Test was used to evaluate the null hypothesis that there is no difference between the distribution of sense of classroom community data ($M = 28.84$, $SD = 6.24$, $N = 169$) and a normal distribution. Test results were statistically significant at the .05 level, providing evidence to reject the null hypothesis. Consequently, it was concluded that classroom community scores are not normally distributed.

	C	D
1		
2		
3		
4	Mean	28.84024
5	Median	29.
6	Kurtosis	1.95117
7	Alternative Kurtosis (Fisher's)	-1.04417

	A	B	C	D
9		Test Statistics	p-level	Conclusion: (5%)
10	Kolmogorov-Smirnov/Lilliefor Test	0.E+0	1.	No evidence against normality
11	Shapiro-Wilk W	0.96562	0.00034	Reject Normality
12	D'Agostino Skewness	0.39925	0.68971	Accept Normality
13	D'Agostino Kurtosis	-5.86891	0.	Reject Normality
14	D'Agostino Omnibus	34.60354	0.	Reject Normality

Note: The Kolmogorov-Smirnov Test results generated by StatPlus include the Lillefors correction, which is not included in the Excel results using the operators and functions procedure provided above. The Shapiro-Wilk W Test is an alternative normality test and is often used with small sample sizes ($N < 50$). The W statistic is the ratio of the best estimator of the variance (based on the square of a linear combination of the order statistics) to the usual corrected sum of squares estimator of the variance (Shapiro & Wilk, 1965).

4.3: Comparing Two Independent Samples

F-TEST OF EQUALITY OF VARIANCE

The *F*-test of Equality of Variance is a parametric procedure that tests the null hypothesis that two groups have the same variance (σ^2) on an interval/ratio scale DV. If the *F*-Test statistic is significant at the .05 level, the researcher rejects H_0 and concludes the groups have unequal variances. This test is typically used to evaluate the assumption of homogeneity of variance, which is a precondition for *t*-tests and ANOVAs.

Degrees of freedom. *df1* is the numerator df (sample size of the group with the largest sample variance − 1) and *df2* is the denominator df (sample size of the group with the smallest variance − 1).

Key Assumptions & Requirements

Variables. DV: one continuous variable on an interval or ratio scale. IV: categorical variable with multiple categories.

Independence of observations.

Normality. The test is fairly robust to violations of normality.

Sample size. Sample size should be sufficiently large. The *F*-test test has lower statistical power when sample size is smaller, which is when unequal variance are most likely to influence Type I error.

Excel Functions Used

COUNT(value1,value2,...). Counts the numbers in the range of numbers.

F.TEST(array1,array2). Returns a 2-tailed probability, where the arrays represent ranges of numbers.

VAR.S(number1,number2,...). Returns the unbiased estimate of population variance, with numbers representing the range of numbers.

F-Test Procedures

Research question and null hypothesis:

Is there a difference in classroom community variances between males and females $\sigma_1^2 \neq \sigma_2^2$?

H_0: The variances of classroom community between males and females are homogeneous, $\sigma_1^2 = \sigma_2^2$.

Task: Use the Excel file Motivation.xlsx located at http://www.watertreepress.com/stats if you want to follow along with the analysis. The Data tab contains the data and the F-Test of Equality of Variance tab contains the F-Test Equality of Variance analysis described below.

1. Open the *Motivation.xlsx file using Excel.*

2. Copy variables gender and c_community from the Excel workbook Data tab to columns A and B on an empty sheet. Copy all 168 variable pairs.

	A	B
1	gender	c_community
2	1	23
3	1	22
4	1	23
5	1	23

3. Enter labels N, n (females), n (males), Variance (females), Variance (males), df1, df2, F, and p-level (2-tailed) in clees C1:C9. Enter formulas =COUNT(A2:A169), =COUNT(A2:A145), =COUNT(A146:A169), =VAR.S(B2:B144), =VAR.S(B146:B169), =D3-1, =D2-1, =D5/D4, and =F.TEST(B2:B145,B146:B169) in cells D1:D9.

	C	D
1	N	=COUNT(A2:A169)
2	n (females)	=COUNT(A2:A145)
3	n (males)	=COUNT(A146:A169)
4	Variance (females)	=VAR.S(B2:B144)
5	Variance (males)	=VAR.S(B146:B169)
6	df1	=D3-1
7	df2	=D2-1
8	F	=D5/D4
9	p-level (2-tailed)	=F.TEST(B2:B145,B146:B169)

	C	D
1	N	168
2	n (females)	144
3	n (males)	24
4	Variance (females)	38.14232247
5	Variance (males)	44.23188406
6	df1	23
7	df2	143
8	F	1.159653665
9	p-level (2-tailed)	0.586512314

Formatted one-sample F-Test output summarizing test results:

	C	D	E	F	G
11	F-Test of Equality of Variance				
12		Value	df1	df2	p-level
13	F	1.159654	23	143	0.586512

The above output shows that the results of the F-Test are not statistically significant since the p-level (2-tailed) > .05 (the assumed à priori significance level).

Automated Procedures

Use the following procedures for Analysis ToolPak.

1. Launch Microsoft Excel for Windows and open the Motivation.xlsx file.

2. Select the Data tab and click the Data Analysis icon to open the Data Analysis dialog. Select Descriptive Statistics and click OK to open the Descriptive Statistics dialog.

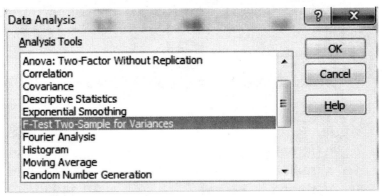

3. Select the Variable 1 Range by highlighting the c_community (classroom community) data in cells F2:F145 for gender = 1 = female and select the Variable 2 Range by highlighting the c_community variable in cells F146:F169 for gender = 2 = male.

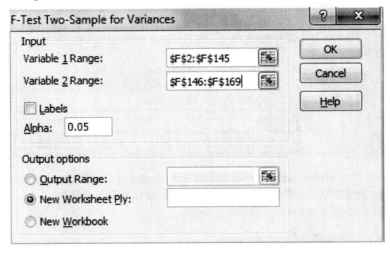

4. Click the OK button to run the procedure.

	A	B	C
1	F-Test Two-Sample for Variances		
2			
3		Variable 1	Variable 2
4	Mean	28.84027778	29.16666667
5	Variance	38.20507964	44.23188406
6	Observations	144	24
7	df	143	23
8	F	0.863745247	
9	P(F<=f) one-tail	0.293256157	
10	F Critical one-tail	0.623020772	

Use the following procedures for StatPlus LE.

1. Launch Microsoft Excel and open the Motivation.xlsx file.

2. Launch StatPlus LE and select Statistics > Basic Statistics and Tables > *F*-Test for Variances from the StatPlus menu bar.

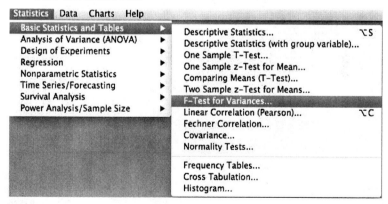

3. Enter the c_community variable in cells F2:F145 for gender = 1 = female in the "Variable #1" box and the

c_community variable in cells F146:F169 for gender = 2 = male in the "Variable #2" box.

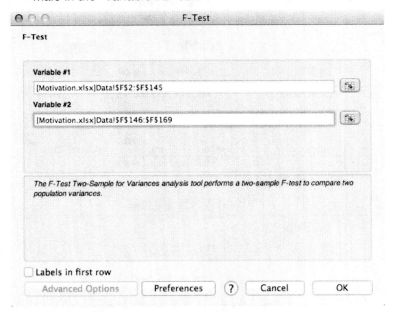

4. Click the OK button to run the procedure.

	A	B	C
1	**F-Test Two-Sample for Variances**		
2	*Descriptive Statistics*		
3	*VAR*	*A*	*B*
4	*Sample size*	144	24
5	*Mean*	28.84028	29.16667
6	*Variance*	38.20508	44.23188
7	*Standard Deviation*	6.18103	6.65071
8	*Mean Standard Error*	0.51509	1.35757

	A	B	C	D
9				
10	Summary			
11	F	1.15775	F Critical value (5%)	1.60508
12	p-level 1-tailed	0.29326	p-level 2-tailed	0.58651
13	H0 (5%)?	accepted		

F-Test Reporting

As a minimum, the following information should be reported in the results section of any report in which the F-Test is used to evaluate the assumption of homogeneity of variance: statistical decision and p-value. Alternatively, the F-statistic and degrees of freedom can also be reported. For example, one might report test results as follows.

The F-Test of Equality of Variance provided evidence that the variance in classroom community scores for male and female groups were statistically equivalent, $F(23,143) = 1.16$, $p = .59$.

INDEPENDENT T-TEST

The Independent t-Test, also known as Student's t-Test and Independent Samples t-Test, is a parametric procedure that assesses whether the means of two independent groups are statistically different from each other. Independent means that each sample consists of a different set of cases and the composition of one sample is not influenced by the composition of the other sample (Diekhoff, 1992). Groups can be formed by randomly assigning research participants to groups or conditions in an experiment or one can use naturally occurring groups, e.g., males and females.

Excel data entry for the Independent t-Test is accomplished by entering the IV (the grouping variable) and DV as separate columns in an Excel spreadsheet. The IV must be entered as numerical data, e.g., treatment group = 1, control group = 2.

One can compute the t-value using the following formula:

$$t = \frac{\overline{X}_1 - \overline{X}_2}{S_{\overline{X}_1 - \overline{X}_2}}$$

where $\overline{X}_1 - \overline{X}_2$ is the difference in means of group 1 and group 2, and $S_{\overline{X}_1 - \overline{X}_2}$ is the estimated standard error of the difference (i.e., using the pooled difference to allow the larger group to be weighted more).

The formula for the estimated standard error of the difference (equal variances assumed) is shown next:

$$S_{\overline{X}_1 - \overline{X}_2} = \sqrt{\frac{S^2_{pooled}}{n_1} + \frac{S^2_{pooled}}{n_2}}$$

where the following formula is used to calculate pooled variance:

$$S^2_{pooled} = \frac{(df_1)s^2_1 + (df_2)s^2_2}{df_1 + df_2}$$

The formula for estimated standard error of the difference (equal variances not assumed) is shown below:

$$S_{\overline{X}_1 - \overline{X}_2} = \sqrt{\frac{s^2_1}{n_1} + \frac{s^2_2}{n_2}}$$

Degrees of freedom. The degrees of freedom (equal variances assumed) and adjusted degrees of freedom (equal variances not assumed) are as follows:

$$df = n_1 + n_2 - 2$$

$$Adjusted\_df = \frac{(\dfrac{s_1^2}{n_1} + \dfrac{s_2^2}{n_2})}{\dfrac{1}{(n_1-1)}(\dfrac{s_1^2}{n_1})^2 + \dfrac{1}{(n_2-1)}(\dfrac{s_2^2}{n_2})^2}$$

Effect size. Cohen's *d* measures effect size and is often used to report effect size following a significant *t*-test. The formula for Cohen's *d* for the Independent *t*-Test is (Green & Salkind):

$$d = t\sqrt{\frac{N_1 + N_2}{N_1 N_2}}$$

where *N* represents the size of each group. This formula expresses the distance between the means of the two groups in terms of the size of the standard deviation. For example, *d* = .6 would mean that the two group means are 6/10th of a standard deviation apart. By convention, Cohen's *d* values are interpreted as follows:

Small effect size = .20
Medium effect size = .50
Large effect size = .80

Alternatively, *r* can be used as a measure of effect size using the following equation (Rosenthal, 1991; Rosnow & Rosenthal, 2005):

$$r = \sqrt{\frac{t^2}{t^2 + df}}$$

where

Small effect size = .10
Medium effect size = .30
Large effect size = .50

Key Assumptions & Requirements

Random selection of samples (probability samples) to allow for generalization of results to a target population.

Variables. DV: one continuous variable, interval/ratio scale. IV: one categorical IV with two categories; e.g., group (treatment, control).

Independence of observations. Independence of observations means that observations (i.e., measurements) are not acted on by an outside influence common to two or more measurements, e.g., other research participants or previous measurements. Evaluation of this assumption is a procedural issue involving research design, sampling, and measurement. and consists more of a procedural review of the research than it is of statistical analysis. Violation of the independence assumption adversely affects probability statements leading to inaccurate *p*-values and reduced statistical power (Scariano & Davenport, 1987).

Normality. DV is normally distributed in each group. The Independent *t*-Test is robust to mild to moderate violations of normality assuming a sufficiently large sample size. However, it may not be the most powerful test available for a given non-normal distribution. When the two samples are mildly skewed in the same direction, the one-tailed *t*-Test is biased. If the samples are skewed in opposite directions, the Type I error rate can be affected. Glass and Hopkins (1996) report that for the *t*-Test, the probability of a Type II error is largely unaffected by marked non-normality.

Consequently, the condition of normality can be largely disregarded as a prerequisite for using the two-tailed *t*-test. The *t*-Test is robust with respect to failure to meet the normality assumption. For one-tailed tests, accurate probability statements require a sample size of at least 20 in the smaller group (p. 291).

Absence of extreme outliers. Extreme outliers can distort the mean difference and the *t*-statistic. They tend to inflate the variance and depress the value and corresponding statistical significance of the *t*-statistic.

Homogeneity of variance.

Sample size. When sample sizes are large (i.e., when both groups have > 25 participants each) and are approximately equal in size, the robustness of this test to violation of the assumption of normality is improved (Diekhoff, 1992). However, with small sample sizes, violation of assumptions is difficult to detect and the test is less robust to violations of assumptions.

Excel Functions Used

ABS(number). Returns the absolute value of the specified number.

AVERAGE(number1,number2,...). Returns the arithmetic mean, where numbers represent the range of numbers.

COUNT(value1,value2,...). Counts the numbers in the range of numbers.

POWER(number,power). Returns a number raised to the specified power, where number is the base number and power is the exponent.

SQRT(number). Returns the square root of a number.

STDEV.S(number1,number2,...). Returns the unbiased estimate of population standard deviation, where numbers represent the range of numbers.

T.DIST.2T(x,deg_freedom). Returns the 2-tailed *t*-distribution probability, where x is the value to be evaluated and deg_freedom is a number representing the degrees of freedom.

Independent t-Test Procedures

Research question and null hypothesis:

Is there a difference in mean computer confidence posttest between male and female university students, $\mu_1 \neq \mu_2$?

Note: IV is gender (male, female) and DV is computer confidence posttest.

H_0: There is no difference in mean computer confidence posttest between male and female university students, $\mu_1 = \mu_2$.

Alternatively, H_0: The distribution of computer confidence posttest is the same for male and female university students.

Task: Use the Excel file Computer Anxiety.xlsx located at <u>http://</u>

www.watertreepress.com/stats *if you want to follow along with the analysis. The Data tab contains the data and the Independent t-Test tab contains the Independent t-Test analysis described below.*

1. Open the *Computer Anxiety.xlsx file using Excel.*

2. Copy variables gender and comconf2 (computer confidence posttest) from the Excel workbook Data tab to columns A and B on an empty sheet. Copy all 86 cases.

	A	B
1	gender	comconf2
2	1	35
3	1	40
4	2	38
5	2	35

3. Sort cases in ascending order based on gender.

	A	B
1	gender	comconf2
2	1	35
3	1	40
4	1	30
5	1	34

4. Enter labels Males, Females, and Sample in cells C2:C4 and n, M, SD, and Variance in cells D1:G1. Enter formulas for =COUNT(A2:A23, =COUNT(A24:A87), and D2+D3 in cells D2:D4, =AVERAGE(B2:B23), =AVERAGE(B24:B87), and =AVERAGE(B2:B87) in cells E2:E4, =STDEV.S(B2:B23), =STDEV.S(B24:B87), and =STDEV.S(B2:B87) in cells F2:F4, and =POWER(F2,2) and =POWER(F3,2) in cells G2:G3. (Note: Gender = 1 = males and Gender = 2 = females.)

◢	C	D	E
1		n	M
2	Males	=COUNT(A2:A23)	=AVERAGE(B2:B23)
3	Females	=COUNT(A24:A87)	=AVERAGE(B24:B87)
4	Sample	=D2+D3	=AVERAGE(B2:B87)

◢	F	G
1	SD	Variance
2	=STDEV.S(B2:B23)	=POWER(F2,2)
3	=STDEV.S(B24:B87)	=POWER(F3,2)
4	=STDEV.S(B2:B87)	

◢	C	D	E	F	G
1		n	M	SD	Variance
2	Males	22	31.77273	4.740221	22.4697
3	Females	64	32.78125	5.559116	30.9038
4	Sample	86	32.52326	5.352793	

5.   Enter labels "Equal Variances Assumed" and "Pooled variance" in cells C6 and C7, respectively, and the following formula in cell D7: =((D2-1)*POWER(F2,2)+ (D3-1)*POWER(F3,2))/((D2-1)+(D3-1)).

6.   Enter the labels Equal Variances Assumed, Pooled variance, Mean difference, SE difference, df, t (equal variances), p-level (2-tailed), and Cohen's d in cells C6:C13. Enter formulas =((D2-1)*POWER(F2,2)+ (D3-1)*POWER(F3,2))/((D2-1)+(D3-1)), =E2-E3, =SQRT(D7/ D2+D7/D3), =D2+D3-2, =E2-E3)/D9, =T.DIST. 2T(ABS(D11),D10), =D11*SQRT((D2+D3)/(D2*D3)) in cells D7:D13.

	C	D
8	Mean difference	=E2-E3
9	SE difference	=SQRT(D7/D2+D7/D3)
10	df	=D2+D3-2
11	t (equal variances)	=(E2-E3)/D9
12	p-level (2-tailed)	=T.DIST.2T(ABS(D11),D10)
13	Cohen's d	=D11*SQRT((D2+D3)/(D2*D3))

	C	D
6	Equal Variances Assumed	
7	Pooled variance	28.79525162
8	Mean difference	-1.008522727
9	SE difference	1.326197904
10	df	84
11	t (equal variances)	-0.760461711
12	p-level (2-tailed)	0.449107966
13	Cohen's d	-0.187942609

7. Enter labels Equal Variances Not Assumed, Mean difference, SE difference, df numerator in cells C15C18. Enter formulas in cells C16:D18.

	C	D
15	Equal Variances Not Assumed	
16	Mean difference	=E2-E3
17	SE difference	=SQRT(((F2*F2)/D2)+((F3*F3)/D3))
18	df numerator	=POWER((G2/D2+G3/D3),2)

	C	D
15	Equal Variances Not Assumed	
16	Mean difference	-1.008522727
17	SE difference	1.226466985
18	df numerator	2.262681617

8. Enter labels df denominator, Adjusted df, t, p-level (2-tailed), and Cohen's d in cells C19:C23. Enter the formulas =(1/(D2-1))*POWER((G2/D2),2)+(1/(D3-1))*POWER((G3/D3),2), =D18/D19, =D16/D17, =T.DIST.2T(ABS(D21),D20), and =D21*SQRT((D2+D3)/(D2*D3)) in cells D19:D23.

	C	D
20	Adjusted df	=D18/D19
21	t	=D16/D17
22	p-level (2-tailed)	=T.DIST.2T(ABS(D21),D20)
23	Cohen's d	=D21*SQRT((D2+D3)/(D2*D3))

	C	D
19	df denominator	0.053375102
20	Adjusted df	42.39208056
21	t	-0.822299124
22	p-level (2-tailed)	0.415550779
23	Cohen's d	-0.203225278

Formatted independent *t*-test output summarizing test results:

	C	D	E	F	G
25	Independent t-Test				
26	Equal Variances Assumed				
27		t	df	p-level (2-tailed)	Cohen's d
28	Computer Confidence Posttest	-0.7605	84	0.449	-0.188
29	Equal Variances Not Assumed				
30	Computer Confidence Posttest	-0.8223	42.392	0.416	-0.203

These results show that the difference in computer confidence posttest between males and females is not significant because the *p*-level (two-tailed) is above the criterion of the researcher's *à priori* significance level of .05.

Automated Procedures

Use the following procedures for Analysis ToolPak.

1.   Launch Microsoft Excel for Windows and open the Computer Anxiety.xlsx file. Go to the Independent *t*-Test sheet.

2.   Select the Data tab and click the Data Analysis icon to open the Data Analysis dialog. Select t-Test:Two-Sample Assuming Unequal Variances and click OK to open the *t*-Test dialog. Alternatively, Select *t*-Test:Two-Sample Assuming Equal Variances and click OK.

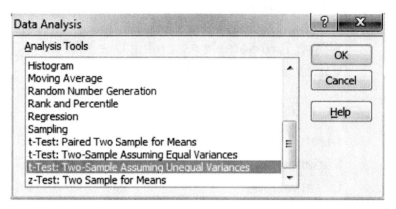

3. Select the Variable 1 Range by highlighting the comconf2 (computer confidence posttest) data for gender = 1 = male in cells B2:B23. Select the Variable 2 Range by highlighting the comconf2 for gender = 2 = female in cells B24:B87. Do not check Labels.

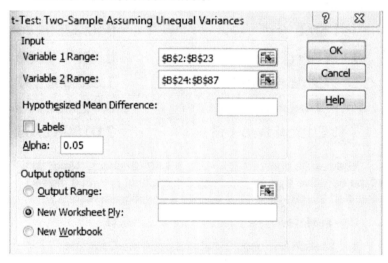

4. Click the OK button to run the procedure.

	A	B	C
1	t-Test: Two-Sample Assuming Unequal Variances		
2			
3		Variable 1	Variable 2
4	Mean	31.7727273	32.78125
5	Variance	22.469697	30.9037698
6	Observations	22	64

	A	B
7	Hypothesized Mean Difference	0
8	df	42
9	t Stat	-0.822299124
10	P(T<=t) one-tail	0.207775389
11	t Critical one-tail	1.681952357
12	P(T<=t) two-tail	0.415550779
13	t Critical two-tail	2.018081703

The results show $t(42) = -.82$, $p = .42$ (2-tailed). (Note: Use of the negative sign for the t-value is optional provided the text identified the direction of difference for significant results.)

Use the following procedures for StatPlus LE.

1.   Launch Microsoft Excel and open the Computer Anxiety.xlsx file. Go to the Independent t-Test sheet.

2.   Launch StatPlus LE and select Statistics > Basic Statistics and Tables > Comparing Means (T-Test) from the StatPlus menu bar.

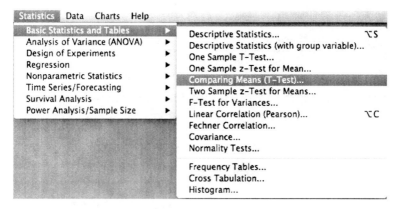

3. Select the Variable #1 range by highlighting the comconf2 (computer confidence posttest) data for gender = 1 = male in cells B2:B23. Select the Variable #2 range by highlighting the comconf2 data for gender = 2 = female in cells B24:B87. Select Two Sample T-Test Assuming Unequal Variances (heteroscedastic). Do not select Labels in first row.

4. Click the OK button to run the procedure.

	A	B	C	D
1	**Comparing Means [t-test assuming unequal variances (heteroscedastic)]**			
2	*Descriptive Statistics*			
3	*VAR*	*Sample size*	*Mean*	*Variance*
4		22	31.77273	22.4697
5		64	32.78125	30.90377

	A	B	C	D
7	Summary			
8	Degrees Of Freedom	42	Hypothesized Mean Difference	0.E+0
9	Test Statistics	0.8223	Pooled Variance	28.79525
10				
11	Two-tailed distribution			
12	p-level	0.41555	t Critical Value (5%)	2.01808
13				
14	One-tailed distribution			
15	p-level	0.20778	t Critical Value (5%)	1.68195

The results show $t(42) = .82$, $p = .42$ (2-tailed).

Independent t-Test Reporting

As a minimum, the following information should be reported in the results section of any report: null hypothesis that is being evaluated, descriptive statistics (e.g., *M, SD, N, n*), statistical test used (i.e., Independent *t*-Test), results of evaluation of test assumptions, and test results. For example, one might report test results as follows.

An Independent *t*-Test (unequal variances assumed) was conducted to evaluate the null hypothesis that there is no difference in computer confidence posttest between male and female university students ($N = 86$). Test results provided evidence that the difference in computer confidence posttest between the male group ($M = 31.77$, $SD = 4.74$) and the female group ($M = 32.78$, $SD = 5.56$) was not statistically significant, $t(42.39) = .82$, $p = .42$ (2-tailed), $d = .20$. Therefore, there was insufficient evidence to reject the null hypothesis.

(Note: all assumptions require evaluation and reporting before test results can be relied upon.)

MANN-WHITNEY U TEST

The Mann-Whitney U Test is a nonparametric procedure that determines if ranked scores in two independent groups differ. It is also used to analyze interval or ratio scale variables that are not normally distributed. This test is equivalent to the Kruskal-Wallis H Test when two independent groups are compared. It is a useful nonparametric test when the normality assumption of the Independent t-Test is not tenable. The formula for U is the smaller of the following two values:

$$U_1 = R_1 - \frac{n_1(n_1 + 1)}{2}$$

$$U_2 = R_2 - \frac{n_2(n_2 + 1)}{2}$$

where R_1 and R_2 are the sum of ranks for groups 1 and 2.

Degrees of freedom. Degrees of freedom = $k - 1$, where k = number of groups.

Effect size. An approximation of the r coefficient can be obtained using the value of z, as reported by Excel, using the following formula (Rosenthal, 1991):

$$r = \frac{z}{\sqrt{N}}$$

where N = total number of cases and z = the z-value displayed in Excel output.

Alternatively, the difference in mean ranks between groups can be used for effect size.

Key Assumptions & Requirements

Random selection of samples (probability samples) to allow for generalization of results to a target population.

Variables. DV: one continuous variable measured on the ordinal, interval, or ratio scale. IV: one categorical variable with two categories; e.g., group (treatment, control).

Distributions of each group have the same shape.

Independence of observations.

Excel Functions Used

ABS(number). Returns the absolute value of a number.

COUNT(value1,value2,...). Counts the numbers in the range of numbers.

NORMSDIST(z). Returns the standard normal cumulative distribution function, where z is the number for the desired distribution.

MEDIAN(number1,number2,...). Returns the median of a range of numbers.

MIN(number1,number2,...). Returns the smallest number in the range of numbers.

RANK.AVG(number,ref,order). Returns the rank of a number in a list, where number = the number to be ranked, ref = the list of numbers upon which the rankings are based, and 0 indicates the reference list is sorted in descending order.

SQRT(number). Returns the square root of a number.

SUM(number1,number2,...). Adds the range of numbers.

Mann-Whitney U Test Procedures

Research question and null hypothesis:

Are the ranks of computer knowledge pretest dispersed differently between male and female university students?

H_0: There is no difference in how the ranks of computer knowledge pretest are dispersed between male and female university students.

Task: Use the Excel file Computer Anxiety.xlsx located at http://www.watertreepress.com/stats if you want to follow along with the analysis. The Data tab contains the data and the Mann-Whitney U Test tab contains the Mann-Whitney U Test analysis described below.

1. Open the *Computer Anxiety.xlsx* file using Excel.

2. Copy gender and comkow data from Excel workbook Data tab and paste the data in columns A and B of an empty sheet. Copy all 92 cases.

	A	B
1	gender	comknow
2	1	14
3	1	4
4	2	5
5	2	10

3. Enter label Ranks in cell C1. Enter formula =RANK.AVG(B2,$B$2:$B$93,1) in cell C2. Fill Down to cell C93.

	C
1	Ranks
2	=RANK.AVG(B2,$B$2:$B$93,1)
3	=RANK.AVG(B3,$B$2:$B$93,1)
4	=RANK.AVG(B4,$B$2:$B$93,1)
5	=RANK.AVG(B5,$B$2:$B$93,1)

	C
1	Ranks
2	70
3	22.5
4	40.5
5	81

4. Sort cases by gender is ascending order.

	A	B	C
1	gender	comknow	Ranks
2	1	14	70
3	1	4	22.5
4	1	7	40.5
5	1	17	81

5. Enter labels Male, Female, and Total in cells D2:D4 and labels N and Median in cells E1:F1. Enter formulas =COUNTIF(A2:A93,1), COUNTIF(A2:A93,2) and =E2+E3 in cells E2:E4. Enter formulas =MEDIAN(B2:B25) and =MEDIAN(B26:B93) in cvells F2:F3.

	D	E	F
1		N	Median
2	Male	=COUNTIF(A2:A93,1)	=MEDIAN(B2:B25)
3	Female	=COUNTIF(A2:A93,2)	=MEDIAN(B26:B93)
4	Total	=E2+E3	

6. Enter labels Mean Rank and Sum of Ranks in cells G1:H1. Enter formulas =AVERAGE(C2:C25) and =AVERAGE(C26:C93) in cells G2:G3 and formulas =SUM(C2:C25) and =SUM(C26:C93) in cells H2:H3.

	G	H
1	Mean Rank	Sum of Ranks
2	=AVERAGE(C2:C25)	=SUM(C2:C25)
3	=AVERAGE(C26:C93)	=SUM(C26:C93)

	D	E	F	G	H
1		N	Median	Mean Rank	Sum of Ranks
2	Male	24	10.5	52.5	1260
3	Female	68	8	44.38235	3018
4	Total	92			

7. Enter labels df, U1, U2, U, Z, p-level, r, and Difference in

ranks in cells D5:D12. Enter formulas =COUNT(E2:E3)-1,
=E2*E3+E2*(E2+1)/2-H2, =E2*E3+E3*(E3+1)/2-H3,
=MIN(E6:E7, =(E8-E2*E3/2)/SQRT(E2*E3*(E2+E3+1)/
12), =(1-NORMSDIST(ABS(E9)))*2, =E9/SQRT(E4), and
=G2-G3 in cells E5:E12.

	D	E
5	df	=COUNT(E2:E3)-1
6	U1	=E2*E3+E2*(E2+1)/2-H2
7	U2	=E2*E3+E3*(E3+1)/2-H3
8	U	=MIN(E6:E7)
9	Z	=(E8-E2*E3/2)/SQRT(E2*E3*(E2+E3+1)/12)
10	p-level	=(1-NORMSDIST(ABS(E9)))*2
11	r	=E9/SQRT(E4)
12	Difference in mean ranks	=G2-G3

	D	E
5	df	1
6	U1	672
7	U2	960
8	U	672
9	Z	-1.280417389
10	p-level	0.200398381
11	r	-0.133492741
12	Difference in mean ranks	8.117647059

Formatted Mann-Whitney U Test output summarizing test
results:

	D	E
14	Mann-Whitney U Test	
15		Computer Knowledge
16	Mann-Whitney U	672
17	df	1
18	Z	-1.280417389
19	r	-0.133492741
20	p-level (2-tailed)	0.200398381

The above output shows that the Mann-Whitney U test is not significant since the p-level > .05 (the assumed à priori significance level).

Automated Procedures

Use the following procedures for StatPlus Pro.

1.   Launch Microsoft Excel and open the Computer Anxiety.xlsx file. Go to the Mann-Whitney U Test sheet.

2.   Launch StatPlus Pro and select Statistics > Nonparametric Statistics > Comparing Two Independent Samples (Mann-Whitney, Runs Test) from the StatPlus menu bar.

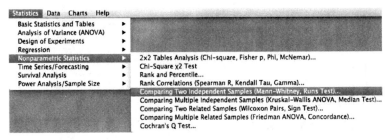

3.   Select the Variable #1 range by highlighting the comknow (computer knowledge pretest) data for gender = 1 = male in cells B2:B25 and select the Variable #2 range by highlighting the comknow data for gender = 2 = female in cells B26:B93. Do not check Labels in first row.

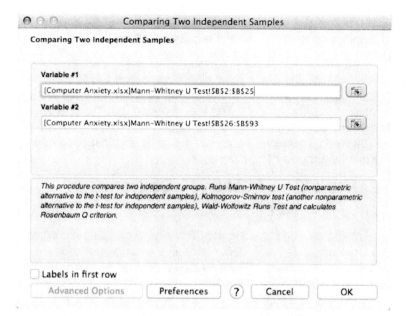

Comparing Two Independent Samples

4. Click the OK button to run the procedure.

	A	B	C	D
1	**Comparing Two Independent Samples**			
2	Sample size #1	24	Sample size #2	68
3	Mann-Whitney U Test			
4	W1 Sum of Ranks (series 1)	1,260.	U (larger)	672.
5	W2 Sum of Ranks (series 2)	3,018.	U	960.
6	Mean W1	1,116.	Mean W2	3,162.
7	Standard Deviation W	112.22011	Multiplicity Factor	3,438.
8	Z	1.28042	p-level	0.2004

The results show $U(1) = 672.00$, $z = 1.28$, $p = .20$ (2-tailed).

Mann-Whitney U Test Reporting

As a minimum, the following information should be reported in the results section of any report: null hypothesis that is being evaluated, descriptive statistics (e.g., median, mean rank, range, N, n), statistical test used (i.e., Mann-Whitney U Test), results of evaluation of test assumptions if violated, and test results. For example, one might report test results as follows.

The Mann-Whitney U Test was conducted to evaluate the null hypothesis that there is no difference in how the ranks of computer knowledge pretest are dispersed between male and female university students. The test revealed that the difference between groups was not significant $U(1) = 672.00$, $z = 1.28$, $p =. 20$ (2-tailed). Therefore, there was insufficient evidence to reject the null hypothesis of no difference.

PEARSON CHI-SQUARE (X^2) CONTINGENCY TABLE ANALYSIS

Chi-Square (χ^2) Contingency Table Analysis, also known as the Chi-Square Test of Independence, is a nonparametric procedure to determine if frequencies produced by cross-classifying observations simultaneously across two categorical variables are independent. For example, do males and females (the first categorical variable) differ in their opinions regarding some issue (favor versus not favor; the second categorical variable)? If the null hypothesis cannot be rejected there would be no difference between gender and the issue. If the null hypotheses were rejected the inference is that there is a difference between gender and the issue, e.g., females tend to favor the issue and males tend to not favor the issue.

The dataset represents a R x C contingency table, where R is the number of rows (categories of one variable) and C is the number of columns (categories of the second variable). For example, two dichotomous variables will produce a 2 x 2 table. By convention, the row variable is considered the DV and the column variable is viewed as the IV. The process that summarizes categorical data in this way to produce a contingency table also goes by the name of crosstabulations or crosstabs.

Contingency tables show frequencies produced by cross-classifying observations, e.g., students described simultaneously according to computer ownership and gender.

Below is the formula for the test statistic:

$$\chi^2 = \sum\left(\frac{(O-E)^2}{E}\right)$$

where O = observed frequency and E = expected frequency.

Degrees of freedom. The degrees of freedom = (number of rows − 1) x (number of columns − 1).

Effect size. Phi is frequently used to report effect size for 2 x 2 contingency tables. For a 2 x 2 table phi can be interpreted as small effect = .1, medium effect = .3, large effect = .5 and OR can be interpreted as small effect = 1.49, medium effect = 3.45, large effect = 9. Cramér's *V* is used as a measure of effect size for larger tables. Cohen (1988) proposed the following standards for interpreting Cramér's *V* in this situation:

For df = 1, small effect = 0.10, medium effect = 0.30, large effect = 0.50
For df = 2, small effect = 0.07, medium effect = 0.21, large effect = 0.35
For df = 3, small effect = 0.06, medium effect = 0.17, large effect = 0.29

(Note: For 2 x 2 tables, Cramér's *V* equals phi.)

Key Assumptions & Requirements

Random selection of samples (probability samples) to allow for generalization of results to a target population.

Variables. Variables must be reported in raw frequencies (not percentages). Values/categories of the variable must be mutually exclusive and exhaustive.

Independence of observations.

Sample size. Observed frequencies must be sufficiently large. Each cell has an expected frequency of five or more (some statisticians prefer 10 or more while others will accept a less stringent standard of no counts less than 2 and 80% of counts > 5). If the sample size is very small, the χ^2 value is overestimated; if it is very large, the χ^2 value is underestimated.

Note: One can sometimes combine columns/rows to increase expected counts that are too low. However, such action may reduce interpretability. Avoid combining cells in order to produce significant results.

Excel Functions Used

CHISQ.DIST.R(x,deg_freedom). Returns the right-tailed p-level of the chi-square distribution, where x is the chi-square value to be evaluated and deg_freedom is a number reflecting degrees of freedom.

IF(logical_test,value_if_true,value_if_false). Returns one value if the condition is TRUE and a different value if the condition is FALSE.

POWER(number,power). Raises a number to the specified power, e.g., 2 = squared.

SUM(number1,number2,...). Adds the range of numbers.

Pearson Chi-Square (χ^2) Contingency Table Analysis Procedures

Research question and null hypothesis:

Are the proportions associated with computer ownership different for male and female university students?

Alternatively, one may also ask: Is computer ownership related to whether a university student is male or female? Is computer ownership for male and female university students independent?

H_0: The proportions associated with computer ownership are the same for male and female university students.

Task: Use the Excel file Computer Anxiety.xlsx located at http://www.watertreepress.com/stats if you want to follow along with the analysis. The Data tab contains the data and the Pearson Chi-Square (χ^2) Contingency Table *tab contains the Pearson Chi-Square (χ^2) Contingency Table Analysis described below.*

1. Open the *Computer Anxiety.xlsx* file using Excel.

2. Copy gender (1 = male, 2 = female) and comown (1 = yes, 2 = no) data from the Excel workbook Data tab and paste the data in columns A and B of an empty sheet.

	A	B
1	gender	comown
2	1	1
3	1	1
4	2	1
5	2	1

3. Sort cases by gender in ascending order.

4. Enter the following formulas in columns C through F:

    a. male, yes: Enter =IF(B2=1,1,0) in cell C2. Fill down to cell C25.

    b. male, no: Enter =IF(B2=2,1,0) in cell D2. Fill down to cell D25.

    c. female, yes: Enter =IF(B26=1,1,0) in cell E26. Fill down to cell E93.

    d. Enter =IF(B26=2,1,0) in cell F26. Fill down to cell F93.

5. Enter labels Yes, No, and Totals in cells G2:G4 and labels Male, Female, and Totals in cells H1:J1. Enter formulas=SUM(C2:C25), =SUM(D2:D25, and =SUM(H2:H3) in cells H2:H4, =SUM(E26:E93), =SUM(F26:F93), and =SUM(I2:I3) in cells I2:I4, and =SUM(H2:I2), =SUM(H3:I3), and =SUM(J2:J3) in cells J2:J4 to create a crosstabulation.

	G	H	I	J
1		Male	Female	Totals
2	Yes	=SUM(C2:C25)	=SUM(E26:E93)	=SUM(H2:I2)
3	No	=SUM(D2:D25)	=SUM(F26:F93)	=SUM(H3:I3)
4	Totals	=SUM(H2:H3)	=SUM(I2:I3)	=SUM(J2:J3)

⊿	G	H	I	J
1		Male	Female	Totals
2	Yes	18	45	63
3	No	6	23	29
4	Totals	24	68	92

6. Enter labels Yes and No in cells G7:G8 and Male
   Expected and Female Expected in cells H6:I6. Enter
   formulas =$J2*H$4/$J$4 and =$J3*H$4/$J$4 in cells
   H7:H8 and =$J2*I$4/$J$4 and =$J3*I$4/$J$4 in cells I7:I8
   to create an expected frequencies table.

⊿	G	H	I
6		Male Expected	Female Expected
7	Yes	=$J2*H$4/$J$4	=$J2*I$4/$J$4
8	No	=$J3*H$4/$J$4	=$J3*I$4/$J$4

⊿	G	H	I
6		Male Expected	Female Expected
7	Yes	16.43478261	46.56521739
8	No	7.565217391	21.43478261

7. Create a calculation table by entering label (Observed –
   Expected)-squared/Expected in cell J6. Also enter
   formulas =POWER((H2-H7),2)/H7 and =POWER((H3-H8),
   2)/H8 in cells J7:J8 and =POWER((I2-I7),2)/I7 and
   =POWER((I3-I8),2)/I8 in cells K7:K8.

⊿	J	K
6	(Observed - Expected)-squared/Expected	
7	=POWER((H2-H7),2)/H7	=POWER((I2-I7),2)/I7
8	=POWER((H3-H8),2)/H8	=POWER((I3-I8),2)/I8

◢	J	K
6	(Observed - Expected)-squared/Expected	
7	0.149068323	0.052612349
8	0.323838081	0.114295793

8. Finally, create a test statistics table in columns G and H as follows. Enter labels Proportion owning computers, Chi-square, df, and p-level in cells G10:G13. Enter formulas =J2/J4, =SUM(J7:K8), =(2-1)*(2-1), and =CHISQ.DIST.RT(H11,H12) in cells H10:H13.

◢	G	H
10	Proportion owning computers	=J2/J4
11	Chi-square	=SUM(J7:K8)
12	df	=(2-1)*(2-1)
13	p-level	=CHISQ.DIST.RT(H11,H12)

The degrees of freedom = (number of rows − 1) x (number of columns − 1) = (2 − 1) x (2 − 1).

◢	G	H
10	Proportion owning computers	0.684782609
11	Chi-square	0.639814547
12	df	1
13	p-level	0.423777961

Formatted Pearson χ^2 contingency table analysis output summarizing test results:

	G	H	I	J
15	Pearson Chi-Square Contingency Table Analysis			
16		Value	df	p-level
17	Chi-Square	0.6398145	1	0.423778

The above output shows that the test was not significant since the *p*-level > .05 (the assumed *à priori* significance level).

Automated Procedures

Use the following procedures for StatPlus Pro.

1.   Launch Microsoft Excel and open the Computer Anxiety.xlsx file. Go to the Chi-Square Contingency Table sheet.

2.   Launch StatPlus Pro and select Statistics > Nonparametric Statistics > Chi-Square χ^2 Test > Count Cases Classified By Row And Column from the StatPlus menu bar.

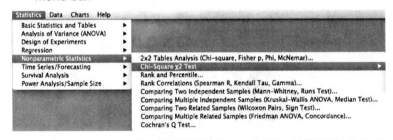

3.   Select the Row Variable range by highlighting the gender data in cells A1:A93 and select the Column Variable range by highlighting the comown (computer ownership) data in cells B1:B93. Check Labels in first row.

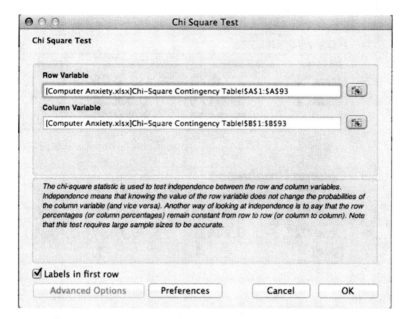

4. Click the OK button to run the procedure.

	A	B	C	D
1	**Chi Square Test**			
2				
3	*Observed Frequencies*			
4	**VARS**	**Column "1"**	**Column "2"**	**Total**
5	**Row "1"**	18.	6.	24.
6	**Row "2"**	45.	23.	68.
7	**Total**	63.	29.	92.
8				
9				
10	*Expected Frequencies*			
11	**VARS**	**Column "1"**	**Column "2"**	
12	**Row "1"**	16.43478	7.56522	
13	**Row "2"**	46.56522	21.43478	

	A	B	C	D
16	*Row Proportions*			
17	**VARS**	**Column "1"**	**Column "2"**	**Total**
18	**Row "1"**	0.75	0.25	1.
19	**Row "2"**	0.66176	0.33824	1.
20	**Total**	0.68478	0.31522	1.
21				
22				
23	*Column Proportions*			
24	**VARS**	**Column "1"**	**Column "2"**	**Total**
25	**Row "1"**	0.28571	0.2069	0.26087
26	**Row "2"**	0.71429	0.7931	0.73913
27	**Total**	1.	1.	1.
28				
29				
30	*Proportions of Total*			
31	**VARS**	**Column "1"**	**Column "2"**	**Total**
32	**Row "1"**	0.19565	0.06522	0.26087
33	**Row "2"**	0.48913	0.25	0.73913
34	**Total**	0.68478	0.31522	1.

	A	B	C	D
37	*Chi-squared Values*			
38	**VARS**	**Column "1"**	**Column "2"**	
39	**Row "1"**	0.14907	0.32384	
40	**Row "2"**	0.05261	0.1143	
41				
42				
43	*Summary*			
44	Chi-square	0.63981		
45	d.f.	1		
46	p-level > X	0.42378		

The results show $\chi^2(1) = .64$, $p = .42$.

Pearson Chi-Square (χ^2) Contingency Table Analysis Reporting

As a minimum, the following information should be reported in the results section of any report: null hypothesis that is being evaluated, descriptive statistics (e.g., observed frequency counts, proportion, N), statistical test used (i.e.,Pearson χ^2 contingency table analysis), results of evaluation of test assumptions if violated, and test results (i.e., correlation coefficient and p-level). For example, one might report test results as follows.

A two-way Pearson χ^2 contingency table analysis was conducted to evaluate the null hypothesis that computer ownership is independent of student gender. The two variables were computer ownership (yes = 63, no = 29) and student gender (male = 24, female = 68), $N = 92$. The proportion of students in the sample who own computers was 68.48%.

The Pearson χ^2 contingency table analysis was not significant, $\chi^2(1, N = 92) = .64$, $p = .42$. Consequently, there was insufficient evidence to reject the null hypothesis. Consequently, test results provided evidence that computer ownership was independent of student gender.

(Note: post-hoc pairwise comparisons would be used to evaluate differences among proportions for tables larger than 2x2 following a significant omnibus test.)

4.4: Comparing Multiple Independent Samples

POST HOC MULTIPLE COMPARISON TESTS

Key Point
A significant multiple independent samples test, e.g., ANOVA or Kruskal-Wallis *H* test, provides evidence that there is a significant difference between groups, but it does not identify pairwise differences (i.e., differences between pairs of groups).

Post hoc (or follow-up) multiple comparison tests are used following a significant omnibus test – e.g., one-way ANOVA or Kruskal-Wallis *H* Test – in order to determine which groups differ from each other when there are three or more groups. A post hoc test following a significant independent *t*-test is not required because this test only involves two groups and if the *t*-test is significant it is clear what two groups are different. However, in a test involving three or more groups, a significant omnibus test only provides evidence to the researcher that the groups differ, not how the groups differ. In a three group test the researcher does not know if group A differs significantly from group B and group C or if group B differs significantly from group C. Hence there is a need to conduct post hoc tests to identify pairwise differences.

Here is a partial list of the post hoc multiple comparison tests one can use when the assumption of homogeneity of variance is met for an ANOVA (Norusis, 2011).

- The Bonferroni test sets the α error rate to the experimentwise error rate (usually .05) divided by the total number of comparisons to control for Type I error when multiple comparisons are being made. The Bonferroni test is used in the ANOVA example using Excel operators and functions provided in this book. The following formulas are used for this test in analyzing each pairwise comparison.

$$\overline{X}_{Difference} = \overline{X}_i - \overline{X}_k$$

$$SE = (\sqrt{MS_W})(\sqrt{\frac{1}{n_1} + \frac{1}{n_2}})$$

$$t = \frac{\overline{X}_{Difference}}{SE}$$

The t-distribution is then used to compute the lower and upper bounds of the confidence interval.

$$Lower\_Bound = \overline{X}_{Difference} - (t_{Critical})(SE)$$

$$Upper\_Bound = \overline{X}_{Difference} + (t_{Critical})(SE)$$

where $t_{Critical}$ is the adjusted critical value based on the Bonferroni correction of familywise Type I error rate.

- The Tukey-Kramer Test is preferred when the number of groups is large as it is a conservative pairwise comparison test and researchers prefer to be conservative when the large number of groups threatens to inflate Type I errors. It is used for unequal sample sizes. A different critical difference is calculated for each pair of means and is used to evaluate the significance of the difference between each pair of means based on the different sample sizes. It is included in StatPlus ANOVA output.

- The Scheffé Test is a widely-used method for controlling Type I errors in post hoc testing of differences in group means. It works by first requiring the overall F-test of the null hypothesis be rejected. If the null hypothesis is not rejected overall, then it is not rejected for any comparison null hypothesis. While the Scheffé Test maintains an experimentwise .05 significance level in the face of multiple comparisons, it does so at the cost of a loss in statistical power (more Type II errors may be made). The Scheffé test is very conservative, more conservation than Tukey-Kramer. It is included in StatPlus ANOVA output.

$$F_{Scheffe} = \frac{(\overline{X}_1 - \overline{X}_2)^2}{S_W^2 (\frac{1}{n_1} + \frac{1}{n_2})}$$

$$F_{ScheffeCritical} = (k-1)(F_{ANOVACritical})$$

- The Least Significant Difference (LSD) Test, also called Fisher's LSD Test, is based on the t-statistic and thus can be considered a form of t-test. It compares all possible pairs of means after the F-test rejects the null hypothesis that groups do not differ. LSD is the most liberal of the post-hoc tests (it is most likely to reject the null hypothesis). It controls the experimentwise Type I error rate at a selected α level, but only for the omnibus (overall) test of the null hypothesis. Many researchers recommend against any use of LSD on the grounds that it has poor control of experimentwise α significance and better alternatives exist. The LSD test is included in StatPlus ANOVA output.

The Mann-Whitney U Test is appropriate for pairwise post hoc comparisons following a significant Kruskal-Wallis H Test.

ONE-WAY BETWEEN SUBJECTS ANOVA

Between subjects Analysis of Variance (ANOVA) is a parametric procedure that assesses whether the means of multiple independent groups are statistically different from each other (Keppel, 2004). This analysis is appropriate whenever one wants to compare the means of three or more groups (the independent t-test is used to compare the means of two independent groups). Since both t-test and ANOVA are based on similar mathematical models, both tests produce identical p-values when two means are compared.

An ANOVA with one IV is a one-way ANOVA. A factorial ANOVA is used when there is more than one IV, e.g., a two-way ANOVA is a factorial ANOVA with two IVs. When a DV is measured for independent groups where each group is exposed to a different intervention, the set of interventions or conditions is called a between subjects factor (IV). The groups correspond to interventions that are categories or levels of this IV.

Between subjects ANOVA measures three sources of variation in the data and compares their relative sizes:

1. Total variation; that is, the sum of the squares of the differences of each mean with the grand mean (the grand mean is the total of all the data divided by the total sample size).

$$SS_{Total} = \sum (\overline{X}_{Group} - \overline{X}_{GM})^2$$

where GM = grand mean.

2. Between groups variation; that is, how much variation occurs due to interaction between groups.

$$SS_{Between} = n \sum (\overline{X}_{Group} - \overline{X}_{GM})^2$$

The mean square between groups is the variance between groups.

$$MS_{Between} = \frac{SS_{Between}}{dfn}$$

where dfn = between group variation = number of groups − 1.

3. Within groups variation; that is, how much variation occurs within each group.

$$SS_{Within} = \sum (X - \overline{X}_{Group})^2$$

The mean square within groups is the variance between groups.

$$MS_{Within} = \frac{SS_{Within}}{dfd}$$

where dfd = within group variation = total number of participants − number of groups.

The F-statistic is the ratio of the between groups variation and the within groups variation:

$$F = \frac{MS_{Between}}{MS_{Within}}$$

If the computed F-statistic is approximately 1.0 or less, differences in group means are only random variations. If the computed F-statistic is greater than 1, then there is more variation between groups than within groups, from which one infers that the grouping variable (IV) does make a difference when the results are statistically significant. In other words, a large value of F indicates relatively more difference between groups than within groups (evidence to reject H_0).

A significant ANOVA (i.e., $p <= .05$) tells one that there is a high probability (i.e., 95% or higher) that at least one difference exists somewhere between groups. ANOVA does not identify where the pairwise differences lie. Post hoc multiple comparison test analysis is needed to determine which mean(s) is(are) different.

Key Point
Do not conduct post hoc multiple comparison tests if the ANOVA results are not statistically significant.

Degrees of freedom. Two degrees of freedom parameters are associated with ANOVA: *dfn* (between group variation) = $a - 1$ and *dfd* (within group variation) = $N - a$, where a is the number of groups and N is the total number of participants in all groups.

Effect size. Eta squared (η^2) is used to measure ANOVA effect size.

$$\eta^2 = \frac{SS_{Between}}{SS_{Total}}$$

A common rule of thumb is that eta squared values of .01, .06, and .14 represent small, medium, and large effect sizes.

Post hoc tests. Post hoc multiple comparison tests identify significant pairwise differences. The Bonferroni test is an appropriate post hoc test to use.

Key Assumptions & Requirements

Random selection of samples (probability samples) to allow for generalization of results to a target population.

Variables. DV: one continuous variable, interval/ratio scale. IV: one categorical variables with multiple categories; e.g., Group (Treatment A, Treatment B, Control).

Independence of observations. Independence of observations means that observations (i.e., measurements) are not acted on by an outside influence common to two or more measurements, e.g., other research participants or previous measurements. Evaluation of this assumption is a procedural issue involving research design, sampling, and measurement. and consists more of a procedural review of the research than it is of statistical analysis. Violation of the independence assumption adversely affects probability statements leading to inaccurate p-values and reduced statistical power (Scariano & Davenport, 1987).

Multivariate normality. The DV is normally distributed in each subpopulation or cell. This is necessary because ANOVA uses probability values regarding group differences. These probabilities will be incorrect if the data are not normal. For a one-way ANOVA, checking each group for normality is usually the best option to evaluate normality.

Glass and Hopkins (1996) report that for ANOVAs,

Non-normality has negligible consequences on Type I and Type II error probabilities unless the populations are highly skewed, the n's are very small, or one-tailed tests are employed (p. 403).

Absence of extreme outliers. Outliers contribute to non-normality and unequal variance.

Homogeneity of variance. ANOVA requires equal variance among groups because variability is pooled to create an error term. If variances are not equal, the one pooled error term will be too large for some groups and too small for other groups, resulting in incorrect probabilities. Glass and Hopkins (1996) assert that violations of the ANOVA homogeneity of variance assumption have negligible consequences on the accuracy of the probability statements when the n's are equal (p. 405).

Sample size. When sample sizes are relatively large and approximately equal in size, this test is fairly robust to violations of the assumptions of normality and homogeneity of variance provided distributions are symmetric (Diekhoff, 1992). This means that although power is decreased, the probability of a Type I error is as low or lower than it would be if its assumptions were met. There are exceptions to this rule. For example, a combination of unequal sample sizes and a violation of the assumption of homogeneity of variance can lead to an inflated Type I error rate.

Excel Functions Used

AVERAGE(number1,number2,...). Returns the arithmetic mean, where numbers represent the range of numbers.

COUNT(value1,value2,...). Counts the numbers in the range of numbers.

COUNTA(value1,value2,...). Counts the cells with non-empty values in the range of values.

DEVSQ(number1,number2,...). Returns the sum of squares of deviations of data from the sample mean.

F.DIST.RT(x,deg_freedom1,deg_freedom2). Returns the right-tailed F-distribution probability, where x is the F-value to be evaluated, deg_freedom1 is the between groups df, and deg_freedom2 is the within groups df.

SQRT(number). Returns the square root of a number.

SUM(number1,number2,...). Adds the range of numbers.

T.INV.2T(probability, deg_freedom). Returns the 2-tailed inverse of the t-distribution, where probability is the probability value and deg_freedom is a number representing degrees of freedom.

VAR.S(number1,number2,...). Returns the unbiased estimate of population variance, with numbers representing the range of numbers.

One-Way Between Subjects ANOVA Procedures

Research question and null hypothesis:

Is there a difference in computer anxiety posttest between graduate students based on enrolled class? The IV is class (class 1, class 2, class 3, class 4) and the DV is computer confidence posttest.

H_0: There is no difference in computer anxiety posttest between graduate students based on enrolled class.

Task: Use the Excel file Computer Anxiety.xlsx located at http://www.watertreepress.com/stats if you want to follow along with the analysis. The Data tab contains the data and the One-Way Between Subjects ANOVA tab contains the ANOVA analysis described below.

1. Open the *Computer Anxiety.xlsx file using Excel.*

2. Copy variables class and comanx2 (computer anxiety posttest) from the Excel workbook Data tab to columns A and B on an empty sheet. Copy all cases.

	A	B
1	class	comanx2
2	4	32
3	4	29
4	1	37
5	2	53

3. Sort cases in ascending order based on class.

	A	B
1	class	comanx2
2	1	37
3	1	51
4	1	38
5	1	59

4. Enter labels Class 1, Class 2, Class 3, and Class 4 in cells C2:C5 and n, Sum, Mean, SD, and Variance in cells D1:H1. Enter formulas =COUNT(A2:A38), =COUNT(A39:A55), =COUNT(A56:A73), and =COUNT(A74:A87) in cells D2:D5. Enter formulas =SUM(B2:B38), =SUM(B39:B55), =SUM(B56:B73), and =SUM(B74:B87) in cells E2:E5. Enter formulas =AVERAGE(B2:B38), =AVERAGE(B39:B55), =AVERAGE(B56:B73), and =AVERAGE(B74:B87) in cells F2:F5. Enter formulas =STDEV.S(B2:B38), =STDEV.S(B39:B55), =STDEV.S(B56:B73), and =STDEV.S(B74:B87) in cells G2:G5. Finally, enter formulas =VAR.S(B2:B38), VAR.S(B39:B55), =VAR.S(B56:B73), and VAR.S(B74:B87) in cells H2:H5.

	C	D	E
1		n	Sum
2	Class 1	=COUNT(A2:A38)	=SUM(B2:B38)
3	Class 2	=COUNT(A39:A55)	=SUM(B39:B55)
4	Class 3	=COUNT(A56:A73)	=SUM(B56:B73)
5	Class 4	=COUNT(A74:A87)	=SUM(B74:B87)

	F	G	H
1	Mean	SD	Variance
2	=AVERAGE(B2:B38)	=STDEV.S(B2:B38)	=VAR.S(B2:B38)
3	=AVERAGE(B39:B55)	=STDEV.S(B39:B55)	=VAR.S(B39:B55)
4	=AVERAGE(B56:B73)	=STDEV.S(B56:B73)	=VAR.S(B56:B73)
5	=AVERAGE(B74:B87)	=STDEV.S(B74:B87)	=VAR.S(B74:B87)

	C	D	E	F	G	H
1		n	Sum	Mean	SD	Variance
2	Class 1	36	1650	44.5946	9.12098	83.19219
3	Class 2	17	880	51.7647	10.3774	107.6912
4	Class 3	18	956	53.1111	10.7643	115.8693
5	Class 4	14	542	38.7143	10.5643	111.6044

5. Enter labels # groups, N, Grand mean, dfn, and dfd in cells C7:C11. Enter formulas =COUNT(D2:D5), =SUM(D2:D5), =AVERAGE(B2:B87), =D7-1, and D8-D7 in cells D7:D11.

	C	D
7	# groups	=COUNT(D2:D5)
8	N	=SUM(D2:D5)
9	Grand mean	=AVERAGE(B2:B87)
10	dfn	=D7-1
11	dfd	=D8-D7

C	D
7	# groups	4
8	N	85
9	Grand mean	46.8372093
10	dfn	3
11	dfd	81

6. Enter label SSb in cell C12 and formula =D14-DEVSQ(B2:B38)-DEVSQ(B39:B55)-DEVSQ(B56:B73)-DEVSQ(B74:B87) in cell D12.

C	D
12	SSb	2231.108267

7. Enter labels SSw, SS (total), MSb, MSw, F, p-level, and eta-squared in cells C13:C19. Enter formulas =D14-D12, =DEVSQ(B2:B87), =D12/D10, =D13/D11, =D15/D16, =F.DIST.RT(D17,D10,D11), and =D12/D14 in cells D13:D19.

C	D
13	SSw	=D14-D12
14	SS (total)	=DEVSQ(B2:B87)
15	MSb	=D12/D10
16	MSw	=D13/D11
17	F	=D15/D16
18	p-level	=F.DIST.RT(D17,D10,D11)
19	eta-squared	=D12/D14

	C	D
13	SSw	8138.612663
14	SS (total)	10369.72093
15	MSb	743.7027557
16	MSw	99.25137394
17	F	7.493123029
18	p-level	0.000171023
19	eta-squared	0.215156057

Sum of squares between, within, and total (SSb, SSw, and SS (total)) are the sum of squared differences from the mean.

Mean square between and within (MSb and MSw) are estimates of variance across groups and are calculated as the sum of squares divided by its appropriate degrees of freedom.

Eta-squared is the effect size statistic.

8. Enter label Post Hoc Multiple Comparison Tests in cell I7 and labels Dependent Variable: Computer Anxiety Posttest, Independent Variable: Class, Test: Scheffé, Alpha, and F critical in cells I9:I13. Enter formulas 0.05 and =(D7-1)*F.INV.RT(J12,K3,K4) in cells J12:J13.

	I	J
12	Alpha	0.05
13	F critical	=(D7-1)*F.INV.RT(J12,K3,K4)

◢	I	J	K
7	Post Hoc Multiple Comparison Tests		
8			
9	Dependent Variable: Computer Anxiety Posttest		
10	Independent Variable: Class		
11	Test: Scheffe		
12	Alpha	0.05	
13	F critical	8.147809668	

9. Enter labels Group Comparison, Mean Difference,
Standard Error, Mean Difference Squared, MSw, 1/n+1/n,
and F in cells I15:O15. Enter labels 1 vs 2, 1 vs 3, 1 vs 4, 2
vs 3, 2 vs 4, and 3 vs 4 in cells I16:I21. Enter formulas
=F2-F3, =F2-F4, =F2-F5, =F3-F4, =F3-F5, and =F4-F5 in
cells J16:J21 to calculate mean pairwise differences. Enter
formulas =SQRT($I$4)*SQRT((1/D2)+(1/D3)), =SQRT($I
$4)*SQRT((1/D2)+(1/D4)), =SQRT($I$4)*SQRT((1/D2)+(1/
D5)), =SQRT($I$4)*SQRT((1/D3)+(1/D4)), =SQRT($I
$4)*SQRT((1/D3)+(1/D5)) and =SQRT($I$4)*SQRT((1/
D4)+(1/D5)) in cells K16:K21 to calculate pairwise
standard error. Enter formula =POWER(J16,2) in cell L16
and Fill Down to cell L21 to calculate difference squared.
Enter formula =$L$4 in cells M16:M21 to insert the ANOVA
mean square (within) statistic. Insert formulas =1/D2+1/D3,
=1/D2+1/D4, =1/D2+1/D5, =1/D3+1/D4, =1/D3+1/D5, and
=1/D4+1/D5 in cells N16:N21 to facilitate calculation of
Scheffé F. Finally, enter formula =L16(M16*N16) in cell
O16 and Fill Down to cell O21 to calculate Scheffé F.

	J	K
15	Mean Difference	Standard Error
16	=F2-F3	=SQRT($L$4)*SQRT((1/D2)+(1/D3))
17	=F2-F4	=SQRT($L$4)*SQRT((1/D2)+(1/D4))
18	=F2-F5	=SQRT($L$4)*SQRT((1/D2)+(1/D5))
19	=F3-F4	=SQRT($L$4)*SQRT((1/D3)+(1/D4))
20	=F3-F5	=SQRT($L$4)*SQRT((1/D3)+(1/D5))
21	=F4-F5	=SQRT($L$4)*SQRT((1/D4)+(1/D5))

	L	M	N	O
15	Difference Squared	MSw	1/n+1/n	F
16	=POWER(J16,2)	=$L$4	=1/D2+1/D3	=L16/(M16*N16)
17	=POWER(J17,2)	=$L$4	=1/D2+1/D4	=L17/(M17*N17)
18	=POWER(J18,2)	=$L$4	=1/D2+1/D5	=L18/(M18*N18)
19	=POWER(J19,2)	=$L$4	=1/D3+1/D4	=L19/(M19*N19)
20	=POWER(J20,2)	=$L$4	=1/D3+1/D5	=L20/(M20*N20)
21	=POWER(J21,2)	=$L$4	=1/D4+1/D5	=L21/(M21*N21)

Formatted ANOVA output summarizing test results:

	M	N	O	P	Q	R	S
1	One-Way Between Subjects ANOVA						
2	Source	Sum of Squares	df	Mean Square	F	p-level	Eta-Squared
3	class	2231.1083	3	743.703	7.493	0.0002	0.2152
4	Error	8138.6127	82	99.2514			
5	Total	10369.721					

The above output shows that the ANOVA is significant since the p-level is >= .05 (the assumed à priori significance level). Effect size, measured by eta-squared, is .22. Since the ANOVA is significant, post hoc multiple comparison tests are required to identify pairwise differences.

	I	J	K	L	M	N	O
15	Group Comparison	Mean Difference	Standard Error	Mean Difference Squared	MSw	1/n+1/n	F
16	1 vs 2	-7.17011	2.91904	51.4105	99.251	0.0859	6.0335
17	1 vs 3	-8.51652	2.86294	72.53105	99.251	0.0826	8.8491
18	1 vs 4	5.880309	3.126	34.57803	99.251	0.0985	3.5385
19	2 vs 3	-1.34641	3.36931	1.812807	99.251	0.1144	0.1597
20	2 vs 4	13.05042	3.59551	170.3135	99.251	0.1303	13.174
21	3 vs 4	14.39683	3.55012	207.2686	99.251	0.127	16.446

The Scheffé test results identifies the following significant pairwise differences because the *F*-value is greater than the Scheffé F critical value of 8.15: 1 vs 3, 2 vs 4, and 3 vs 4. Remaining pairwise differences are not significant.

Automated Procedures

Use the following procedures for Analysis ToolPak.

1. Launch Microsoft Excel for Windows and open the Computer Anxiety.xlsx file. Go to the One-Way Between Subjects ANOVA sheet.

2. Select the Data tab and click the Data Analysis icon to open the Data Analysis dialog. Select Anova: Single Factor and click OK to open the Anova: Single Factor dialog.

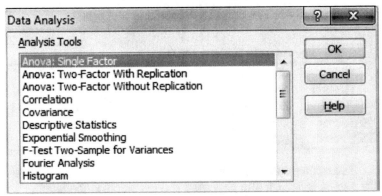

3. Select the Input Range by highlighting the comconf2 (computer confidence posttest) data disaggregated by Class and arranged in columns in cells Q1:T38. Select Labels in First Row.

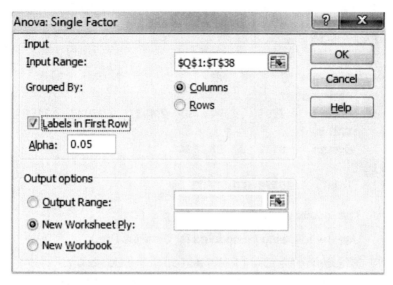

4. Click the OK button to run the procedure.

	A	B	C	D	E
1	Anova: Single Factor				
2					
3	SUMMARY				
4	Groups	Count	Sum	Average	Variance
5	Class 1	37	1650	44.59459	83.19219
6	Class 2	17	880	51.76471	107.6912
7	Class 3	18	956	53.11111	115.8693
8	Class 4	14	542	38.71429	111.6044

	A	B	C	D	E	F	G
11	ANOVA						
12	Source of Variation	SS	df	MS	F	P-value	F crit
13	Between Groups	2231	3	743.703	7.4931	0.00017	2.71594
14	Within Groups	8139	82	99.2514			
15							
16	Total	10370	85				

The results show $F(3,82) = 7.49$, $p < .001$.

Use the following procedures for StatPlus Pro.

1. Launch Microsoft Excel and open the Computer Anxiety.xlsx file. Go to the Go to the One-Way Between Subjects ANOVA sheet.

2. Launch StatPlus Pro and select Statistics > Analysis of Variance (ANOVA) > One-way ANOVA with post-hoc tests (unstacked) from the StatPlus menu bar.

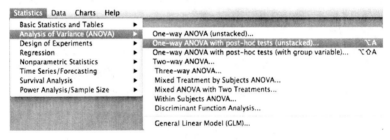

3. Select the Variables range by highlighting the comconf2 (computer confidence posttest) data arranged in cells Q1:T38 by class (i.e., unstacked format). Select Labels in first row.

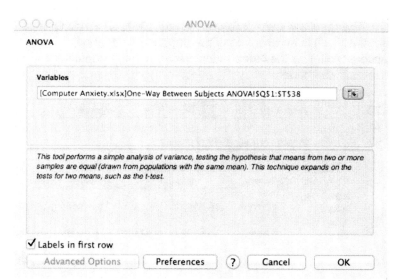

4. Click the OK button to run the procedure.

	A	B	C	D	E
1	**Analysis of Variance (One-Way)**				
2					
3	*Descriptive Statistics*				
4	*Groups*	*Sample size*	*Sum*	*Mean*	*Variance*
5	Class 1	37	1,650.	44.59459	76,576.
6	Class 2	17	880.	51.76471	47,276.
7	Class 3	18	956.	53.11111	52,744.
8	Class 4	14	542.	38.71429	22,434.
9					
10	Total	86		46.83721	121.99672

	A	B	C	D	E	F	G	H
12	ANOVA							
13	Source of Variation	d.f.	SS	MS	F	p-level	F crit	Omega Sqr.
14	Between Groups	3	2,231.10827	743.70276	7.49312	0.00017	2.71594	0.18467
15	Within Groups	82	8,138.61266	99.25137				
16								
17	Total	85	10,369.72093					

The results show $F(3,82) = 7.49$, $p < .001$, $\omega^2 = .18$. Omega squared (ω^2) is an estimate of the dependent variance accounted for by the independent variable in the population for a fixed effects model.

	A	B	C	D	E	F
23	Comparisons among groups (Factor 1 - Factor #1)					
24						
25	Scheffe contrasts among pairs of means					
26	Group vs Group (Contrast)	Difference	95% Confidence Interval		Test Statistics	p-level
27	Class 1 vs Class 2	-7.17011	-15.50232	1.1621	2.01118	0.11878
28	Class 1 vs Class 3	-8.51652	-16.6886	-0.34443	2.9497	0.0375
29	Class 1 vs Class 4	5.88031	-3.04265	14.80327	1.17951	0.32268
30	Class 2 vs Class 3	-1.34641	-10.9639	8.27109	0.05323	0.9837
31	Class 2 vs Class 4	13.05042	2.78726	23.31358	4.39144	0.00645
32	Class 3 vs Class 4	14.39683	4.26323	24.53042	5.48184	0.00175

	A	B	C	D	E
33	Tukey-Kramer Test for Differences Between Means				
34	Groups	Difference	Test Statistics	p-level	Accepted?
35	Class 1 vs Class 2	-7.17011	3.47377	0.07472	rejected
36	Class 1 vs Class 3	-8.51652	4.20692	0.01981	accepted
37	Class 1 vs Class 4	5.88031	2.66028	0.24417	rejected
38	Class 2 vs Class 3	-1.34641	0.56513	0.97831	rejected
39	Class 2 vs Class 4	13.05042	5.13309	0.00273	accepted
40	Class 3 vs Class 4	14.39683	5.73507	0.00063	accepted

	A	B	C	D	E	F
41	Bonferroni Test for Differences Between Means					
42	Alpha/N	0.00833				
43	Group vs Group (Contrast)	Difference	95% Confidence Interval		Test Statistics	p-level
44	Class 1 vs Class 2	-7.17011	-15.06252	0.7223	2.45633	0.09689
45	Class 1 vs Class 3	-8.51652	-16.25725	-0.77578	2.97474	0.02311
46	Class 1 vs Class 4	5.88031	-2.57167	14.33228	1.8811	0.38105
47	Class 2 vs Class 3	-1.34641	-10.45626	7.76345	0.39961	1.
48	Class 2 vs Class 4	13.05042	3.32899	22.77185	3.62964	0.00295
49	Class 3 vs Class 4	14.39683	4.79812	23.99553	4.05531	0.00068

Bonferroni post hoc tests show significant pairwise differences between Class 1 vs Class 3, Class 2 vs Class 4, and Class 3 vs Class 4.

	A	B	C	D	E
50	Fisher LSD				
51	Group vs Group (Contrast)	Difference	Test Statistics	p-level	Accepted?
52	Class 1 vs Class 2	-7.17011	2.45633	0.0161	accepted
53	Class 1 vs Class 3	-8.51652	2.97474	0.00383	accepted
54	Class 1 vs Class 4	5.88031	1.8811	0.06342	rejected
55	Class 2 vs Class 3	-1.34641	0.39961	0.69046	rejected
56	Class 2 vs Class 4	13.05042	3.62964	0.00049	accepted
57	Class 3 vs Class 4	14.39683	4.05531	0.00011	accepted

One-Way Between Subjects ANOVA Reporting

As a minimum, the following information should be reported in the results section of any report: null hypothesis that is evaluated, descriptive statistics (e.g., *M, SD, N, n*), statistical test used (i.e., one-way between subjects ANOVA), results of evaluation of ANOVA assumptions, and ANOVA results. For a test one should also report effect size (e.g., eta squared, η^2) and the results of post hoc multiple comparison tests if ANOVA results are significant. For example, one might report test results as follows.

A one-way between subjects ANOVA was conducted to evaluate the following null hypotheses: There is no difference in computer confidence posttest between graduate students based on enrolled class. The ANOVA was significant, $F(3,82) = 7.49$, $p < .001$, $\eta^2 = .22$. Consequently, there was sufficient evidence to reject the null hypothesis of no difference in computer computer anxiety posttest between graduate students based on enrolled class. Post hoc Scheffé multiple comparison tests revealed three pairwise significant differences: 1 vs 3 (computer anxiety lower in class 1), 2 vs 4 (computer anxiety lower in class 4), and 3 vs 4 (computer anxiety lower in class 4).

(Note: all assumptions require evaluation and reporting before test results can be relied upon.)

KRUSKAL-WALLIS H TEST

The Kruskal-Wallis H Test is a nonparametric procedure that compares total ranks between multiple independent groups when the DV is either ordinal or interval/ratio scale. It is an extension of the Mann-Whitney U Test for multiple groups and is the nonparametric version of one-way between subjects analysis of variance. The formula using squares of the average ranks is provided below:

$$H = \frac{12}{N(N+1)} \sum n_i (\bar{r})^2 - 3(N+1)$$

where N = total sample size, n = the sample size of each group, and r = sum of ranks of each group.

Degrees of freedom. Degrees of freedom = $k - 1$, where k = number of groups.

Post hoc multiple comparison tests. For pairwise post hoc comparisons, the Mann-Whitney U test is appropriate following a significant Kruskal-Wallis H test.

Effect size. Effect size for the Kruskal-Wallis H test is reported in conjunction with post hoc tests following a significant Kruskal-Wallis *H* test. That is, report effect size using the *r* coefficient with the Mann-Whitney *U* test. An approximation of the *r* coefficient can be obtained using the value of *z* and the following formula (Rosenthal, 1991):

$$ r = \frac{z}{\sqrt{N}} $$

where *N* = total number of cases and *z* = *z*-value displayed in Mann-Whitney U test Excel output.

Alternatively, the difference in mean ranks between groups can be used for effect size.

Key Assumptions & Requirements

Random selection of samples (probability samples) to allow for generalization of results to a target population.

Variables. DV: one continuous variable measured on the ordinal, interval, or ratio scale. IV: one categorical variable with multiple categories.

Distributions of each group have the same shape. For example, Fagerland and Sandvik (2009) point out that if groups vary on skewness (a mix of negative and positive skewed distributions) or groups have different variances, test results will be inaccurate.

Independence of observations.

Sample size. Adequate cell size, e.g., $n > 5$ in each group.

Excel Functions Used

CHISQ.DIST.RT(x,deg_freedom). Returns the right-tailed *p*-level of the chi-square distribution, where x is the chi-square value to be evaluated and deg_freedom is a number reflecting degrees of freedom.

COUNT(value1,value2,...). Counts the numbers in the range of numbers.

MEDIAN(number1,number2,...). Returns the median of a

range of numbers.

POWER(number,power). Returns a number raised to the specified power, where number is the base number and power is the exponent.

RANK.AVG(number,ref,order). Returns the rank of a number in a list, where number = the number to be ranked, ref = the list of numbers upon which the rankings are based, and 0 indicates the reference list is sorted in descending order.

SQRT(number). Returns the square root of a number.

SUM(number1,number2,...). Adds the range of numbers.

Kruskal-Wallis H Test Procedures

Research question and null hypothesis:

Is there a difference in the sum of ranks of computer knowledge pretest among four undergraduate computer literacy classes?

H_0: There is no difference between the sum of ranks of computer knowledge pretest among four undergraduate computer literacy classes.

Task: Use the Excel file Computer Anxiety.xlsx located at http://www.watertreepress.com/stats if you want to follow along with the analysis. The Data tab contains the data and the Kruskal-Wallis H Test *tab contains the* Kruskal-Wallis H Test *analysis described below.*

1. Open the *Computer Anxiety.xlsx file using Excel.*

2. Copy class and comkow data from the Excel workbook Data tab and paste the data in columns A and B of an empty sheet.

	A	B
1	class	comknow
2	4	14
3	4	4
4	1	5
5	2	10

3. Enter label Ranks in cell C1 and formula
   =RANK.AVG(B2$B$2:$B$93,0) in cell C2 (note the
   relative and fixed addresses). Fill Down to cell C93.

	C
1	Ranks
2	=RANK.AVG(B2,$B$2:$B$93,0)
3	=RANK.AVG(B3,$B$2:$B$93,0)
4	=RANK.AVG(B4,$B$2:$B$93,0)
5	=RANK.AVG(B5,$B$2:$B$93,0)

	C	D
1	Ranks	
2	23	
3	70.5	
4	63.5	
5	40.5	

4. Sort cases in ascending order by class.

	A	B	C
1	class	comknow	Ranks
2	1	5	63.5
3	1	1	88
4	1	2	81
5	1	6	56.5

5. Enter labels Class 1, Class 2, Class 3, and Class 4 in cells D2:D5 and n in cell E1. Enter formulas =COUNT(A2:A40, =COUNT(A41:A59, =COUNT(A60:A79), =COUNT(A80:A93 in cells E1:E5.

	D	E
1		n
2	Class 1	=COUNT(A2:A40)
3	Class 2	=COUNT(A41:A59)
4	Class 3	=COUNT(A60:A79)
5	Class 4	=COUNT(A80:A93)

	D	E
1		n
2	Class 1	39
3	Class 2	19
4	Class 3	20
5	Class 4	14

6. Enter the labels Median, Sum of Ranks, and Mean Rank in cells F1:H1. Enter formulas =MEDIAN(B2:B40), =MEDIAN(B41:B59), =MEDIAN(B60:B79), and =MEDIAN(B80:B93) in cells F2:F5. Enter formulas =SUM(C2:C40), =SUM(C41:C59), =SUM(C60:C79), and =SUM(C80:C93) in cells G2:G5. Enter formulas =AVERAGE(C2:C40), =AVERAGE(C41:C59),

=AVERAGE(C60:C79), and =AVERAGE(C80:C93) in cells H2:H5.

	F	G	H
1	Median	Sum of Ranks	Mean Rank
2	=MEDIAN(B2:B40)	=SUM(C2:C40)	=AVERAGE(C2:C40)
3	=MEDIAN(B41:B59)	=SUM(C41:C59)	=AVERAGE(C41:C59)
4	=MEDIAN(B60:B79)	=SUM(C60:C79)	=AVERAGE(C60:C79)
5	=MEDIAN(B80:B93)	=SUM(C80:C93)	=AVERAGE(C80:C93)

	F	G	H
1	Median	Sum of Ranks	Mean Rank
2	7	1906	48.87179487
3	10	956	50.31578947
4	6	965.5	48.275
5	11.5	450.5	32.17857143

7. Enter labels N and df in cells D6:D7. Enter formulas =SUM(E2:E5) and =COUNT(E2:E5) − 1 in cells E6:E7.

	D	E
6	N	=SUM(E2:E5)
7	df	=COUNT(E2:E5)-1

	D	E
6	N	92
7	df	3

8. Enter the letter H (the Kruskal-Wallis H statistic) in cell D8 and the formula =(12/(E6*(E6+1)))*(POWER(G2,2)/ E2+POWER(G3,2)/E3+POWER(G4,2)/ E4+POWER(G5,2)/E5)-3*(E6+1) in cell E8. The general formula is =(12/(N*(N+1)))* (POWER(SR_1,2)/ n_1+POWER(SR_2,2)/n_2+ ... +POWER(SR_n,2)/n_n)−3*(N + 1), where N = total sample size, SR = sum of ranks for each group, and n = group sample size.

	D	E
8	H	4.811353003

9. Finally, enter the label *p*-level and formula
=CHISQ.DIST.RT(E8,E7) in cells D9:E9.

	D	E
9	p-level	=CHISQ.DIST.RT(E8,E7)

	D	E
9	p-level	0.186143578

Formatted Kruskal-Wallis *H* test output summarizing test results:

	D	E	F	G
11	Kruskal-Wallis H Test			
12		H	df	p-level
13	Computer Knowledge	4.811353	3	0.186144

Excel output includes the Kruskal-Wallis *H* statistic, degrees of freedom, and the calculated *p*-level. The above output shows that the Kruskal-Wallis *H* test is not significant since the *p*-level is > .05 the assumed *à priori* significance level).

Automated Procedures

Use the following procedures for StatPlus Pro.

1. Launch Microsoft Excel and open the Computer Anxiety.xlsx file. Go to the Go to the Kruskal-Wallis *H* Test sheet.

2. Launch StatPlus Pro and select Statistics > Nonparametric Statistics > Comparing Multiple Independent Samples (Kruskal-Wallis ANOVA, Median Test) from the StatPlus menu bar.

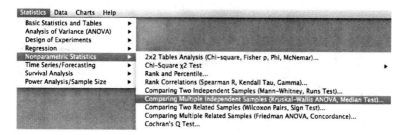

3. Select the Variables range by highlighting the comknow (computer knowledge pretest) data arranged in cells J1:M40 by class (i.e., unstacked format). Select Labels in first row.

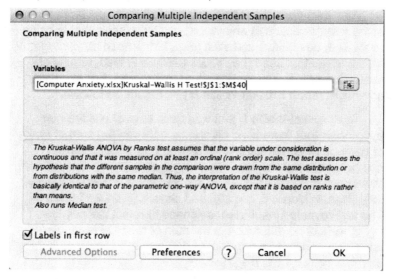

4. Click the OK button to run the procedure.

	A	B	C	D
1	**Comparing Multiple Independent Samples**			
2		**Sample size**	**Sum of Ranks**	
3	Class 1	39	1,721.	
4	Class 2	19	811.	
5	Class 3	20	894.5	
6	Class 4	14	851.5	

	A	B	C	D
8	Kruskal-Wallis ANOVA			
9	H	4.81135	N	92
10	Degrees Of Freedom	3	p-level	0.18614
11	H (corrected)	4.83269		

The test results show $H(3) = 4.81$, $p = .19$.

Kruskal-Wallis H Test Reporting

As a minimum, the following information should be reported in the results section of any report: null hypothesis that is being evaluated, descriptive statistics (e.g., Mdn, mean rank, range, N, n), statistical test used (i.e., Kruskal-Wallis H test), results of evaluation of test assumptions, and test results. For example, one might report Kruskal-Wallis H test results as follows.

The Kruskal-Wallis H test was used to evaluate the null hypothesis that there is no difference between the sum of ranks of computer knowledge pretest among four undergraduate computer literacy classes. The sample consisted of the following four classes: class 1 (Mdn = 7, $n = 39$), class 2 (Mdn = 10, $n = 19$), class 3 (Mdn = 6, $n = 20$), and class 4 (Mdn = 11.5, $n = 14$). The test revealed insufficient evidence to reject the null hypothesis of no difference in the sum of ranks of computer knowledge pretest among four undergraduate computer literacy classes, $H(3) = 4.81$, $p = .19$.

4.5: Comparing Two Dependent Samples

DEPENDENT T-TEST

The Dependent t-Test, also called the Paired-Samples t-Test, dependent samples t-test, and t-test for correlated groups, is a parametric procedure that compares mean scores obtained from two dependent (related) samples. In other words, each case in one sample has a unique corresponding member in the other sample. For example, the DV is test score and the IV is observation (pretest, posttest) in which each case has a pretest and a paired posttest score. The Dependent t-Test will show whether the differences observed in the two observations will be found reliably in repeated samples.

Dependent or related data are obtained by:

- Measuring participants from the same sample on two different occasions (i.e., using a repeated-measures or within subjects design).

- Using a matching procedure by pairing research participants and dividing them so one member of the pair is assigned to each group.

Excel data entry for the Dependent t-Test is fairly straightforward. Each observation, e.g., pretest, posttest, is entered in Excel as a separate column.

The following formula is used to calculate t:

$$t = \frac{\overline{X}_1 - \overline{X}_2}{\dfrac{S_{\overline{X}_1 - \overline{X}_2}}{\sqrt{N}}}$$

where $\overline{X}_1 - \overline{X}_2$ is the difference in means of sample 1 and sample 2, $S_{\overline{X}_1 - \overline{X}_2}$ is the estimated standard error of the difference (i.e., the standard deviation of difference scores), and $\sqrt{N}$ is the square root of the number of paired observations.

Degrees of freedom. The degrees of freedom for this test are $N - 1$.

Effect size. Effect size can be determined by calculating Cohen's *d*. The formula for Cohen's *d* for a dependent *t*-test is (Green & Salkind, 2008):

$$d = \frac{t}{\sqrt{N}}$$

where *N* represents the number of cases in the analysis. By convention, Cohen's *d* values are interpreted as follows:

Small effect size = .20
Medium effect size = .50
Large effect size = .80

Alternatively, *r* can be used as a measure of effect size using the following equation (Rosenthal, 1991; Rosnow & Rosenthal, 2005):

$$r = \sqrt{\frac{t^2}{t^2 + df}}$$

where

Small effect size = .10
Medium effect size = .30
Large effect size = .50

Key Assumptions & Requirements

Random selection of samples (probability samples) to allow for generalization of results to a target population.

Variables. IV: a dichotomous categorical variable. DV: an interval or ratio scale variable. The data are dependent.

Normality. The sampling distribution of the differences between scores is normally distributed. (The two related groups themselves do not need to be normally distributed.) Note: the normality assumption for a dependent t-test pertains to difference scores. The dependent t-test is robust to mild to moderate violations of normality assuming a sufficiently large sample size, e.g., $N > 30$. However, it may not be the most powerful test available for a given non-normal distribution.

Excel Functions Used

ABS(number). Returns the absolute value of the specified number.

AVERAGE(number1,number2,...). Returns the arithmetic mean, where numbers represent the range of numbers.

COUNT(value1,value2,...). Counts the numbers in the range of numbers.

SQRT(number). Returns the square root of a number.

STDEV.S(number1,number2,...). Returns the unbiased estimate of population standard deviation, where numbers represent the range of numbers.

T.DIST.2T(x,deg_freedom). Returns the 2-tailed t-distribution probability, where x is the value to be evaluated and deg_freedom is a number representing the degrees of freedom.

Dependent t-Test Procedures

Research question and null hypothesis:

Is there a difference between computer confidence pretest and computer confidence posttest among university students, $\mu_1 - \mu_2 \neq 0$?

Note: IV is observation (pretest, posttest) and DV is computer confidence.

H_0: There is no difference between computer confidence pretest and computer confidence posttest among university students, $\mu_1 - \mu_2 = 0$.

Task: Use the Excel file Computer Anxiety.xlsx located at http://www.watertreepress.com/stats if you want to follow along with the analysis. The Data tab contains the data and the Dependent t-Test tab contains the Dependent t-Test analysis described below.

1. Open the *Computer Anxiety.xlsx file using Excel.*

2. Copy variables comconf1 (computer confidence pretest) and comconf2 (computer confidence posttest) from the Excel workbook Data tab to columns A and B on an empty sheet. Copy all 86 cases.

	A	B
1	comconf1	comconf2
2	32	35
3	38	40
4	33	38
5	23	35

3. Enter label Difference in cell C1 and calculate difference scores (comconf1 − comconf2) in cells C2:C87.

	A	B	C
1	comconf1	comconf2	Difference
2	32	35	-3
3	38	40	-2
4	33	38	-5
5	23	35	-12

4. Enter labels comconf1 and comconf2 in cells D2:D3 and n, Mean, and SD in cells E1:G1. Enter formulas =COUNT(A2:A87)and =COUNT(B2:B87) in cells E2:E3, =AVERAGE(A2:A87) and AVERAGE(B2:B87) in cells F2:F3, and =STDV.S(A2:A87) and =STDEV.S(B2:B87) in cells G2:G3.

	D	E
1		n
2	comconf1	=COUNT(A2:A87)
3	comconf2	=COUNT(B2:B87)

	F	G
1	Mean	SD
2	=AVERAGE(A2:A87)	=STDEV.S(A2:A87)
3	=AVERAGE(B2:B87)	=STDEV.S(B2:B87)

	D	E	F	G
1		n	Mean	SD
2	comconf1	86	31.0930233	5.79985
3	comconf2	86	32.5232558	5.35279

5. Finally, enter labels N, Mean difference, SD mean difference, SE mean, df, t, p-level (2-tailed), and Cohen's d in cells D4:D11. Enter formulas =E2, =AVERAGE(C2:C87), =STDEV.S(C2:C87), =E6/SQRT(E4), =E4-1, =(F2-F3)/(E6/SQRT(E4)), =T.DIST.2T(ABS(E9),E8), and =E9/SQRT(E4) in cells E4:E11.

	D	E
4	N	=E2
5	Mean difference	=AVERAGE(C2:C87)
6	SD mean difference	=STDEV.S(C2:C87)
7	SE mean	=E6/SQRT(E4)
8	df	=E4-1
9	t	=(F2-F3)/(E6/SQRT(E4))
10	p-level (2-tailed)	=T.DIST.2T(ABS(E9),E8)
11	Cohen's d	=E9/SQRT(E4)

	D	E
4	N	86
5	Mean difference	-1.430232558
6	SD mean difference	4.383231947
7	SE mean	0.472656056
8	df	85
9	t	-3.025947809
10	p-level (2-tailed)	0.00327887
11	Cohen's d	-0.326296344

The standard error of the mean (SE mean) is the standard deviation of the sampling distribution of the mean. It is a measure of the stability of the sample means.

Formatted dependent t-test output summarizing test results:

	D	E	F	G	H	I	J	K
13	Dependent t-Test							
14		Mean	SD	SE Mean	t	df	p-level	Cohen's d
15	comconf1 - comconf2	-1.43	4.383	0.4727	-3.026	85	0.003	-0.3263

These results show that the difference between groups is significant since the p-level <= .05 (the assumed à priori significance level).

Automated Procedures

Use the following procedures for Analysis ToolPak.

1. Launch Microsoft Excel for Windows and open the Computer Anxiety.xlsx file. Go to the Dependent t-Test sheet.

2. Select the Data tab and click the Data Analysis icon to open the Data Analysis dialog. Select t-Test: Paired Two-Sample for Means and click OK to open the t-Test dialog.

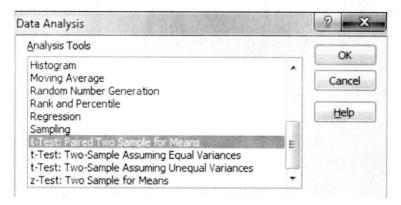

3. Select the Variable 1 Range by highlighting the comconf1 (computer confidence pretest) data in cells A1:A87 and select the Variable 2 Range by highlighting the comconf2 (computer confidence posttest) data in cells B1:B87. Click the OK button to run the procedure.

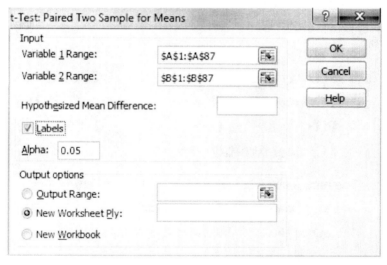

4. Excel places the following output in a new sheet.

⊿	A	B	C
1	t-Test: Paired Two Sample for Means		
2			
3		comconf1	comconf2
4	Mean	31.0930233	32.52325581
5	Variance	33.6383037	28.65239398
6	Observations	86	86
7	Pearson Correlation	0.6937896	

⊿	A	B
8	Hypothesized Mean Difference	0
9	df	85
10	t Stat	-3.025947809
11	P(T<=t) one-tail	0.001639435
12	t Critical one-tail	1.6629785
13	P(T<=t) two-tail	0.00327887
14	t Critical two-tail	1.988267907

The results show $t(85) = -3.03$, $p = .003$ (2-tailed).

Use the following procedures for StatPlus LE.

1. Launch Microsoft Excel and open the Computer Anxiety.xlsx file. Go to the Dependent t-Test sheet.

2. Launch StatPlus LE and select Statistics > Basic Statistics and Tables > Comparing Means (T-Test) from the StatPlus menu bar.

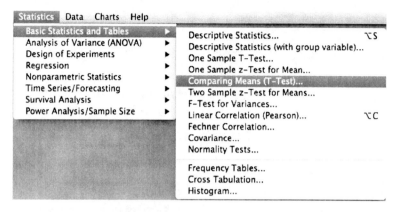

3. Select the Variable #1 range by highlighting the comconf1 (computer confidence pretest) data and select the Variable #2 range by highlighting the comconf2 (computer confidence posttest) data. Select Paired Two Sample T-Test.

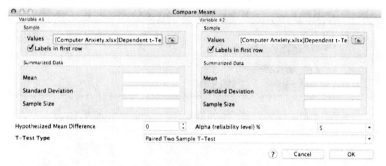

4. Click the OK button to run the procedure.

	A	B	C	D
1	**Comparing Means [Paired two-sample t-test]**			
2	*Descriptive Statistics*			
3	*VAR*	*Sample size*	*Mean*	*Variance*
4		86	31.09302	33.6383
5		86	32.52326	28.65239

	A	B	C	D
7	Summary			
8	Degrees Of Freedom	85	Hypothesized	0.E+0
9	Test Statistics	3.02595	Pooled Variance	31.14535
10				
11	Two-tailed distribution			
12	p-level	0.00328	t Critical Value (5%)	1.98827
13				
14	One-tailed distribution			
15	p-level	0.00164	t Critical Value (5%)	1.66298
16	Pearson Correlation Coefficient	0.69379		

The results show $t(85) = 3.03$, $p = .003$ (2-tailed) and Pearson $r = .69$.

Dependent t-Test Reporting

As a minimum, the following information should be reported in the results section of any report: null hypothesis that is being evaluated, descriptive statistics (e.g., *M, SD, N*), statistical test used (i.e., dependent *t*-test), results of evaluation of test assumptions, and test results. For example, one might report test results as follows.

A dependent *t*-test was conducted to evaluate the null hypothesis that there is no difference between computer confidence pretest and computer confidence posttest among university students ($N = 86$). The results of the test provided evidence that computer confidence posttest ($M = 32.52$, $SD = 5.35$) was significantly higher than computer confidence pretest ($M = 31.09$, $SD = 5.80$), $t(85) = 3.03$, $p = .003$, $d = .33$.

Therefore, there was sufficient evidence to reject the null hypothesis. Effect size as measured by Cohen's *d* was small.

(Note: assumptions require evaluation and reporting before test results can be relied upon.)

WILCOXON MATCHED-PAIR SIGNED RANKS TEST

The Wilcoxon Matched-Pair Signed Ranks Test (also called the Wilcoxon Matched Pair Test and the Wilcoxon Signed Ranks Test) is a nonparametric procedure that compares differences between data pairs of dependent data from two dependent samples.

Relevant formulas are provided as follows:

$$W = Min(NegativeSR, PositiveSR)$$

$$z = \frac{W - \frac{N(N+1)}{4}}{\sqrt{\frac{N(N+1)(2N+1)}{24}}}$$

where SR = sum of ranks and *N* = sample size less ties.

Effect size. An approximation of the *r* coefficient can be obtained using the value of *z* and the following formula (Rosenthal, 1991):

$$r = \frac{z}{\sqrt{N}}$$

Alternatively, the difference in mean ranks between groups can be used for effect size.

Key Assumptions & Requirements

Random selection of samples (probability samples) to allow for generalization of results to a target population.

Variables. DV: one continuous variable that is ordinal, interval, or ratio scale. IV: one dichotomous variable. Use of dependent (i.e., related) data.

Distribution of difference scores between pairs of observations is continuous and symmetrical in the population.

Independence of observations except for the matched pairs. Scores for each matched pair of scores must be independent of other matched pairs of scores.

Sample size. A relatively large sample size is required for accurate results, e.g., $N > 30$.

Excel Functions Used

ABS(number). Returns the absolute value of the specified number.

AVERAGEIF(range, criteria). Returns the average values of cells in the range that meet the given criteria.

COUNT(value1,value2,...). Counts the numbers in the range of numbers.

COUNTIF(range,criteria). Counts the number within a given range that meet the criteria).

MIN(number1,number2,...). Returns the smallest number in the range of numbers.

NORM.S.DIST(z,cumulative). Returns the standard normal distribution.

RANK.AVG(number,ref,order). Returns the rank of a number in a list, where number = the number to be ranked, ref = the list of numbers upon which the rankings are based, and 0 indicates the reference list is sorted in descending order.

SQRT(number). Returns the square root of a number.

SUM(number1,number2,...). Adds the range of numbers.

Wilcoxon Matched-Pair Signed Ranks Test Procedures

Research question and null hypothesis:

Is there a difference in ranks between computer anxiety pretest and computer anxiety posttest among university students? The IV is observation (pretest, posttest) and the DV is computer anxiety score.

H_0: *There is no difference in ranks between computer anxiety pretest and computer anxiety posttest among university students.*

Task: Use the Excel file Computer Anxiety.xlsx located at http://www.watertreepress.com/stats if you want to follow along with the analysis. The Data tab contains the data and the Wilcoxon Signed Ranks Test *tab contains the* Wilcoxon Matched-Pair Signed Ranks Test *analysis described below.*

1. Open the *Computer Anxiety.xlsx file using Excel.*

2. Copy comanx1 and comanx2 data from the Excel workbook Data tab and paste the data in columns A and B of an empty sheet.

	A	B
1	comanx1	comanx2
2	41	32
3	36	29
4	78	37
5	70	53

3. Enter labels Difference and Absolute Difference in cells C1:D1. Enter formulas =B2-A2, and =IF(OR(C2=0,C2=""),"",ABS(C2)) in cells C2:D2 and Fill Down to cells C87:D87.

	C	D
1	Difference	Absolute Difference
2	=B2-A2	=IF(OR(C2=0,C2=""),"",ABS(C2))
3	=B3-A3	=IF(OR(C3=0,C3=""),"",ABS(C3))
4	=B4-A4	=IF(OR(C4=0,C4=""),"",ABS(C4))
5	=B5-A5	=IF(OR(C5=0,C5=""),"",ABS(C5))

	C	D
1	Difference	Absolute Difference
2	-9	9
3	-7	7
4	-41	41
5	-17	17

4. Enter label Rank in cell E1 and formula
   =If(D2<>"",RANK.AVG(D2,D:D,1),"") in cell E2 and Fill
   Down to cell E87.

	E
1	Rank
2	=IF(D2<>"",RANK.AVG(D2,D:D,1),"")
3	=IF(D3<>"",RANK.AVG(D3,D:D,1),"")
4	=IF(D4<>"",RANK.AVG(D4,D:D,1),"")
5	=IF(D5<>"",RANK.AVG(D5,D:D,1),"")

	E
1	Rank
2	45.5
3	38.5
4	83
5	69

5. Enter labels Negative Signed Rank and Positive Signed
   Rank in cells F1:G1. Enter formulas =IF(C2<0,E2,"" and
   =IF(C2>0,E2,"" in cells F1:G2 and Fill Down to cells
   F87:G87.

	F	G
1	Negative Signed Rank	Positive Signed Rank
2	=IF(C2<0,E2,"")	=IF(C2>0,E2,"")
3	=IF(C3<0,E3,"")	=IF(C3>0,E3,"")
4	=IF(C4<0,E4,"")	=IF(C4>0,E4,"")
5	=IF(C5<0,E5,"")	=IF(C5>0,E5,"")
6	=IF(C6<0,E6,"")	=IF(C6>0,E6,"")

	F	G
1	Negative Signed Rank	Positive Signed Rank
2	45.5	
3	38.5	
4	83	
5	69	
6		3

6. Enter labels Negative Ranks and Positive Ranks in cells H2:H3 and N, Mean Rank, and Sum of Ranks in cells I1:K1. Enter formulas =COUNTIF(F2:F87,">0"), =COUNTIF(G2:G87,">0"), =AVERAGEIF(F2:F87,">0"), =AVERAGEIF(G2:G87,">0"), =SUM(F2:F87), and =SUM(G2:G87)) in cells I2:K3.

	H	I
1		N
2	Negative Ranks	=COUNTIF(F2:F87,">0")
3	Positive Ranks	=COUNTIF(G2:G87,">0")

	J	K
1	Mean Rank	Sum of Ranks
2	=AVERAGEIF(F2:F87,">0")	=SUM(F2:F87)
3	=AVERAGEIF(G2:G87,">0")	=SUM(G2:G87)

◢	H	I	J	K
1		N	Mean Rank	Sum of Ranks
2	Negative Ranks	60	49.2	2952
3	Positive Ranks	23	23.2173913	534

7. Finally, enter labels W, N, N less ties, Z, p-level (2-tailed), and r in cells H5:H10. Enter formulas =MIN(K2:K3), =COUNT(A2:A87), =COUNT(D2:D87), =(I5-I7*(I7+1)/4/SQRT((I7*(I7+1)*(2*I7+1)/24)), =NORM.S.DIST(I8,TRUE), and =I8/SQRT(I7) in cells I5:I10.

◢	H	I
5	W	=MIN(K2:K3)
6	N	=COUNT(A2:A87)
7	N less ties	=COUNT(D2:D87)
8	Z	=(I5-I7*(I7+1)/4)/SQRT((I7*(I7+1)*(2*I7+1)/24))
9	p-level (2-tailed)	=2*NORM.S.DIST(I8,TRUE)
10	r	=I8/SQRT(I7)

◢	H	I
5	W	534
6	N	86
7	N less ties	83
8	Z	-5.489022322
9	p-level (2-tailed)	0.00000004
10	r	-0.602498473

Formatted Wilcoxon Matched-Pair Signed Ranks Test output summarizing test results:

	H	I
12	Wilcoxon Matched-Pair Signed Ranks Test	
13		comanx2 - comanx1
14	z	-5.489022322
15	p-level (2-tailed)	0.00000004
16	r	-0.602498473

The above output shows that the Wilcoxon test is significant using the z-approximation since the significance level <= .05 (the assumed *à priori* significance level). The r-approximation is a measure of effect size.

Automated Procedures

Use the following procedures for StatPlus Pro.

1. Launch Microsoft Excel and open the Computer Anxiety.xlsx file. Go to the Wilcoxon Signed Ranks Test sheet.

2. Launch StatPlus Pro and select Statistics > Nonparametric Tests > Comparing Two Related Samples (Wilcoxon Pairs, Sign Test) from the StatPlus menu bar.

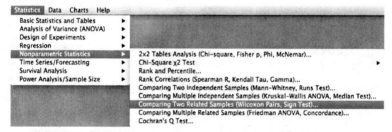

3. Select the Variable #1 range by highlighting the comanx1 (computer anxiety pretest) data in cells A1:A87 and select the Variable #2 range by highlighting the comanx2 (computer anxiety posttest) data in cells B1:B87. Check Labels in first row.

4. Click the OK button to run the procedure.

	A	B	C	D	E	F
1		**Wilcoxon Matched Pairs Test**				
2	*N*	86	*T*	534.	*Z*	5.48902
3	*p-level*	0.				

The results show test results are significant using the *z*-approximation, *z* = 5.49, p < .001 (2-tailed).

Wilcoxon Matched-Pair Signed Ranks Test Reporting

As a minimum, the following information should be reported in the results section of any report: null hypothesis that is being evaluated, descriptive statistics (e.g., mean median, range, mean ranks of negative and positive differences, *N*), statistical test used (i.e., Wilcoxon Matched-Pair Signed Ranks Test), results of evaluation of test assumptions, and test results. For example, one might report results as follows.

The Wilcoxon Matched-Pair Signed Ranks Test was used to evaluate the null hypothesis that there is no difference in ranks between computer anxiety pretest and computer anxiety posttest among university students. The sample ($N = 86$) consisted of 60 negative rank difference scores with a mean rank of 49.20, 23 positive rank difference scores with a mean rank of 23.33, and 3 ties between the pretest ($Mdn = 52.50$) and posttest ($Mdn = 47.00$).

Test results were significant using the z-approximation, $z = 5.49$, $p < .001$, indicating a significant decrease in ranks between computer anxiety pretest and computer anxiety posttest among university students. Effect size using the r-approximation was . 60, suggesting a moderate effect size.

(Note: when reporting z results one may ignore the negative sign provided the direction of difference is noted in the results.)

RELATED SAMPLES SIGN TEST

The Related Samples Sign Test is a nonparametric procedure that compares the signs of the differences between data pairs of dependent data (e.g., pretest-posttest observations) or median differences of independent paired observations. It does not measure magnitude of differences. It tests for a median difference of zero meaning that the number of negative and positive difference scores is equal. The Related Samples Sign Test is used with nominal or ordinal data and may be used with interval data, but the Wilcoxon matched-pair signed ranks test is preferred in this situation. Wilcoxon's signed rank test is more powerful than the Related Samples Sign Test and is generally preferred. The test uses the binomial distribution. However, the normal approximation to the binomial may be used when the probability of success is 0.5.

$$Z = \frac{X_{Smaller} + 0.5 - (X_{Positives} + X_{Negatives})/2}{(\sqrt{X_{Positives} + X_{Negatives}})/2}$$

where $X_{Smaller}$ = the smaller of positive differences and negatives differences between observation pair, $X_{Positives}$ = number of positive differences, and $X_{Negatives}$ = number of negative differences.

As an example, a Related Samples Sign Test can be used to determine if there is a difference between the ratings that raters each give on two products when the ratings represent ordinal or nominal data.

Effect size. The proportion of positive or negative difference scores in comparison to total scores can be reported as effect size.

Key Assumptions & Requirements

Random selection of samples (probability samples) to allow for generalization of results to a target population.

Variables. DV: one continuous variable that is ordinal, interval, or ratio scale. IV: one dichotomous variable. Use of dependent (i.e., related) data.

Distribution of difference scores between pairs of observations is continuous and symmetrical in the population.

Independence of observations except for the matched pairs. Scores for each matched pair of scores must be independent of other matched pairs of scores.

Sample size. Large sample size, $N > 25$, because paired differences equalling 0 are omitted from the analysis; having a relatively large number of paired differences equal to 0 can significantly reduce the effective sample size.

Excel Functions Used

COUNT(value1,value2,...). Counts the numbers in the range of numbers.

COUNTIF(range,criteria). Counts the number within a given range that meet the criteria).

IF(logical_test,value_if_true,value_if_false). Returns one value if the condition is TRUE and a different value if the condition is FALSE.

MAX(number1,number2,...). Returns the maximum value in a set of numbers.

MEDIAN(number1,number2,...). Returns the median of a range of numbers.

MIN(number1,number2,...). Returns the smallest number in the range of numbers.

NORM.S.DIST(z,cumulative). Returns the standard normal distribution.

SQRT(number). Returns the square root of a number.

Related Samples Sign Test Procedures

Research question and null hypothesis:

Are the number of positive difference scores and negative difference scores in computer anxiety different between pretest and posttest?

Note: the researcher used a pretest/posttest design.

H_0: The number of positive difference scores and negative difference scores in computer anxiety are equal between pretest and posttest.

Task: Use the Excel file Computer Anxiety.xlsx located at http://www.watertreepress.com/stats if you want to follow along with the analysis. The Data tab contains the data and the Related Samples Sign Test tab contains the Related Samples Sign Test analysis described below.

1. Open the Computer Anxiety.xlsx file using Excel.

2. Copy comanx1 and comanx2 data from the Excel workbook Data tab and paste the data in columns A and B of an empty sheet.

	A	B
1	comanx1	comanx2
2	41	32
3	36	29
4	78	37
5	70	53

3. Enter labels Difference and Sign in cells C1:D1. Enter formula =B2-A2 in cell C2 and =IF(C2<0,"-",IF(C2=0,"Tie",IF(C2>0,"+"))) in cell D2. Fill Down to cells C87:D87.

	C	D
1	Difference	Sign
2	=B2-A2	=IF(C2<0,"-",IF(C2=0,"Tie",IF(C2>0,"+")))
3	=B3-A3	=IF(C3<0,"-",IF(C3=0,"Tie",IF(C3>0,"+")))
4	=B4-A4	=IF(C4<0,"-",IF(C4=0,"Tie",IF(C4>0,"+")))
5	=B5-A5	=IF(C5<0,"-",IF(C5=0,"Tie",IF(C5>0,"+")))

	C	D
1	Difference	Sign
2	-9	-
3	-7	-
4	-41	-
5	-17	-

4. Enter labels comanx1 and comanx2 in cells F2:F3 and Median and Range in cells G1:H1. Enter formulas =MEDIAN(A2:A87) and =MEDIAN(B2:B87) in cells G2.G3. Enter formulas =MAX(A2:A87)-MIN(A2:A87) and =MAX(B2:B87)-MIN(B2:B87) in cells H2:H3.

	F	G	H
1		Median	Range
2	comanx1	=MEDIAN(A2:A87)	=MAX(A2:A87)-MIN(A2:A87)
3	comanx2	=MEDIAN(B2:B87)	=MAX(B2:B87)-MIN(B2:B87)

	F	G	H
1		Median	Range
2	comanx1	53	65
3	comanx2	47	52

5. Enter labels N, #negatives, # positives, # ties, Smaller + or -, Z, and p-level (2-tailed) in cells F5:F11. Enter formulas =COUNT(A2:A7), COUNTIF(D2:D87,"-"), =COUNTIF(D2:D87,"+"), =COUNTIF(D2:D87,"Tie"), =MIN(G6:G7), =(G9+0.5-(G6+G7)/2)/(SQRT(G6+G7)/2), and =2*NORM.S.DIST(G10,TRUE) in cells G5:G11.

	F	G
5	N	=COUNT(A2:A87)
6	# negatives	=COUNTIF(D2:D87,"-")
7	# positives	=COUNTIF(D2:D87,"+")
8	# ties	=COUNTIF(D2:D87,"Tie")
9	Smaller + or -	=MIN(G6:G7)
10	Z	=(G9+0.5-(G6+G7)/2)/(SQRT(G6+G7)/2)
11	p-level (2-tailed)	=2*NORM.S.DIST(G10,TRUE)

	F	G
5	N	86
6	# negatives	60
7	# positives	23
8	# ties	3
9	Smaller + or -	23
10	Z	-3.95151336
11	p-level (2-tailed)	7.76585E-05

Formatted Related Samples Sign Test output summarizing test results:

	F	G
13	Related Samples Sign Test	
14		comanx1 - comanx2
15	Z	-3.95151336
16	p-level (2-sided)	7.76585E-05

The above output shows that the Related Samples Sign Test is significant using the z-approximation since the significance level <= .05 (the assumed à priori significance level).

Automated Procedures

Use the following procedures for StatPlus Pro.

1. Launch Microsoft Excel and open the Computer Anxiety.xlsx file. Go to the Related Samples Sign Test sheet.

2. Launch StatPlus Pro and select Statistics > Nonparametric Tests > Comparing Two Related Samples (Wilcoxon Pairs, Sign Test) from the StatPlus menu bar.

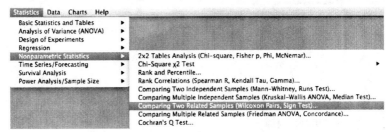

3. Select the Variable #1 range by highlighting the comanx1 (computer anxiety pretest) data in cells A1:A87 and select the Variable #2 range by highlighting the comanx2 (computer anxiety posttest) data in cells B1:B87. Check Labels in first row.

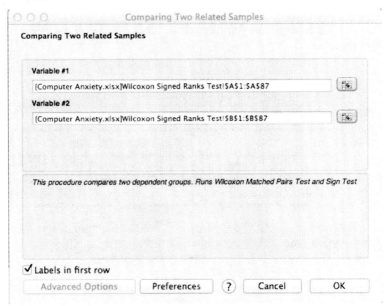

4. Click the OK button to run the procedure.

	A	B	C	D	E	F
5				**Sign Test**		
6	N		83	Z	3.95151 *p-level*	0.00008

The results show test results are significant using the *z*-approximation, *z* = 3.95, p < .001.

Related Samples Sign Test Reporting

As a minimum, the following information should be reported in the results section of any report: null hypothesis that is being evaluated, descriptive statistics (e.g., mean and/or median, *SD* and/or range, negative and positive differences, *N*), statistical test used (i.e., Related Samples Sign Test), results of evaluation of test assumptions, and test results. For example, one might report results as follows.

The Related Samples Sign Test was used to evaluate the null hypothesis that the number of positive difference scores and negative difference scores in computer anxiety are equal between pretest and posttest. The sample (*N* = 86) consisted of 60 negative difference scores, 23 positive difference scores, and 3 ties between the pretest (*M* = 53.49, *Mdn* = 52.50, *SD* = 15.12) and posttest (*M* = 46.84, *Mdn* = 47.00, *SD* = 11.05).

The test demonstrated that the number of positive difference scores was significantly less than the number of negative difference scores in computer anxiety between pretest and posttest using the *z*-approximation, *z* = –3.95, *p* < .001, suggesting a significant reduction in computer anxiety at the posttest. The proportion of negative difference scores in comparison to total scores, a measure of effect size, was .70.

MCNEMAR TEST

The McNemar Test is a nonparametric chi-square procedure that compares proportions obtained from a 2 x 2 contingency table where the row variable (A) is the DV and the column variable (B) is the IV. The McNemar Test is used to test if there is a statistically significant difference between the probability of a (0,1) pair and the probability of a (1,0) pair. Below is a crosstabulation table showing the data structure:

		\multicolumn{2}{c}{B}	Totals
		0	1	Totals
A	0	a	b	a + b
	1	c	d	c + d
Totals		a + c	b + d	N

Sample proportions are obtained using the following formulas:

- $P(A) = (a + b)/N$
- $P(B) = (a + c)/N$

Dichotomous variables are employed where data are coded as "1" for those participants that display the property defined by the variable in question and "0" for those who do not display that property. The test addresses two possible outcomes (presence/absence of a characteristic) on each measurement. The test is often used for the situation where one tests for the presence (1) or absence (0) of something and variable A is the state at the first observation and variable B is the state at the second observation.

The formulas for the McNemar chi-square and Z statistics are as follows:

$$\chi^2 = \frac{(b-c)^2}{b+c}$$

$$Z = \frac{(b-c)}{\sqrt{(b+c)}}$$

Degrees of freedom. The McNemar Test has one degree of freedom.

Effect size. Phi is frequently used to report effect size for the McNemar Test. Phi can be interpreted as small effect = .1, medium effect = .3, large effect = .5

Key Assumptions & Requirements

Random selection of samples (probability samples) to allow for generalization of results to a target population.

Variables. Two dichotomous variables coded in the same manner forming a 2x2 contingency table (the row variable is the DV and the column variable is the IV). Uses dependent data.

Distribution of difference scores between pairs of observations is symmetrical in the population.

Independence of observations except for the matched pairs. Scores for each matched pair of scores must be independent of other matched pairs of scores.

Sample size. Large sample size.

Excel Functions Used

ABS(number). Returns the absolute value of a number.

CHISQ.DIST.RT(x,deg_freedom). Returns the right-tailed probability of the chi-square distribution, where x is the value that is evaluated and deg_freedom is the number of degrees of freedom.

COUNTIFS(range1, criteria1, range2, criteria2,...). Counts the number of cells in a range that meet specific criteria, where range is the reference to cells with the data and criteria identifies the criteria for the data to be included in the count.

NORM.S.DIST(z,cumulative). Returns the standard normal distribution.

POWER(number,power). Returns a number raised to the specified power, where number is the base number and power is the exponent.

SQRT(number). returns the square root of a number.

SUM(number1,number2,...). Adds the range of numbers.

McNemar Test Procedures

Research question and null hypothesis:

Did online student favorability toward longer summer residencies change between observation 1 and observation 2?

H_0: There was no change in student favorability toward longer summer residencies between observation 1 and observation 2.

Note: The McNemar Test determines whether or not the difference between P(A) and P(B) is statistically significant.

Task: Use the Excel file Survey.xlsx located at http://www.watertreepress.com/stats if you want to follow along with the analysis. The Data tab contains the data and the McNemarTest tab contains the McNemar Test analysis described below.

1. Open the *Survey.xlsx file using Excel.*

2. Copy variables obs1 (observation 1) and obs2 (observation 2) from the Excel workbook Data tab to columns A and B on an empty sheet. Copy all 105 variable pairs.

	A	B
1	obs1	obs2
2	0	0
3	0	0
4	1	0
5	1	1

3. Sort column A in ascending order.

4. Enter labels a, b, c, and d in cells D1:D4. Enter formulas =COUNTIF(B2:B42,0), =COUNTIF(B2:B42,1), =COUNTIF(B43:B106,0), and =COUNTIF(B43:B106,1)in cells E1:E4.

	D	E
1	a	=COUNTIF(B2:B42,0)
2	b	=COUNTIF(B2:B42,1)
3	c	=COUNTIF(B43:B106,0)
4	d	=COUNTIF(B43:B106,1)

5. Next, enter the labels N, P(A), and P(B)) in cells D5:D7. Enter formulas =SUM(E1:E4), =(E1+E2)/E5, and

=(E1+E3)/E5 in cells E5:E7 to display total sample size and the sample proportions:

	D	E
5	N	=SUM(E1:E4)
6	P(A)	=(E1+E2)/E5
7	P(B)	=(E1+E3)/E5

6. Enter the labels Z, p-level, Chi-square,and p-level in cells D8:D11. Enter formulas =(E2-E3)/SQRT(E2+E3), =2*(1-NORM.S.DIST(ABS(E8),TRUE)), =POWER((E3-E2),2)/(E3+E2), and =CHISQ.DIST.RT(E10,1) in cells E8:E11.

	D	E
8	Z	=(E2-E3)/SQRT(E2+E3)
9	p-level	=2*(1-NORM.S.DIST(ABS(E8),TRUE))
10	Chi-square	=POWER((E3-E2),2)/(E3+E2)
11	p-level	=CHISQ.DIST.RT(E10,1)

	D	E
1	a	29
2	b	12
3	c	8
4	d	56
5	N	105
6	P(A)	0.39047619
7	P(B)	0.352380952
8	Z	0.894427191
9	p-level	0.37109337
10	Chi-square	0.8
11	p-level	0.37109337

The numbers a, b, c, d represent cells in the following crosstabulation table.

		Obs2		Totals
		Not Favor	Favor	
Obs1	Not Favor	29	12	41
	Favor	8	56	64
	Totals	37	68	105

Note: Data are coded as follows: 0 = Not Favor, 1 = Favor.

Sample proportions are obtained using the following formulas: $P(A) = (a + b)/N$ and $P(B) = (a + c)/N$.

Formatted McNemar Test output summarizing test results:

	D	E	F
13	McNemar Test		
14		Value	p-level (2-sided)
15	Z	0.894427191	0.37109337
16	Chi-square	0.8	0.37109337
17	N		

The above output shows a nonsignificant McNemar Test since the p-level > .05 (the assumed à priori significance level).

Automated Procedures

Use the following procedures for StatPlus Pro.

1. Launch Microsoft Excel and open the Survey.xlsx file. Go to the McNemar Test sheet.

2. Launch StatPlus Pro and select Statistics > Nonparametric Tests > 2 x 2 Tables Analysis (Chi-square, Fisher p, Phi, McNemar) from the StatPlus menu bar.

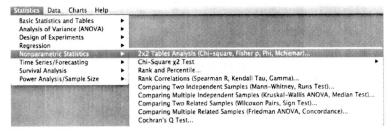

3. Enter values for A, B, C, and D from the values provided in cells D1:E4. Uncheck Labels in first row.

4. Click the OK button to run the procedure.

	A	B	C	D
1	2x2 Tables Analysis			
2	Alpha value (for confidence interval)	0.05		
3				
4		Column 1	Column 2	Row totals
5	Frequencies, row 1	29.	8.	37.
6	Percent of total	0.27619	0.07619	0.35238
7	Frequencies, row 2	12.	56.	68.
8	Percent of total	0.11429	0.53333	0.64762
9	Column totals	41.	64.	105.
10	Percent of total	0.39048	0.60952	

The above output displays a 2 x 2 crosstabulation showing frequency counts and percents for each cell.

	A	B	C
12	**Statistics**	**Value**	**p-level**
13	Chi-square (df=1)	37.13313	0.
14	Yates corrected Chi-square	34.62528	0.
15	Mantel-Haenszel	36.77948	0.
16	McNemar Test (d.f.=1)	0.8	0.37109

The results show $\chi^2(1, N = 105) = .80$, $p = .37$ (2-sided).

McNemar Test Reporting

As a minimum, the following information should be reported in the results section of any report: null hypothesis that is being evaluated, descriptive statistics (e.g., observed frequency counts and/or probabilities of success by category, N), statistical test used (i.e., McNemar Test), results of evaluation of test assumptions, and test results. For example, one might report test results as follows.

The McNemar Test was used to evaluate the null hypothesis that there was no change in online student favorability toward longer summer residencies between observation 1 and observation 2 ($N = 105$). The percent of students who favored longer residencies at observation 1 was 39.05% and the percent of students who favored longer residencies at observation 2 was 35.24%. The McNemar Test provided insufficient evidence to reject the null hypothesis of no difference in preference, $\chi^2(1, N = 105) = .80$, $p = .37$ (2-sided).

4.6: Comparing Multiple Dependent Samples

ONE-WAY WITHIN SUBJECTS ANOVA

Within subjects Analysis of Variance (ANOVA), also known as a Repeated Measures ANOVA, is a parametric procedure that assesses whether the means of multiple dependent groups are statistically different from each other. It is associated with time-series research designs and three or more repeated measurements (a Dependent t-Test is used if there are only two repeated measurements).

Within subjects ANOVA measures three sources of variation in the data and compares their relative sizes:

1. Total variation; that is, the sum of the squares of the differences of each mean with the grand mean (the grand mean is the total of all the data divided by the total sample size).

$$SS_{Total} = \sum (\overline{X}_{Group} - \overline{X}_{GM})^2$$

where GM = grand mean.

2. Between observation variation; that is, how much variation occurs due to interaction between observations.

$$SS_{Between} = k \sum (\overline{X}_{Group} - \overline{X}_{GM})^2$$

where k = number of observations (i.e., repeated measurements).

The mean square between groups is the variance between groups.

$$MS_{Between} = \frac{SS_{Between}}{dfn}$$

where dfn = between group variation = number of groups − 1.

3. Participant variation; that is, the variation in scores for each individual.

$$SS_{Participants} = n\sum(X - \overline{X})^2$$

The mean square within groups is the variance between groups.

$$MS_{Participants} = \frac{SS_{Participants}}{dfd}$$

where dfd = within group variation = total number of participants − number of groups.

The F-statistic is the ratio of the between groups variation and the within groups variation:

$$F = \frac{MS_{Between}}{MS_{Participants}}$$

If the computed F-statistic is approximately 1.0 or less, differences in group means are only random variations. If the computed F-statistic is greater than 1, then there is more variation between groups than within groups, from which one infers that the grouping variable (IV) does make a difference when the results are statistically significant. In other words, a large value of F indicates relatively more difference between groups than within groups (evidence to reject H_0).

A significant ANOVA (i.e., $p <= .05$) tells one that there is a high probability (i.e., 95% or higher) that at least one difference exists somewhere between groups. ANOVA does not identify where the pairwise differences lie. Post hoc analysis is needed to determine which mean(s) is(are) different.

Key Point
Do not conduct post hoc tests if the ANOVA results are not statistically significant.

Degrees of freedom. Three degrees of freedom parameters are associated with within subjects ANOVA. The degrees of freedom for between groups is $k - 1$, where k = the number of groups; the degrees of freedom for participants is $n - 1$, where n is the number of cases in each group; and the degrees of freedom for within groups (error) is $(k - 1)(n - 1)$.

Effect size. The effect size statistic typically used with one-way within subjects ANOVA is partial eta squared (η_p^2).

$$\eta_p^2 = \frac{SS_{Between}}{SS_{Between} + SS_{Error}}$$

A common rule of thumb is that eta squared values of .01, .06, and .14 represent small, medium, and large effect sizes.

Key Assumptions & Requirements

Random selection of samples (probability samples) to allow for generalization of results to a target population.

Variables. DV: one continuous variable, interval/ratio scale. IV: one or more categorical variables with multiple categories; e.g., Group (Treatment A, Treatment B, Control). At least one IV must be a within subjects variable.

Multivariate normality. The distributions of the differences in the DV between two or more related groups are approximately normally distributed.

Absence of extreme outliers in the differences between related groups.

Sphericity. The variance of the difference between all pairs of means is constant across all combinations of related groups.

Sphericity is tenable when the variance of the difference between the estimated means for any pair of groups is the same as for any other pair. To correct the univariate F-test results to compensate for departures from sphericity, the researcher uses the Huynh-Feldt or Greenhouse-Geisser epsilon (ε) adjustment, provided by multiplying the between-groups degrees of freedom by the value of ε. Degrees of freedom should be corrected based on the value of epsilon (ε). If $\varepsilon > 0.75$, use the Huynh-Feldt adjustment; if $\varepsilon < 0.75$, use the Greenhouse-Geisser adjustment.

Excel Functions Used

AVERAGE(number1,number2,...). Returns the arithmetic mean, where numbers represent the range of numbers.

COUNT(value1,value2,...). Counts the numbers in the range of numbers.

COUNTA(value1,value2,...). Counts the cells with non-empty values in the range of values.

COVARIANCE.S(array1,array2). Returns the sample covariance, where each array is a range of numbers.

DEVSQ(number1,number2,...). Returns the sum of squares of deviations of data from the sample mean.

F.DIST.RT(x,deg_freedom1,deg_freedom2). Returns the right-tailed F-distribution probability, where x is the F-value to be evaluated, deg_freedom1 is the between groups df, and deg_freedom2 is the within groups df.

POWER(number,power). Returns a number raised to the specified power, where number is the base number and power is the exponent.

STDEV.S(number1,number2,...). Returns the unbiased estimate of population standard deviation, where numbers represent the range of numbers.

SUM(number1,number2,...). Adds the range of numbers.

SUMSQ(number1,number2,...). Returns the sum of squares of the numbers.

One-Way Within Subjects ANOVA Procedures

Research question and null hypothesis:

Is there a difference in mean computer confidence over time (observation 1, observation 2, and observation 3, $\mu_1 \neq \mu_2 \neq \mu_3$? The IV is observation (observation 1, observation 2, observation 3) and the DV is computer confidence.

H_0: There is no difference in mean computer confidence over time (observation 1, observation 2, and observation 3), $\mu_1 = \mu_2 = \mu_3$.

Task: Use the Excel file Computer Anxiety.xlsx located at http:// www.watertreepress.com/stats if you want to follow along with the analysis. The Data tab contains the data and the One-Way Within Subjects ANOVA tab contains the ANOVA analysis described below.

1. Open the *Computer Anxiety.xlsx* file using Excel.

2. Copy variables comconf1, comconf2, and comconf3 from the Excel workbook Data tab to columns A, B, and C on an empty sheet. Copy the 75 cases with labels having no missing data in cells A1:C:76.

	A	B	C
1	comconf1	comconf2	comconf3
2	32	35	35
3	38	40	39
4	33	38	36
5	23	35	36

3. Enter the label Case means in Cell D1. Enter formula =AVERAGE(A2:C2 in cell D2 and Fill Down to cell D76 to calculate case means in column D.

	D	E
1	Case Means	
2	=AVERAGE(A2:C2)	
3	=AVERAGE(A3:C3)	
4	=AVERAGE(A4:C4)	
5	=AVERAGE(A5:C5)	

⬜	D	E
1	Case Means	
2	34	
3	39	
4	35.66666667	
5	31.33333333	

4. Enter labels comconf1, comconf2, comconf3, and Grand Mean in cells E2:E5 and Obs Means and Obs SD in cells F1:G1. Enter formula =AVERAGE(A2:A76), =AVERAGE(B2:B76), and =AVERAGE(C2:C76) in cells F2:F4. Enter formulas =STDEV.S(A2:A76), =STDEV.S(B2:B76), and =STDEV.S(C2:C76) in cells G2:G4.

⬜	E	F	G
1		Obs Means	Obs SD
2	comconf1	=AVERAGE(A2:A76)	=STDEV.S(A2:A76)
3	comconf2	=AVERAGE(B2:B76)	=STDEV.S(B2:B76)
4	comconf3	=AVERAGE(C2:C76)	=STDEV.S(C2:C76)

⬜	E	F	G
1		Obs Means	Obs SD
2	comconf1	31.26666667	5.834041141
3	comconf2	32.44	5.373206803
4	comconf3	33.49333333	3.818069886

5. Enter labels # observations, N, Grand mean (GM), SS-between, SS participants, SS total, and SS error in cells E6:E12. and formulas in cells E6:F12 as shown below. Enter formulas =COUNTA(E2:E4), =COUNT(A2:A76), =AVERAGE(F2:F4), =F11-DEVSQ(A2:A76)-DEVSQ(B2:B76)-DEVSQ(C2:C76), =F6*DEVSQ(D2:D76), =DEVSQ(A2:C76), and =F11-F9-F10 in cells F6:F12.

	E	F
6	# observations	=COUNTA(E2:E4)
7	N	=COUNT(A2:A76)
8	Grand mean (GM)	=AVERAGE(F2:F4)
9	SS between	=F11-DEVSQ(A2:A76)-DEVSQ(B2:B76)-DEVSQ(C2:C76)
10	SS participants	=F6*DEVSQ(D2:D76)
11	SS total	=DEVSQ(A2:C76)
12	SS error	=F11-F9-F10

	E	F
6	# observations	3
7	N	75
8	Grand mean (GM)	32.4
9	SS between	186.1066667
10	SS participants	4494.666667
11	SS total	5920
12	SS error	1239.226667

6. Enter labels Sphericity Assumed, df between, df participants, df error, MSb, MSp, F, p-level, and Eta-squared in cells E14:E22. Enter formulas =F6-1, =F7-1, =(F6-1)*(F7-1), =F9/F15, =F12/F17, =F18/F19, =F.DIST.RT(F20,F15,F17), and =F9/(F9+F12) in cells in cells F15:F22 to display sphericity assumed statistics.

🔺	E	F
14	Sphericity Assumed	
15	df between	=F6-1
16	df participants	=F7-1
17	df error	=(F6-1)*(F7-1)
18	MSb	=F9/F15
19	MSp	=F12/F17
20	F	=F18/F19
21	p-level	=F.DIST.RT(F20,F15,F17)
22	Eta-squared	=F9/(F9+F12)

🔺	E	F
14	Sphericity Assumed	
15	df between	2
16	df participants	74
17	df error	148
18	MSb	93.05333333
19	MSp	8.373153153
20	F	11.11329646
21	p-level	0.000032
22	Eta-squared	0.130570627

7. Enter labels comconf1, comconf2, comconf3, Mean, and Mean-GM in cells H3:H7, SAMPLE COVARIANCE MATRIX in cell I1, and comconf1, comconf2, comconf3, and Mean in cells I2:L2. Enter formulas=COVARIANCE.S(A2:A76,A2:A76), =COVARIANCE.S(B2:B76,A2:A76), =COVARIANCE.S(C2:C76,A2:A76), =AVERAGE(I3:I5), and =I6-$L$6 in cells I3:I7. Enter formulas =COVARIANCE.S(A2:A76,B2:B76), =COVARIANCE.S(B2:B76,B2:B76),

=COVARIANCE.S(C2:C76,B2:B76), =AVERAGE(J3:J5),
and =J6-$L$6 in cells J3:J7. Enter formulas
=COVARIANCE.S(A2:A76,C2:C76),
=COVARIANCE.S(B2:B76,C2:C76),
=COVARIANCE.S(C2:C76,C2:C76), =AVERAGE(J3:J5),
and =J6-$L$6 in cells K3:K7. Enter formulas
=AVERAGE(I3:K3) in cell L3 and Fill Down to cell L6.

	H	I
1		SAMPLE COVARIANCE MATRIX
2		comconf1
3	comconf1	=COVARIANCE.S(A2:A76,A2:A76)
4	comconf2	=COVARIANCE.S(B2:B76,A2:A76)
5	comconf3	=COVARIANCE.S(C2:C76,A2:A76)
6	Mean	=AVERAGE(I3:I5)
7	Mean-GM	=I6-$L$6

	J
1	
2	comconf2
3	=COVARIANCE.S(A2:A76,B2:B76)
4	=COVARIANCE.S(B2:B76,B2:B76)
5	=COVARIANCE.S(C2:C76,B2:B76)
6	=AVERAGE(J3:J5)
7	=J6-$L$6

	K
1	
2	comconf3
3	=COVARIANCE.S(A2:A76,C2:C76)
4	=COVARIANCE.S(B2:B76,C2:C76)
5	=COVARIANCE.S(C2:C76,C2:C76)
6	=AVERAGE(K3:K5)
7	=K6-$L$6

	L
1	
2	Mean
3	=AVERAGE(I3:K3)
4	=AVERAGE(I4:K4)
5	=AVERAGE(I5:K5)
6	=AVERAGE(I6:K6)
7	

	I	J	K	L
1	SAMPLE COVARIANCE MATRIX			
2	comconf1	comconf2	comconf3	Mean
3	34.036036	21.0162162	13.393694	22.8153
4	21.0162162	28.8713514	17.955676	22.6144
5	13.3936937	17.9556757	14.577658	15.309
6	22.8153153	22.6144144	15.309009	20.2462
7	2.56906907	2.36816817	-4.937237	

8.   Enter label Diagonal in cell H13 and POPULATION COVARIANCE MATRIX in cell I9. Enter formulas =I3-$L3-I$6+$L$6, =I4-$L4-I$6+$L$6, =I5-$L5-I$6+$L$6, and =I10 in cells I10:I13. Enter formulas =J3-$L3-J$6+$L$6, =J4-$L4-J$6+$L$6, =J5-$L5-J$6+$L$6, and =J11 in cells J10:J13. Enter formulas =K3-$L3-K$6+$L$6, =K4-$L4-K$6+$L$6, =K5-$L5-K$6+$L$6, and =K12 in cells K10:K13.

	H	I
9		POPULATION COVARIANCE MATRIX
10		=I3-$L3-I$6+$L$6
11		=I4-$L4-I$6+$L$6
12		=I5-$L5-I$6+$L$6
13	Diagonal	=I10

	J	K
9		
10	=J3-$L3-J$6+$L$6	=K3-$L3-K$6+$L$6
11	=J4-$L4-J$6+$L$6	=K4-$L4-K$6+$L$6
12	=J5-$L5-J$6+$L$6	=K5-$L5-K$6+$L$6
13	=J11	=K12

	H	I	J	K
9		POPULATION COVARIANCE MATRIX		
10		8.6516517	-4.167	-4.484384
11		-4.167267	3.8888	0.2784985
12		-4.484384	0.2785	4.2058859
13	Diagonal	8.6516517	3.8888	4.2058859

9. Enter label Sphericity Not Assumed in cell E24 and Greenhouse-Geisser, Numerator, Denominator, Epsilon, df between, df error, MSb, MSp, F, p-level, and Eta-squared in cells E26:E36. Enter formulas =POWER(SUM(I13:K13),2), =(F6-1)*SUMSQ(I10:K12), =F27/F28, =F29*F17, =F9/F30, =F12/F31, =F32/F33, =F.DIST.RT(F34, F30, F31), and =F9/(F9+F12) in cells F27:F36.

	E	F
24	Sphericity Not Assumed	
25		
26	Greenhouse -Geisser	
27	Numerator	=POWER(SUM(I13:K13),2)
28	Denominator	=(F6-1)*SUMSQ(I10:K12)
29	Epsilon	=F27/F28
30	df between	=F29*F15
31	df error	=F29*F17
32	MSb	=F9/F30
33	MSp	=F12/F31
34	F	=F32/F33
35	p-level	=F.DIST.RT(F34,F30,F31)
36	Eta-squared	=F9/(F9+F12)

	E	F
24	Sphericity Not Assumed	
25		
26	Greenhouse - Geisser	
27	Numerator	280.4387749
28	Denominator	365.5396746
29	Epsilon	0.767191072
30	df between	1.534382144
31	df error	113.5442787
32	MSb	121.2909492
33	MSp	10.91403883
34	F	11.11329646
35	p-level	0.00115952
36	Eta-squared	0.130570627

10. Enter labels Hunyh-Feldt, Numerator, Denominator, Epsilon, df between, df error, MSb, MSw, F, p-level, and Eta-squared in cells E38:E48. Enter formulas in cells E38:F48 as shown below to display sphericity not assumed (Hunyh-Feldt) statistics. Enter formulas ==F7*(F6-1)*F29-2, =(F6-1)*F7-1-(F6-1)*F29), =F39/F40, =F41*F15, =F41*F17, =F9/F42, =F12/F43, =F44/F45, =F.DIST.RT(F46, F42, F43), and =F9/(F9+F12) in cells F39:F48.

	E	F
38	Hunyh-Feldt	
39	Numerator	=F7*(F6-1)*F29-2
40	Denominator	=(F6-1)*(F7-1-(F6-1)*F29)
41	Epsilon	=F39/F40
42	df between	=F41*F15
43	df error	=F41*F17
44	MSb	=F9/F42
45	MSp	=F12/F43
46	F	=F44/F45
47	p-level	=F.DIST.RT(F46,F42,F43)
48	Eta-squared	=F9/(F9+F12)

	E	F
38	Hunyh-Feldt	
39	Numerator	113.0786608
40	Denominator	144.9312357
41	Epsilon	0.780222843
42	df between	1.560445687
43	df error	115.4729808
44	MSb	119.2650717
45	MSp	10.73174571
46	F	11.11329646
47	p-level	0.001153791
48	Eta-squared	0.130570627

11. Create a profile chart (i.e., line chart) displaying computer confidence means across the three observations. See Chapter 2 for the procedures.

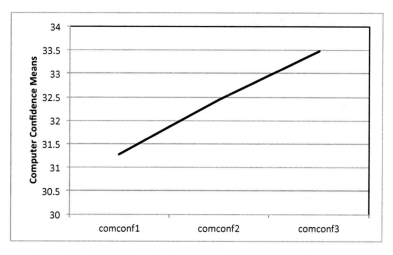

Formatted ANOVA output summarizing test results:

	H	I	J	K	L	M	N
15	One-Way Within Subjects ANOVA						
16	Source of Variation	SS	df	MS	F	p-level	Eta-Squared
17	Obs						
18	Sphericity Assumed	186.10667	2	93.0533	11.113	0.000032	0.1306
19	Greenhouse-Geisser	186.10667	1.5344	121.291	11.113	0.00116	0.1306
20	Hunyh-Feldt	186.10667	1.5604	119.265	11.113	0.00115	0.1306
21	Error						
22	Sphericity Assumed	1239.2267	148	8.37315			
23	Greenhouse-Geisser	1239.2267	113.54	10.914			
24	Hunyh-Feldt	1239.2267	115.47	10.7317			

The above output shows that the ANOVA results are significant for both sphericity assumed and sphericity not assumed since both results show that the difference between observations is significant since the p-level <= .05 (the assumed à priori significance level). Since $\varepsilon > 0.75$, use the Huynh-Feldt correction to report results.

Automated Procedures

Use the following procedures for StatPlus Pro.

1. Launch Microsoft Excel and open the Computer Anxiety.xlsx file. Go to the One-Way Within Subjects ANOVA sheet.

2. Launch StatPlus Pro and select Statistics > Analysis of Variance (ANOVA) > Within Subjects ANOVA from the StatPlus menu bar.

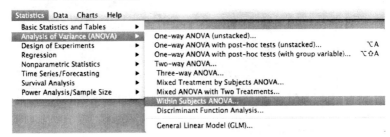

3. Select the Variables range by highlighting the comconf1 (computer confidence pretest), comconf2 (computer confidence posttest), and comconf3 (computer confidence delayed test) data arranged in cells A1:C76. Select Labels in first row.

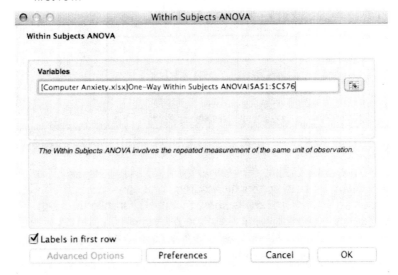

4. Click the OK button to run the procedure.

	A	B	C	D	E	F
1			Within Subjects ANOVA			
2						
3	ANOVA					
4	Source of Variation	d.f.	SS	MS	F	p-level
5	Subjects	74.	4,494.66667	93.05333		
6	Within Subjects - Total	150.	1,425.33333	9.50222		
7	Treatments	2.	186.10667	93.05333	11.1133	0.00003
8	Residuals	148.	1,239.22667	8.37315		
9						
10	Total	224.	5,920.	26.42857		

The results show that $F(2,148) = 11.11$, $p < .001$ (sphericity assumed).

	A	B	C
13	Summary		
14	Treatments	Mean	Standard Deviation
15	comconf1	31.26667	5.83404
16	comconf2	32.44	5.37321
17	comconf3	33.49333	3.81807
18	Total	32.4	5.14087

The above output provides the descriptive statistics (M and SD) for each of the three observations as well as for the total.

	A	B
21	Reliability Estimates	
22	Unadjusted Total Reliability	0.84356
23	Unadjusted Item Reliability	0.64252
24	Adjusted Total Reliability (Cronbach)	0.86214
25	Adjusted Item Reliability	0.67582

Reliability estimates are provided to support a reliability design in which the reliability of a measurement is estimated using multiple measurements of the same attribute. A one-way within subjects ANOVA is used to estimate the reliability of a

single measurement when the levels of the within subjects factor
represent the multiple measurements.

	A	B	C	D
28	Variance-Covariance Matrix Box Test For Homogeneity			
29				
30	Sample Covariance Matrix			
31	VARS	comconf1	comconf2	comconf3
32	comconf1	34.03604	21.01622	13.39369
33	comconf2	21.01622	28.87135	17.95568
34	comconf3	13.39369	17.95568	14.57766
35				
36	Assumed Population Covariance Matrix			
37	VARS	comconf1	comconf2	comconf3
38	comconf1	25.82835	3.27285	3.27285
39	comconf2	3.27285	25.82835	3.27285
40	comconf3	3.27285	3.27285	25.82835

	A	B
42	Variance-Covariance Matrix Determinant	1,842.09895
43	Homogeneity Matrix Determinant	16,470.31387
44	Chi-square	480.75973
45	Degrees Of Freedom	4
46	p-level	0.E+0

One-Way Within Subjects ANOVA Reporting

As a minimum, the following information should be reported
in the results section of any report: null hypothesis(es) that are
being evaluated, descriptive statistics (e.g., M, SD, N, n),
statistical test used (e.g., One-Way Within Subjects ANOVA),
results of evaluation of ANOVA assumptions, ANOVA test results
to include partial eta squared, and the results of post hoc
multiple comparison tests if ANOVA results are significant (adjust
alpha using either the Bonferroni correction or the Holm's
sequential Bonferroni correction). Also include a profile plot. For
example, one might report test results as follows.

A one-way within subjects ANOVA was conducted to evaluate the null hypothesis that there is no difference in mean computer confidence over time. The sample ($N = 75$) consisted of observation 1 ($M = 31.27$, $SD = 5.83$), observation 2 ($M = 32.44$, $SD = 5.37$), and observation 3 ($M = 33.49$, $SD = 3.82$). Higher scores reflect stronger feelings of computer confidence. The ANOVA provided evidence that the null hypothesis of no difference in mean computer confidence over time can be rejected, $F(1.56, 115.47) = 11.11$, $p < .001$, $\eta^2 = .13$, based on sphericity not assumed and using the Hunyh-Feldt adjustment. A profile plot shows a mostly linear trend in computer confidence means along the three observations.

(Note: assumptions require evaluation and reporting before test results can be relied upon. Post hoc results are also required.)

FRIEDMAN TEST

The Friedman Test, also known as the Friedman One-Way ANOVA, is a nonparametric procedure that compares average rank of groups between multiple sets of dependent data when the DV is either ordinal or interval/ratio. It is an extension of the Wilcoxon matched-pair signed ranks test. It is frequently used for continuous data when the one-way within subjects ANOVA cannot be conducted because of a significant violation of the assumption of normality. The test uses the ranks of the data rather than their raw values to calculate the statistic.

$$F_R = \frac{12}{rc(c+1)} \sum R^2 - 3r(c+1)$$

where R^2 = sum of rank total squares, r = number of cases, and c = number of repeated measures.

The dependent data should be the result of either repeated observations of the same group or matching multiple groups as part of an experimental design.

Degrees of freedom. Repeated measures − 1.

Post hoc multiple comparison tests. For pairwise post hoc comparisons, the Wilcoxon Signed-Ranks Test is appropriate following a significant Friedman test.

Effect size. Kendall's *W* (Kendall's coefficient of concordance) can be used as an effect size statistic. The coefficient ranges from 0 to 1, with stronger relationships indicated by higher values. (See Automated Procedures below.)

Key Assumptions & Requirements

Random selection of samples (probability samples) to allow for generalization of results to a target population.

Variables. DV: one continuous variable that is ordinal, interval, or ratio scale. IV: one categorical variable with multiple categories. Use of dependent (i.e., related) data.

Distribution of difference scores between pairs of observations is continuous and symmetrical in the population.

Independence of observations except for the matched pairs. Scores for each matched pair of scores must be independent of other matched pairs of scores.

Sample size. A relative large sample size is required for accurate results, e.g., $N > 30$.

Excel Functions Used

AVERAGE(number1,number2,...). Returns the arithmetic mean, where numbers represent the range of numbers.

CHISQ.DIST.RT(x,deg_freedom). Returns the right-tailed probability of the chi-square distribution, where x is the value that is evaluated and deg_freedom is the number of degrees of freedom.

COUNT(value1,value2,...). Counts the numbers in the range of numbers.

MEDIAN(number1,number2,...). Returns the median of a range of numbers.

POWER(number,power). Returns a number raised to the specified power, where number is the base number and power is the exponent.

RANK.AVG(number,ref,order). Returns the rank of a number in a list, where number = the number to be ranked, ref = the list of numbers upon which the rankings are based, and 0 indicates the reference list is sorted in descending order.

SUM(number1,number2,...). Adds the range of numbers.

Friedman Test Procedures

Research question and null hypothesis:

Is there a difference in average computer anxiety rank among undergraduate students based on observation (end of year 1, end of year 2, end of year 3)?

H_0: There is no difference in average computer anxiety rank among undergraduate students based on observation (end of year 1, end of year 2, end of year 3).

Task: Use the Excel file Computer Anxiety.xlsx located at http:// www.watertreepress.com/stats if you want to follow along with the analysis. The Data tab contains the data and the Friedman Test *tab contains the* Friedman Test *analysis described below.*

1. Open the *Computer Anxiety.xlsx file using Excel.*

2. Copy variables comanx1 (computer anxiety pretest), comanx2 (computer anxiety posttest), and comanx3 (computer anxiety delayed test) from the Excel workbook Data tab to columns A, B, and C on an empty sheet. Copy all 75 cases.

	A	B	C
1	comanx1	comanx2	comanx3
2	41	32	29
3	36	29	25
4	78	37	41
5	70	53	44

3. Enter labels Ranks1, Ranks2, and Ranks3 in cells G1:I1. Enter formula =(COUNT($A2:$C2)+1+RANK.AVG(A2,$A2:$C2,0))/2 in cell G2, then Fill Right and Fill Down in order to convert raw scores to ranks for each variable.

	G
1	Ranks1
2	=(COUNT($A2:$C2)+1+RANK.AVG(A2,$A2:$C2,1)-RANK.AVG(A2,$A2:$C2,0))/2

	H
1	Ranks2
2	=(COUNT($A2:$C2)+1+RANK.AVG(B2,$A2:$C2,1)-RANK.AVG(B2,$A2:$C2,0))/2

	I
1	Ranks3
2	=(COUNT($A2:$C2)+1+RANK.AVG(C2,$A2:$C2,1)-RANK.AVG(C2,$A2:$C2,0))/2

	G	H	I
	Ranks1	Ranks2	Ranks3
1			
2	3	2	1
3	3	2	1
4	3	1	2
5	3	2	1

4. Enter labels comanx1, comanx2, and comanx3 in cells D2:D4 and Obs Median and Mean Rank in cells E1:F1. Enter formulas =MEDIAN(A2:A76, =MEDIAN(B2:B76, =MEDIAN(C2:C76), =AVERAGE(G2:G76), =AVERAGE(H2:H76), and =AVERAGE(I2:I76) in cells E2:F4 in order to display descriptive statistics.

	D	E	F
1		Obs Median	Mean Rank
2	comanx1	=MEDIAN(A2:A76)	=AVERAGE(G2:G76)
3	comanx2	=MEDIAN(B2:B76)	=AVERAGE(H2:H76)
4	comanx3	=MEDIAN(C2:C76)	=AVERAGE(I2:I76)

	D	E	F
1		Obs Median	Mean Rank
2	comanx1	53	2.5
3	comanx2	47	1.97333333
4	comanx3	44	1.52666667

5. Enter labels Sum of ranks 1, Sum of ranks 2, Sum of ranks 3, SS1, SS2, and SS3 in cels D6:D11. Enter formulas =SUM(G2:G76), =SUM(H2:H76), =SUM(I2:I76),

=POWER(E6,2), =POWER(E7,2), and =POWER(E8,2) in cells E6:E11 in order to display sum of ranks and sum of squares for each observation.

	D	E
6	Sum of ranks 1	=SUM(G2:G76)
7	Sum of ranks 2	=SUM(H2:H76)
8	Sum of ranks 3	=SUM(I2:I76)
9	SS1	=POWER(E6,2)
10	SS2	=POWER(E7,2)
11	SS3	=POWER(E8,2)

	D	E
6	Sum of ranks 1	187.5
7	Sum of ranks 2	148
8	Sum of ranks 3	114.5
9	SS1	35156.25
10	SS2	21904
11	SS3	13110.25

6. Enter labels N, # observations, Sum of rank total squares, DF, Friedman chi-square, and p-level in cells D12:D17. Enter formulas =COUNT(A2:A76), =COUNT(A2:C2), =SUM(E9:E11), =E13-1, =(12/(E12*E13*(E13+1))*E14)-3*E12*(E13+1), and =CHISQ.DIST.RT(E16,E15) in cells E12:E17.

	D	E
12	N	=COUNT(A2:A76)
13	# observations	=COUNT(A2:C2)
14	Sum of rank total squares	=SUM(E9:E11)
15	DF	=E13-1
16	Friedman chi-square	=(12/(E12*E13*(E13+1))*E14)-3*E12*(E13+1)
17	p-level	=CHISQ.DIST.RT(E16,E15)

	D	E
12	N	75
13	# observations	3
14	Sum of rank total squares	70170.5
15	DF	2
16	Friedman chi-square	35.60666667
17	p-level	0.000000019

7. Construct a profile plot (line chart) of computer anxiety mean ranks (cells F2:F4) across the three observations. See Chapter 2 for a description of procedures.

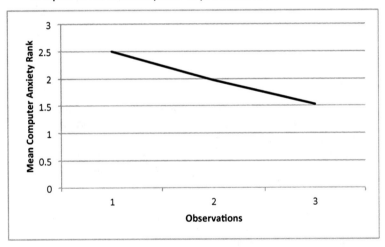

The profile plot indicates a mostly linear trend line among the three observations

Formatted Friedman test output summarizing test results:

	D	E
19	Friedman Test Statistics	
20	N	75
21	Chi-Square	35.60666667
22	df	2
23	p-level	0.000000019

The above output shows that the Friedman Test results are significant since the *p*-level <= .05 (the assumed *à priori* significance level). Consequently, post hoc pairwise comparison tests are required using the Wilcoxon Signed Ranks Test in order to identify the statistical significance of pairwise differences. Identify significant pairwise differences using the Bonferroni correction or the Holm's sequential Bonferroni correction.

Automated Procedures

Use the following procedures for StatPlus Pro.

1. Launch Microsoft Excel and open the Computer Anxiety.xlsx file. Go to the Friedman Test sheet.

2. Launch StatPlus Pro and select Statistics > Nonparametric Statistics > Comparing Multiple Related Samples (Friedman ANOVA, Concordance) from the StatPlus menu bar.

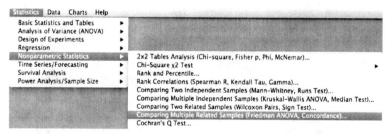

3. Select the Variables range by highlighting the comanx1 (computer anxiety pretest), comanx2 (computer anxiety posttest), and comanx3 (computer anxiety delayed test) data arranged in cells A1:C76. Select Labels in first row.

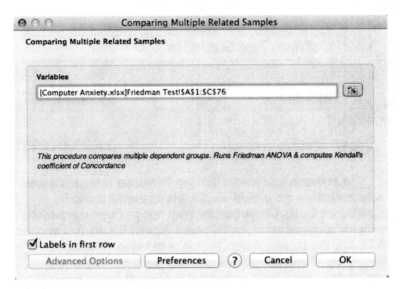

4. Click the OK button to run the procedure.

	A	B	C	D
1	**Comparing Multiple Related Samples**			
2				
3	N	75	Degrees Of Freedom	2
4	Chi-square	36.96194	p-level	0.
5	Kendall Coeff. of Concordance	0.24641	Average rank	0.23623
6		Average rank	Sum of Ranks	Mean
7	comanx1	2.5	187.5	53.69333
8	comanx2	1.97333	148.	46.78667
9	comanx3	1.52667	114.5	43.88

The results show that $\chi^2(2, N = 75) = 36.96$, p < .001. Descriptive statistics are also displayed for each observation.

Kendall's Coefficient of Concordance (Kendall's W) for k related samples from a continuous field is used to assess agreement among observations. Kendall's *W* ranges from 0 (no agreement) to 1 (complete agreement).

Friedman Test Reporting

As a minimum, the following information should be reported in the results section of any report: null hypothesis that is being evaluated, descriptive statistics (e.g., Mdn, mean rank, range, *N*, *n*), statistical test used (i.e., Friedman Test), results of evaluation of test assumptions, and test results, to include post hoc multiple comparison test results if the omnibus test is significant, and a profile plot. For example, one might report test results as follows.

The Friedman Test was used to evaluate the null hypothesis that there was no difference in average computer anxiety rank among undergraduate students based on repeated observations. The sample consisted of the following three observations: end of year 1 (Mdn = 53.00, mean rank = 2.50, range = 65), end of year 2 (Mdn = 47.00, mean rank = 1.97, range = 52), and end of year 3 (Mdn = 44.00, mean rank = 1.53, range = 46). The test provided evidence that the null hypothesis of no difference in average computer anxiety rank among undergraduate students can be rejected, $\chi^2(2, N = 75) = 35.61, p < .001$.

4.7: Correlations

INTRODUCTION

Correlation is a statistical technique that measures and describes the relationship (i.e., association, correlation) between variables. A relationship exists when changes in one variable tend to be accompanied by consistent and predictable changes in the other variable. In other words, if a significant relationship exists, the two variables covary in some nonrandom fashion. The null hypothesis is that there is no relationship between variables (i.e., statistical independence).

A monotonic relationship is one in which the value of one variable increases as the value of the other variable increases or the value of one variable increases as the value of the other variable decreases, but not necessarily in a linear fashion.

A linear relationship means that any given change in one variable produces a corresponding change in the other variable. A plot of their values in a scatterplot approximates a straight line, or values that average out to be a straight line.

Bivariate correlation, multiple correlation, and canonical correlation are related statistical methods for modeling the relationship between two or more random variables. Bivariate correlation refers to a one on one relationship between two variables, multiple correlation refers to a one on many correlation, and canonical correlation refers to a many on many correlation.

There are three additional correlation terms that one is likely to encounter in the professional literature:

- Zero-order correlation is the relationship between two variables, while ignoring the influence of other variables.

- Partial correlation is the relationship between two variables after removing the overlap of a third or more other variables from both variables.

- Semipartial correlation is the relationship between two variables after removing a third variable from just one of the two variables.

Researchers generally choose the measure that is appropriate for the lower scale when selecting a correlation measure to assess the relationship between variables that are measured using different scales of measurement. For example, if one variable is nominal, and the other is interval, one would use a test appropriate for the nominal variable.

The most common errors in interpreting a correlation coefficient are:

• Confusing causality and correlation. Correlation does not imply causation.

• Claiming a relationship exists on the basis of the calculated correlation coefficient when the correlation test is not significant.

• Failing to consider that there may be a third variable related to both of the variables being analyzed that is responsible for the correlation.

• Failing to consider differences in units of analysis. For example, when students are the units of analysis one can expect to obtain one correlation coefficient. However, when an aggregate are the units of analysis, e.g., schools, school districts, or states, the correlation coefficient can differ although the same variables are analyzed. The meaning and interpretation of the correlation coefficient is directly linked to the units of analysis that are used (Glass & Hopkins, 1996).

In conducting correlation analysis, one should be aware of a type of confounding known as Simpson's paradox (also known as the Yule–Simpson effect) in which a relationship that appears in different groups of data disappears when these groups are combined and the reverse trend appears for the aggregated data. Consequently, the researcher needs to understand how the within-group and aggregate comparisons can differ. For example, test scores may rise over time for every ethnic group but the overall average may still decline or remain flat because of the different sizes of each group.

> **Key Point**
> If the results of a correlation test are not significant, there is no relationship, regardless of the correlation coefficient produced by the test.

Strength of Relationship

A correlation measures the strength or degree of the relationship between X and Y as shown in Figure 4.1 below. The strength of relationship (how closely they are related) is usually expressed as a number (correlation coefficient) between −1 and +1. Strength of relationship can also be evaluated using a scatterplot by observing how closely the points are clustered. No relationship will appear as a random shotgun pattern while points will be clustered tightly along a linear trend line for a strong linear relationship.

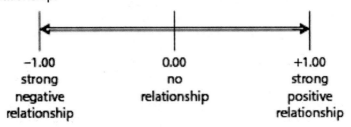

−1.00	0.00	+1.00
strong	no	strong
negative	relationship	positive
relationship		relationship

FIGURE 4.1
Graphic depiction of strength of relationship.

A zero correlation indicates no relationship. As the correlation coefficient moves toward either −1 or +1, the relationship gets stronger until there is a perfect correlation at either extreme. Perfect correlation is referred to as singularity.

A general interpretive guide that is often used to describe strength of statistically significant relationships (i.e., $p \le .05$) is provided below:

     Between 0 and ±0.20 – Very weak

Between ±0.20 and ±0.40 – Weak
Between ±0.40 and ±0.60 – Moderate
Between ±0.60 and ±0.80 – Strong
Between ±0.80 and ±1.00 – Very strong

However, other interpretive guides exist in the professional literature.

- Various Correlation Coefficients, e.g., Pearson *r* (Hinkle, Wiersma, & Jurs, 1998)

  Little if any relationship < .30
  Low relationship = .30 to < .50
  Moderate relationship = .50 to < .70
  High relationship = .70 to < .90
  Very high relationship = .90 and above

- Phi or Cramér's *V* (Rea & Parker, 2005)

  Negligible association < .10
  Weak association = .10 to < .20
  Moderate association = .20 to < .40
  Relatively strong association = .40 to < .60
  Strong association = .60 to < .80
  Very strong association = .80 and higher

Although different researchers may use different adjectives to describe the strength of a given correlation coefficient, the square of the correlation coefficient (i.e., the coefficient of determination) is used to express a standardized percent of variance explained by the relationship. For example, $r = .70$ can be described variously as reflecting a strong or high relationship between variable A and variable B. However, it is interpreted as variable A "accounts for" 49 percent of the variance in variable B; or that variable B accounts for 49 percent of the variance in variable B; or that they share 49 percent of variance in common.

Key Point
Statistical significance does not mean a relationship is not spurious (both variables can be affected by a third, unidentified variable).

Direction of Relationship

Positive linear correlation (a positive number) means that two variables tend to move in the same direction. That is, as one gets larger, so does the other. Negative or inverse linear correlation (a negative number) means that the two variables tend to move in opposite directions. That is, as one gets larger, the other gets smaller. However, in a nonlinear or curvilinear relationship, as the scores of one variable change, the scores of the other variable do not tend to only increase or only decrease. At some point, the scores change their direction of change.

Tests for association can be symmetrical or asymmetrical. If the test is symmetrical, the coefficient of association – e.g., Pearson r – will be the same regardless of which variable is designated the IV (predictor variable). However, if the test is asymmetrical – e.g., Cramér's V – the designation of variables as IV and DV matters. Asymmetric tests measure strength of association in predicting the DV (criterion variable), while symmetric tests measure the strength of association when prediction is done in both directions.

Form of Relationship

The form of a relationship is either linear (see Figure 4.2) or curvilinear (concave up or down; see Figure 4.3).

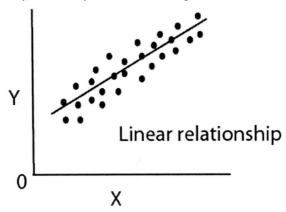

FIGURE 4.2
Chart showing a linear relationship.

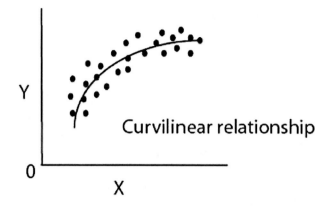

FIGURE 4.3
Chart showing a curvilinear relationship with a concave down orientation.

This book mostly addresses linear relationships, which means that linearity between variables is an assumption for many correlation tests. An example of a curvilinear relationship is age and health care usage. They are related, but the relationship does not follow a straight line. Young children and older people both tend to use much more health care than teenagers or young adults.

Correlation Coefficient Interpretation

Correlation coefficients provide a measure of the strength and direction of relationship between variables. Bivariate correlation coefficients represent the relationship between two variables. The Pearson product-moment correlation coefficient (also known as Pearson *r*) is the most often cited bivariate correlation coefficient used to describe the linear relationship between two interval/ratio scale variables. It's value can range anywhere between −1 (perfect inverse relationship), to 0 (no relationship) to +1 (perfect direct relationship). Linear relationships are depicted with scatterplots representing values clustered around a straight line. The higher the linear correlation, the tighter is the clustering around the straight line. Weak relationships are represented by widely scattered values.

A common scale used to characterize Pearson *r* is the one proposed by Hinkle, Wiersma, and Jurs (1998):

Little if any relationship < .30
Low relationship = .30 to < .50
Moderate relationship = .50 to < .70
High relationship = .70 to < .90
Very high relationship = .90 and above

Additionally, squaring the correlation coefficient produces the coefficient of determination that is useful in interpreting the correlation. The coefficient of determination tells one how much of the variance in y is explained by x. It is the percentage of the variability among scores on one variable that can be attributed to differences in the scores on the other variable. For example, if the bivariate correlation is $r = .7$ (a high relationship), $r^2 = .7 * .7 = .49$. Therefore, 49% of the variation in one variable is related to changes in the second variable. In other words, one variable is said to explain 49% of the variance in the other variable. The coefficient of nondetermination (k^2) is the proportion of total variance in one variable that is not explained from another variable. It is calculated by the formula $1 - r^2$.

Similarly, R is the coefficient of multiple correlation used in the multiple correlation procedure and reflects the relationship between one variable (the DV) and multiple IVs. Also, the coefficient of multiple determination (R^2) is the percent of variance in the DV explained collectively by multiple IVs.

It is important to note that correlation does not imply causation (i.e., a change in x does not cause a change in y), although correlation is one of several preconditions for causation. Consequently, correlation is useful in exploring possible cause and effect relationships, but does not prove causation. In particular, a third lurking or confounding variable, related to both x and y variables, might account for the mathematical correlation between x and y and when this effect is removed the relationship is no longer significant. In such situations the original relationship is said to be spurious, meaning that two variables have no direct causal connection, yet appear to be causally related due to either coincidence or the influence of one or more lurking variables.

Interpretation of correlation coefficients is influenced by the results of the appropriate inferential test. For example, if the test is not significant (i.e., $p > .05$), there is no reliable relationship regardless of the value of the calculated correlation coefficient. Alternatively, a statistically significant correlation may account for very little variation and consequently may be practically unimportant.

Unreliable measurement causes relationships to be under-estimated increasing the risk of Type II errors. Additionally, interpretation of results are influenced by whether of not correlation test assumptions are tenable. For example, restricting the range of scores can have a large impact on the correlation coefficient by artificially reducing its magnitude. Also, outliers can distort the interpretation of data depending on the location of the outlier. The professional literature is mixed regarding the robustness of Pearson r to non-normality, with, for example, Field (2000) stating Pearson r is "extremely robust" (p. 87) and Triola (2010) claiming "data must have a bivariate normal distribution" (p. 520). Departures from normality have a tendency to inflate Type I error and reduce power. Additionally, the maximum possible correlation between variables is limited when their distributions are markedly skewed in opposite directions (Nunnally & Bernstein, 1994).

Generally, different correlation coefficients cannot be compared across different samples as they are based on different computational formulas and some are sensitive to sample size. The interpretation of correlation coefficients is situational and is based on several factors such as the the nature of the specific correlation coefficient, the degree to which correlation assumptions were met, and the possible existence of lurking variables.

PEARSON PRODUCT-MOMENT CORRELATION TEST

The Pearson Product-Moment Correlation Test (also known as Pearson r) is a parametric procedure that determines the strength and direction of the linear relationship between two continuous variables. Pearson r is symmetric, with the same coefficient value obtained regardless of which variable is the IV and which is the DV. It has a value in the range $-1 \leq r \leq 1$. The absolute value of Pearson r can be interpreted as follows (Hinkle, Wiersma, & Jurs, 1998):

Little if any relationship < .30
Low relationship = .30 to < .50
Moderate relationship = .50 to < .70
High relationship = .70 to < .90
Very high relationship = .90 and above

A scatterplot can be used to visually inspect the degree and direction of linear relationship between the two variables. Since Pearson r is symmetric, it makes no difference which variables are displayed on the x- and y-axes. Additionally, one can determine if there is a curvilinear (i.e., nonlinear) component to the relationship that is not captured by the Pearson r correlation coefficient. For example, the relationship between human height and age is mostly a curvilinear relationship over a person's lifespan that would not be adequately captured by Pearson r (points on the scatterplot tend to fall along an arc rather that a straight line) since people increase in height until approximately age 20 and then stop growing. However, the relationship would be mostly linear if the target population were children. The eta correlation coefficient can be used to determine the total degree of relationship (linear plus curvilinear) between two variables.

Excel data entry for this test is fairly straightforward. Each variable is entered in a sheet of the Excel workbook as a separate column.

Pearson r is calculated as follows using raw scores.

$$r = \frac{\sum(X - \bar{X})(Y - \bar{Y})}{\sqrt{\sum(X - \bar{X})^2 \sum(Y - \bar{Y})^2}}$$

However, it is easier to calculate using z-scores because it standardizes both variables to the same scale.

$$r = \frac{\sum(Z_x Z_y)}{N}$$

The p-level for this correlation coefficient can be calculated using the t-distribution and the following t-value.

$$t = \frac{r\sqrt{N-2}}{\sqrt{1-r^2}}$$

Degrees of freedom. The degrees of freedom for this test is $N-2$, where N is the number of cases in the analysis.

Key Assumptions & Requirements

Random selection of samples (probability samples) to allow for generalization of results to a target population.

Variables. Two interval/ratio scale variables. Many researchers support the use of this test with ordinal scale variables that have several levels of responses. For example, Nunnally and Bernstein (1994) assert that this test can be used with ordinal level variables that have more than 11 rank values.

Absence of restricted range (i.e., data range is not truncated in any variable).

Measurement without error.

Bivariate normality. Both variables should have an underlying distribution that is bivariate normal. It indicates that scores on one variable are normally distributed for each value of the other variable, and vice versa. Univariate normality of both variables does not guarantee bivariate normality. A circular or symmetric elliptical pattern in a bivariate scatterplot is evidence of a bivariate normal distribution. The professional literature is mixed regarding the robustness of Pearson r to non-normality, with, for example, Field (2000) stating Pearson r is "extremely robust" (p. 87) and Triola (2010) claiming "data must have a bivariate normal distribution" (p. 520). Departures from normality have a tendency to inflate Type I error and reduce power.

Absence of extreme outliers. Pearson r is very sensitive to outliers. A nonparametric test should be used if outliers are detected.

Independence of observations.

Homoscedasticity. The variability in scores for one variable is roughly the same at all values of a second variable.

Linearity. There is a linear relationship between the two variables. This assumption is best evaluated using a scatterplot.

Excel Functions Used

COUNT(value1,value2,...). Counts the numbers in the range of numbers.

AVERAGE(number1,number2,...). Returns the arithmetic mean, where numbers represent the range of numbers.

PEARSON(array1,array2). Returns the Pearson product-moment correlation coefficient, where array1 and array2 represent the range of numbers for each variable.

POWER(number,power). Returns a number raised to the specified power, where number is the base number and power is the exponent.

STDEV.S(number1,number2,...). Returns the unbiased estimate of population standard deviation, where numbers represent the range of numbers.

SQRT(number). Returns the square root of a number.

T.INV.2T(probability,deg_freedom). Returns the inverse of the t-distribution (2-tailed), where probability is the significance level and deg_freedom is a number representing degrees of freedom.

Pearson Product-Moment Correlation Test Procedures

Research question and null hypothesis:

Is there a relationship between intrinsic motivation and alienation among online university students?

H_0: There is no relationship between intrinsic motivation and alienation among online university students.

Task: Use the Excel file Motivation.xlsx located at http://www.watertreepress.com/stats if you want to follow along with the analysis. The Data tab contains the data and the Pearson r tab contains the Pearson r analysis described below.

1.   Open the *Motivation.xlsx* file using Excel.

2.   Copy variables intr_mot (intrinsic motivation) and alienation from the Excel workbook Data tab to columns A and B on an empty sheet. Copy all 169 cases.

	A	B
1	intr_mot	alienation
2	29	72
3	41	89
4	48	68
5	52	82

3.   Remove case #91 (missing intrinsic motivation datum).

4.   Enter labels intr_mot and alienation in cells C2:C3 and n, Mean, and SD in cells D1:F1. Enter formulas =COUNT(A2:A169) and =COUNT(B2:B169) in cells D2:D3, =AVERAGE(A2:A169) and =AVERAGE(B2:B169) in cells E2:E3, and =STDEV.S(A2:A169) and =STDEV.S(B2:B169) in cells F2:F3.

	C	D
1		n
2	intr_mot	=COUNT(A2:A169)
3	alienation	=COUNT(B2:B169)

	E	F
1	Mean	SD
2	=AVERAGE(A2:A169)	=STDEV.S(A2:A169)
3	=AVERAGE(B2:B169)	=STDEV.S(B2:B169)

	C	D	E	F
1		n	Mean	SD
2	intr_mot	168	55.5	15.37437
3	alienation	168	67.1369	11.27497

5.   Enter labels N, df, Pearson r, r-squared, t, and p-level (2-tailed) in cells C4:C9. Enter formulas =D2, =D4-2, =PEARSON(A2:A169,B2:B169), =POWER(D6,2),

=D6*SQRT(D4-2)/SQRT(1-D7), and =T.DIST.
2T(ABS(D8),D5) in cells D4:D9.

	C	D
4	N	=D2
5	df	=D4-2
6	Pearson r	=PEARSON(A2:A169,B2:B169)
7	r-squared	=POWER(D6,2)
8	t	=D6*SQRT(D4-2)/SQRT(1-D7)
9	p-level (2-tailed)	=T.DIST.2T(ABS(D8),D5)

	C	D
4	N	168
5	df	166
6	Pearson r	-0.179403575
7	r-squared	0.032185643
8	t	-2.349573884
9	p-level (2-tailed)	0.019971315

Formatted Pearson r output summarizing test results:

	C	D	E	F
11	Pearson r			
12		Value	df	p-level 2-tailed)
13	r	-0.1794036	166	0.01997131

The above output shows a slight inverse relationship between intrinsic motivation and alienation. As one variable increases, the other decreases. These results show that this relationship is statistically significant since the t-value < the lower critical value for a 2-tailed test with .05 significance level. (It would also be significant if it were > the upper critical value.)

Automated Procedures

Use the following procedures for Analysis ToolPak.

1. Launch Microsoft Excel for Windows and open the Motivation.xlsx file. Go to the Pearson *r* sheet.

2. Select the Data tab and click the Data Analysis icon to open the Data Analysis dialog. Select Correlation and click OK to open the Correlation dialog.

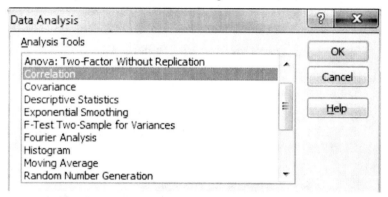

3. Select the Input Range by highlighting the intr_mot (intrinsic motivation) and alienation data in cells A1:B169. Check Labels in First Row.

4. Click the OK button to run the procedure. Excel places the following output in a new sheet.

	A	B	C
1		intr_mot	alienation
2	intr_mot	1	
3	alienation	-0.179403575	1

The result shows Pearson r = -.18.

Use the following procedures for StatPlus LE.

1.   Launch Microsoft Excel and open the Motivation.xlsx file. Go to the Pearson r sheet.

2.   Launch StatPlus LE and select Statistics > Basic Statistics and Tables > Linear Correlation (Pearson) from the StatPlus menu bar.

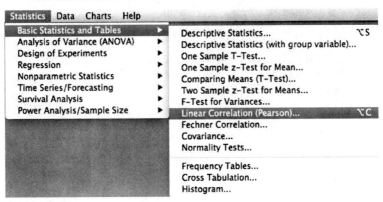

3.   Select the Variables range by highlighting the intr_mot (intrinsic motivation) and alienation data in cells A1:B169. Select Labels in first row.

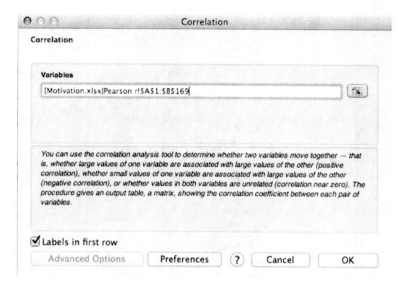

4. Click the OK button to run the procedure.

	A	B	C	D
1	**Correlation Coefficients Matrix**			
2	*Sample size*	168	*Critical value (5%)*	1.97436
3				
4			*intr_mot*	*alienation*
5	**intr_mot**	**Pearson Correlation Coefficient**	*1.*	
6		*R Standard Error*		
7		*t*		
8		*p-value*		
9		*H0 (5%)*		
10	**alienation**	**Pearson Correlation Coefficient**	*-0.1794*	*1.*
11		*R Standard Error*	0.00583	
12		*t*	-2.34957	
13		*p-value*	0.01997	
14		*H0 (5%)*	*rejected*	
15				
16	*R*			
17	*Variable vs. Variable*	*R*		
18	*alienation vs. intr_mot*	-0.1794		

The result shows Pearson $r = -.18$, $p = .02$.

Pearson Product-Moment Correlation Test Reporting

As a minimum, the following information should be reported in the results section of any report: null hypothesis that is being evaluated, descriptive statistics (e.g., *M, SD, N*), statistical test used (i.e., Pearson Product-Moment Correlation Test), results of evaluation of test assumptions, and test results. One might also include a figure of a scatterplot displaying the strength and direction of relationship between the two variables. For example, one might report test results as follows.

The Pearson Product-Moment Correlation Test was conducted to evaluate the null hypothesis that there is no relationship between intrinsic motivation and alienation among online university students ($N = 168$). The results of the test provided evidence that intrinsic motivation is inversely related to alienation, $r(166) = -.18$, $p = .02$ (2-tailed). Therefore, there was sufficient evidence to reject the null hypothesis. The coefficient of determination was .03, indicating that both variables shared only 3 percent of variance in common, which suggests a slight relationship.

(Note: assumptions require evaluation and reporting before test results can be relied upon.)

PARTIAL AND SEMIPARTIAL CORRELATION

Partial correlation is a parametric procedure that determines the correlation between two variables after removing the influences of a third or more variable from the relationship. If the partial correlation approaches 0, the inference is that the original correlation is spurious. That is, the original relationship (i.e., zero-order correlation) is computational only and there is no direct causal link between the original variables because confounding variable(s) were not considered.

One conducts partial correlation when the third variable is related to one or both of the primary variables and when there is a theoretical reason why the third variable would influence the results. The following computational formula is used:

$$r_{12.3} = \frac{r_{12} - r_{13}r_{23}}{\sqrt{1 - r_{13}^2}\sqrt{1 - r_{23}^2}}$$

where $r_{12.3}$ is the partial correlation between variables 1 and 2 while holding variable 3 constant across variables 1 and 2, r_{12} is the correlation between variables 1 and 2, r_{13} is the correlation between variables 1 and 3, and r_{23} is the correlation between variables 2 and 3.

One conducts semipartial correlation to hold variable 3 constant for just variable 1 or for just variable 2. In this case, one computes a semipartial correlation.

$$r_{1(2.3)} = \frac{r_{12} - r_{13}r_{23}}{\sqrt{1 - r_{23}^2}}$$

$$r_{2(1.3)} = \frac{r_{12} - r_{13}r_{23}}{\sqrt{1 - r_{13}^2}}$$

Degrees of freedom. The degrees of freedom for partial correlation is $N - 3$, where N is the number of cases in the analysis.

Key Assumptions & Requirements

Random selection of samples (probability samples) to allow for generalization of results to a target population.

Variables. All variables are continuous. Absence of restricted range (i.e., data range is not truncated in any variable). Many researchers support the use of this test with ordinal level variables that have several levels of responses. For example, Nunnally and Bernstein (1994) assert that this test can be used with ordinal level variables that have more than 11 rank values.

Measurement without error.

Multivariate normality. The variables being compared should have an underlying distribution that is multivariate normal. It indicates that scores on one variable are normally distributed for each value of the other variables, and vice versa.

Absence of extreme outliers.

Independence of observations.

Homoscedasticity. The variability in scores for one variable is roughly the same at all values of a second variable.

Linearity.

Excel Functions Used

ABS(number). Returns the absolute value of a number.

AVERAGE(number1,number2,...). Returns the arithmetic mean, where numbers represent the range of numbers.

COUNT(value1,value2,...). Counts the numbers in the range of numbers.

PEARSON(array1,array2). Returns the Pearson product-moment correlation coefficient, where array1 and array2 represent the range of numbers for each variable.

POWER(number,power). Returns a number raised to the specified power, where number is the base number and power is the exponent.

STDEV.S(number1,number2,...). Returns the unbiased estimate of population standard deviation, where numbers represent the range of numbers.

SQRT(number). Returns the square root of a number.

T.DIST.2T(x,deg_freedom). Returns the 2-tailed t-distribution probability, where x is the value to be evaluated and deg_freedom is a number representing the degrees of freedom.

Partial and Semipartial Correlation Test Procedures

Research question and null hypothesis:

Is there a relationship between external motivation and alienation in online students after controlling for academic self-concept, $r_{12.3} \neq 0$?

H_0: There is no relationship between external motivation and alienation in online students after controlling for academic self-concept, $r_{12.3} = 0$.

Task: Use the Excel file Motivation.xlsx located at http://www.watertreepress.com/stats if you want to follow along with the analysis. The Data tab contains the data and the Partial_Semipartial Correlation tab contains the correlational analysis described below.

1. Open the *Motivation.xlsx* file using Excel.

2. Copy variables extr_mot (extrinsic motivation), alienation, and acad_self_concept (academic self concept) from the Excel workbook Data tab to columns A, B, and C on an empty sheet. Copy all 169 cases.

	A	B	C
1	extr_mot	alienation	acad_self_concept
2	51	72	95
3	73	89	85
4	58	68	89
5	67	82	97

3. Enter labels extr_mot (1), alienation (2), and acad_self_concept (3) in cells D2:D4 and n, Mean, and Standard Deviation in cells E1:G1. Enter formulas =COUNT(A2:A170), =COUNT(B2:B170), and =COUNT(C2:C170) in cells E2:E4, =AVERAGE(A2:A170), =AVERAGE(B2:B170), and =AVERAGE(C2:C170) in cells F2:F4, and =STDEV.S(A2:A170), STDEV.S(B2:B170), and STDEV.S(C2:C170) in cells G2:G4. Note that external motivation and alienation are designated variables 1 and 2, respectively, and a academic self-concept is designated variable 3 (the control variable).

	D	E
1		n
2	extr_mot (1)	=COUNT(A2:A170)
3	alienation (2)	=COUNT(B2:B170)
4	acad_self_concept (3)	=COUNT(C2:C170)

	F	G
1	Mean	Standard Deviation
2	=AVERAGE(A2:A170)	=STDEV.S(C2:C170)
3	=AVERAGE(B2:B170)	=STDEV.S(B2:B170)
4	=AVERAGE(C2:C170)	=STDEV(C2:C170)

	D	E	F	G
1		n	Mean	Standard Deviation
2	extr_mot (1)	169	62.8698	5.69452
3	alienation (2)	169	67.1361	11.2414
4	acad_self_concept (3)	169	95.5503	5.69452

4. Enter labels N and df in cells D6:D7. Enter formulas =COUNT(A2:A170) and =E6-3 in cells E6:E7.

	D	E
6	N	=COUNT(A2:A170)
7	df	=E6-3

	D	E
6	N	169
7	df	166

5. Enter the label Bivariate Correlations in cell E9, r12, r13, and r23 in cells E11:E13, and r, t, and p-level in cells F10:H10. Enter formulas =PEARSON(A2:A170,B2:B170), =PEARSON(A2:A170,C2:C170), and =PEARSON(B2:B170,C2:C170) in cells F11:F13, =F11*SQRT(E6-2)/SQRT(1-POWER(F11,2)), =F12*SQRT(E6-2)/SQRT(1-POWER(F12,2)), and =F13*SQRT(E6-2)/SQRT(1-POWER(F13,2)) in cells G11:G13, and =T.DIST.2T(ABS(G11),(E6-2)), =T.DIST.2T(ABS(G12),(E6-2)), and =T.DIST.2T(ABS(G13),(E6-2)) in cells H11:H13.

	E	F
9	Bivariate Correlations	
10		r
11	r12	=PEARSON(A2:A170,B2:B170)
12	r13	=PEARSON(A2:A170,C2:C170)
13	r23	=PEARSON(B2:B170,C2:C170)

	G
9	
10	t
11	=F11*SQRT(E6-2)/SQRT(1-POWER(F11,2))
12	=F12*SQRT(E6-2)/SQRT(1-POWER(F12,2))
13	=F13*SQRT(E6-2)/SQRT(1-POWER(F13,2))

	H
9	
10	p-level
11	=T.DIST.2T(ABS(G11),(E6-2))
12	=T.DIST.2T(ABS(G12),(E6-2))
13	=T.DIST.2T(ABS(G13),(E6-2))

	E	F	G	H
9	Bivariate Correlations			
10		r	t	p-level
11	r12	0.154309	2.01829	0.045162
12	r13	-0.34844	-4.8039	0.0000034
13	r23	-0.21337	-2.8223	0.005347

Note the significant zero-order correlations.

6. Enter the label Partial Correlation in cell E15 and $r_{12.3}$ in cell E17. Also enter the labels r, t, and p-level in cells F16:H16. Enter the formulas =(F11-(F12*F13))/(SQRT(1-F12*F12)*SQRT(1-F13*F13)), =F17*SQRT(E6-2)/SQRT(1-F17*F17), and =T.DIST.2T(ABS(G17),(E6-3)) in cells

F17:H17.

	F
16	r
17	=(F11-(F12*F13))/(SQRT(1-F12*F12)*SQRT(1-F13*F13))

	G
16	t
17	=F17*SQRT(E6-2)/SQRT(1-F17*F17)

	H
16	p-level
17	=T.DIST.2T(ABS(G17),(E6-3))

	E	F	G	H
15	Partial Correlation			
16		r	t	p-level
17	r12.3	0.08732	1.13275	0.258954

7. Enter the labels Semipartial Correlation in cell E23 and $r_{1(2.3)}$ and $r_{2(1.3)}$ in cells E25:E26. Also enter the labels r, t, and p-level in cells F24:H24. Enter the formulas =(F11-F12*F13)/SQRT(1-F13*F13), =F25*SQRT(E6-3)/SQRT(1-F25*F25), and =T.DIST.2T(ABS(G25),(E6-3)) in cells F25:H25. Also, enter the formulas =(F11-F12*F13)/SQRT(1-F12*F12), =F26*SQRT(E6-3)/SQRT(1-F26*F26), and =T.DIST. 2T(ABS(G26),(E6-3)) in cells F26:H26.

	E	F
23	Semipartial Correlation	
24		r
25	r1(2.3)	=(F11-F12*F13)/SQRT(1-F13*F13)
26	r2(1.3)	=(F11-F12*F13)/SQRT(1-F12*F12)

	G
23	
24	t
25	=F25*SQRT(E6-3)/SQRT(1-F25*F25)
26	=F26*SQRT(E6-3)/SQRT(1-F26*F26)

	H
23	
24	p-level
25	=T.DIST.2T(ABS(G25),(E6-3))
26	=T.DIST.2T(ABS(G26),(E6-3))

	E	F	G	H
23	Semipartial Correlation			
24		r	t	p-level
25	r1(2.3)	0.081848	1.05808	0.291555
26	r2(1.3)	0.085309	1.10315	0.271559

Formatted partial and semipartial correlation test output summarizing test results:

	E	F	G	H
19	Partial Correlation			
20		Value	df	p-level
21	r12.3	0.08732	166	0.258954

	E	F	G	H
28	Semipartial Correlation			
29		Value	df	p-level
30	r1(2.3)	0.081848	166	0.291555
31	r2(1.3)	0.085309	166	0.271559

Excel output displays significant zero-order correlations between variables. However partial and semipartial correlations are not significant since the p-levels > .05 (the assumed *à priori* significance level).

Partial and Semipartial Correlation Test Reporting

As a minimum, the following information should be reported in the results section of any report: null hypothesis that is being evaluated, descriptive statistics (e.g., *M, SD, N*), statistical test used (i.e., partial correlation test), results of evaluation of test assumptions, and test results (i.e., zero-order correlation, partial correlation, and semipartial correlations, as appropriate). For example, one might report results as follows.

Partial correlation analysis was conducted to evaluate the null hypothesis that there is no relationship between external motivation and alienation in online students after controlling for academic self-concept, $r_{12.3} = 0$. Pearson Product-Moment Correlation Coefficients were calculated among the three variables of external motivation ($M = 62.87$, $SD = 5.69$), alienation ($M = 67.14$, $SD = 11.24$), and academic self-concept ($M = 95.55$, *11.24*) among online students ($N = 169$). The bivariate correlation between external motivation and alienation was $r(167) = .15$, $p = .045$; the correlation between external motivation and academic self-concept was $r(167) = -.35$, $p < .001$; and the correlation between alienation and academic self-concept was $r(167) = -.21$, $p = .005$. However, the partial correlation was not significant, $r_{12.3}(166) = .09$, $p = .26$. Consequently, there was insufficient evidence to reject the null hypothesis that there is no relationship between external motivation and alienation in online students after controlling for academic self-concept.

(Note: assumptions require evaluation and reporting before test results can be relied upon.)

RELIABILITY ANALYSIS

Introduction

Reliability refers to the consistency or repeatability of an instrument or observation. Classical reliability theory posits that an observed or measured score (symbolized by x) has two components, (a) a true score (symbolized by t) and (b) an error score (symbolized by e). This relationship is shown by:

$$x = t + e$$

The higher the error the more unreliable the measurement. These errors may come from random inattentiveness, guessing, differential perception, recording errors, etc. on the part of observers or subjects. These measurement errors are assumed to be random in classical test theory.

Accordingly, instrument reliability is the extent to which an item, scale, or instrument will yield the same score when administered in different times, locations, or populations, when the two administrations do not differ in relevant variables. In other words, it pertains to the consistency of measurement. Correlation procedures are used to assess reliability.

The measurement instrument should be both reliable and valid. Figure 4.4 below displays the relationship between reliability and validity. Validity is achieved if the shot pattern is centered on the bullseye, shown on the two targets to the right. Absence of reliability or low reliability results in a dispersed shot pattern, shown on the two top targets. This condition is analogous to a sample with a large variance. Increased reliability decreases the variance in the shot pattern, resulting in a tighter grouping (i.e., increased consistency in hitting the bullseye).

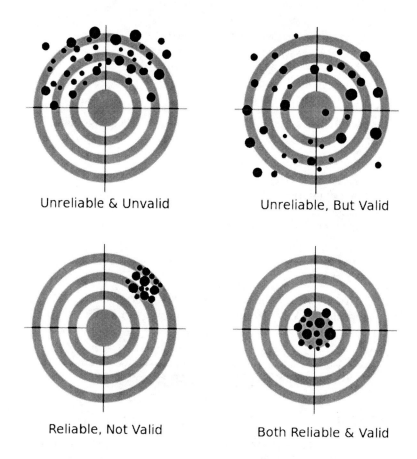

Unreliable & Unvalid

Unreliable, But Valid

Reliable, Not Valid

Both Reliable & Valid

Image: (c) Nevit Dilmen found at Wikimedia commons

FIGURE 4.4
Relationship between reliability and validity.

Internal consistency reliability refers to the ability of each item on an instrument to measure a single construct or dimension. It assumes the equivalence of all items on the instrument. Internal consistency coefficients estimate how consistently individuals respond to the items within a scale. The reliability of the instrument is estimated by how well items that reflect the same construct produce similar results.

Reliability coefficients can be interpreted as follows (Hinkle, Wiersma, & Jurs, 1998):

Very high reliability = .90 and above
High reliability = .70 to < .90
Moderate reliability = .50 to < .70
Low reliability = .30 to < .50
Little if any reliability < .30

George and Mallery (2003) provide the following interpretive guide for internal consistency reliabilities:

Excellent = .90 and above
Good = .80 to < .90
Acceptable = .70 to < .80
Questionable = .50 to < .70
Unacceptable < .50

Key Point
Many social science researchers consider scale reliability below .70 as questionable and avoid using such scales.

Split-Half Internal Consistency Reliability Analysis

Split-half is a popular types of internal consistency reliability that splits the scale into two parts and examines the correlation between the parts. Typically, responses on odd versus even items are employed and total scores on odd items are correlated with the total scores obtained on even items. The correlation obtained, however, represents the reliability coefficient of only half the test, and since reliability is related to the length of the test, a correction must be applied in order to obtain the reliability for the entire test. The Spearman-Brown Prophecy formula is used to make this correction.

$$\rho^* = \frac{k\rho}{1+(k-1)\rho}$$

where ρ^* is the predicted reliability, k is the number of parts combined (2 in split-half reliability analysis), and ρ is the reliability of the current scale.

Key Assumptions & Requirements

Variables. The instrument, representing an additive scale, should consist of multiple interval or ratio scale items. The items measure the same construct and are thus related to each other in a linear manner.

Normality. Each pair of items on the scale should have a bivariate normal distribution. If this assumption is not tenable, Spearman rank order correlation should be considered for the reliability analysis.

Homogeneity of variance. If the variances of the split halves are not approximately equal, the Guttman split-half reliability coefficient should be used.

$$G = 2(1 - \frac{S^2_{half1} + S^2_{half2}}{S^2_{total}})$$

Excel Functions Used

AVERAGE(number1,number2,...). Returns the arithmetic mean, where numbers represent the range of numbers.

CORREL(array1,array2). Returns the correlation coefficient, where the two arrays identify the cell range of values for two variables.

COUNTA(value1,value2,...). Counts the cells with non-empty values in the range of values.

STDEV.S(number1,number2,...). Returns the unbiased estimate of population standard deviation, where numbers represent the range of numbers.

VAR.S(number1,number2,...). Returns the unbiased estimate of population variance, with numbers representing the range of numbers.

Split-Half Internal Consistency Reliability Analysis Procedures

Research question and null hypothesis:

Is the Sense of Classroom Community Index reliable, $r \geq .70$?

H_0: The Sense of Classroom Community Index is not reliable, $r < .70$.

Below is a copy of the Sense of Classroom Community Index.

Directions: Below, you will see a series of statements concerning a specific course or program you are presently taking or have recently completed. Read each statement carefully and place an X in the parentheses to the right of the statement that comes closest to indicate how you feel about the course or program. You may use a pencil or pen. There are no correct or incorrect responses. If you neither agree nor disagree with a statement or are uncertain, place an X in the neutral (N) area. Do not spend too much time on any one statement, but give the response that seems to describe how you feel. Please respond to all items.

Note: each item has the following response set: Strongly Agree (SA), Agree (A), Neutral (N), Disagree (D), Strongly Disagree (SD)

1. I feel that students in this course care about each other

2. I feel that I am encouraged to ask questions

3. I feel connected to others in this course

4. I feel that it is hard to get help when I have a question

5. I do not feel a spirit of community

6. I feel that I receive timely feedback

7. I feel that this course is like a family

8. I feel isolated in this course

9. I feel that I can rely on others in this course

10. I feel uncertain about others in this course

11. I feel that my educational needs are not being met

12. I feel confident that others will support me

Notes:

Items are scored as follows: SA = 4, A = 3, N = 2, D = 1, SD = 0. To obtain the overall Classroom Community Index score, one must add the weights of all 12 items. Total raw scores range from a maximum of 48 to a minimum of 0. Items 4, 5, 8, 10, and 11 are reversed scored.

Task: Use the Excel file Community Index.xlsx located at http://www.watertreepress.com/stats if you want to follow along with the analysis. The Data tab contains the data and the Split-Half Reliability tab contains the split-half reliability analysis described below.

1. Open the *Community Index.xlsx file using Excel.*

2. Copy variables q01 through q12 and Index from the Excel workbook Data tab to columns A and M on an empty sheet. Copy all 346 cases.

3. Enter labels Part 1 - Odd Questions and Part 2 - Even Questions in cells N1:O1. Enter formulas =A2+C2+E2+G2+I2+K2 and =B2+D2+F2+H2+J2+L2 in cells N2:O2 and Fill Down to N347:O347 to display sums of odd questions and even questions for each case.

	N	O
1	Part 1 - Odd Questions	Part 2 - Even Questions
2	=A2+C2+E2+G2+I2+K2	=B2+D2+F2+H2+J2+L2
3	=A3+C3+E3+G3+I3+K3	=B3+D3+F3+H3+J3+L3
4	=A4+C4+E4+G4+I4+K4	=B4+D4+F4+H4+J4+L4
5	=A5+C5+E5+G5+I5+K5	=B5+D5+F5+H5+J5+L5

	N	O
1	Part 1 - Odd Questions	Part 2 - Even Questions
2	22	23
3	18	19
4	18	18
5	16	20

4. Enter labels Scale, Part 1, and Part 2 in cells P2:P4 and Mean, SD, and Variance in cells Q1:S1. Enter formulas =AVERAGE(M2:M347), =AVERAGE(N2:N347), and =AVERAGE(O2:O347) in cells Q2:Q4, =STDEV.S(M2:M347), =STDEV.S(N2:N347), and =STDEV.S(O2:O347) in cells R2:R4, and =VAR.S(M2:M347), =VAR.S(N2:N347), and =VAR.S(O2:O347) in cells S2:S4.

	P	Q
1		Mean
2	Scale	=AVERAGE(M2:M347)
3	Part 1	=AVERAGE(N2:N347)
4	Part 2	=AVERAGE(O2:O347)

	R	S
1	SD	Variance
2	=STDEV.S(M2:M347)	=VAR.S(M2:M347)
3	=STDEV.S(N2:N347)	=VAR.S(N2:N347)
4	=STDEV.S(O2:O347)	=VAR.S(O2:O347)

	P	Q	R	S
1		Mean	SD	Variance
2	Scale	33.650289	8.272652	68.4368
3	Part 1	16.4132948	4.51532	20.3881
4	Part 2	17.2369942	4.293091	18.4306

5. Enter labels q1 through q12 in cells P5:P126. Enter formulas =AVERAGE(A2:A347) and =STDEV.S(A2:A347 in cells Q5:R5. Continue entering formulas to calculate mean and standard deviation for q2 through q12 in cells Q6:R16.

	P	Q	R
5	q1	=AVERAGE(A2:A347)	=STDEV.S(A2:A347)
6	q2	=AVERAGE(B2:B347)	=STDEV.S(B2:B347)
7	q3	=AVERAGE(C2:C347)	=STDEV.S(C2:C347)
8	q4	=AVERAGE(D2:D347)	=STDEV(D2:D347)
9	q5	=AVERAGE(E2:E347)	=STDEV.S(E2:E347)
10	q6	=AVERAGE(F2:F347)	=STDEV.S(F2:F347)
11	q7	=AVERAGE(G2:G347)	=STDEV.S(G2:G347)
12	q8	=AVERAGE(H2:H347)	=STDEV.S(H2:H347)
13	q9	=AVERAGE(I2:I347)	=STDEV.S(I2:I347)
14	q10	=AVERAGE(J2:J347)	=STDEV.S(J2:J347)
15	q11	=AVERAGE(K2:K347)	=STDEV.S(K2:K347)
16	q12	=AVERAGE(L2:L347)	=STDEV.S(L2:L347)

	P	Q	R
5	q1	3.098265896	0.821202652
6	q2	3.248554913	0.869156308
7	q3	2.687861272	0.97844748
8	q4	3.040462428	1.009280883
9	q5	2.664739884	1.039941228
10	q6	2.780346821	1.183591144
11	q7	2.138728324	1.112955382
12	q8	2.73699422	1.045440721
13	q9	2.757225434	0.931893719
14	q10	2.534682081	0.984052277
15	q11	3.066473988	0.98902836
16	q12	2.895953757	0.868539229

6. Finally, enter labels # Items, N, r, Spearman-Brown, and Guttman in cells P18:P22. Enter formulas =COUNTA(A1:L1), =COUNT(A2:A347), =CORREL(N2:N347,O2:O347), 2*Q20/(1+(2-1)*Q20), and =2*(1-((S3+S4)/S2)) in cells Q18:Q22.

	P	Q
18	# Items	=COUNTA(A1:L1)
19	N	=COUNT(A2:A347)
20	r	=CORREL(N2:N347,O2:O347)
21	Spearman-Brown	=2*Q20/(1+(2-1)*Q20)
22	Guttman	=2*(1-((S3+S4)/S2))

	P	Q
18	# Items	12
19	N	346
20	r	0.763954637
21	Spearman-Brown	0.866183995
22	Guttman	0.865558934

Formatted split-half internal consistency reliability analysis output summarizing test results:

	P	Q	R	S	T	U
24	Split-Half Reliability Analysis					
25		N	# Items	r	Spearman-Brown	Guttman
26	Scale	346	12	0.76395	0.86618	0.86556

The above Excel outputs shows that the Sense of Classroom Community Index possesses a high internal consistency reliability of .87 as measured by the split-half reliability procedure with the Guttman adjustment for unequal variances.

Split-Half Internal Consistency Reliability Analysis Reporting

As a minimum, the following information should be reported in the results section of any report to confirm the reliability characteristics of a scale used in the research study: identification of instrument, model used (e.g., split-half), and reliability coefficient. For example, one might report internal consistency reliability results as follows.

The present research, which used the Sense of Classroom Community Index to operationalize classroom community, confirmed the high internal consistency reliability of this instrument. Split-half reliability analysis using Guttman's adjustment to compensate for unequal variances showed that the internal consistency reliability of this instrument was .87.

Cronbach's Alpha Internal Consistency Reliability Analysis

Cronbach's alpha model of internal consistency reliability analysis is based on the average inter-item correlation. It is used as an estimate of the internal consistency reliability of a psychometric test administered to a sample of examinees. Alpha coefficients range in value from 0 to 1 and can be used to describe the reliability of multiple choice formatted questionnaires or scales (e.g. Likert scales). The higher the score, the more reliable is the instrument.

One way to calculate Cronbach's alpha is to use an ANOVA with rows (cases) and columns (items or questions) as sources of variation.

$$Alpha = 1 - \frac{MS_{Error}}{MS_{Between}}$$

Key Assumptions & Requirements

Variables. The instrument, representing an additive scale, should consist of multiple interval or ratio scale items. The items measure the same construct and are thus related to each other in a linear manner. Cronbach's alpha requires that items are not scored dichotomously.

Normality. Each item on the scale should be normally distributed. If this assumption is not tenable, Spearman rank order correlation should be considered for the reliability analysis.

Excel Functions Used

AVERAGE(number1,number2,...). Returns the arithmetic mean, where numbers represent the range of numbers.

COUNT(value1,value2,...). Counts the numbers in the range of numbers.

COUNTA(value1,value2,...). Counts the cells with non-empty values in the range of values.

DEVSQ(number1,number2,...). Returns the sum of squares of deviations of data from the sample mean.

F.DIST.RT(x,deg_freedom1,deg_freedom2). Returns the right-tailed F-distribution probability, where x is the F-value to be evaluated, deg_freedom1 is the between groups df, and deg_freedom2 is the within groups df.

SUM(number1,number2,...). Adds the range of numbers.

VAR.S(number1,number2,...). Returns the unbiased estimate of population variance, with numbers representing the range of numbers.

Cronbach's Alpha Internal Consistency Reliability Analysis Procedures

Research question and null hypothesis:

Is the Sense of Classroom Community Index reliable, $r \geq .70$?

H_0: The Sense of Classroom Community Index is not reliable, $r < .70$.

Below is a copy of the Sense of Classroom Community Index.

Directions: Below, you will see a series of statements concerning a specific course or program you are presently taking or have recently completed. Read each statement carefully and place an X in the parentheses to the right of the statement that comes closest to indicate how you feel about the course or program. You may use a pencil or pen. There are no correct or incorrect responses. If you neither agree nor disagree with a statement or are uncertain, place an X in the neutral (N) area. Do not spend too much time on any one statement, but give the response that seems to describe how you feel. Please respond to all items.

Note: each item has the following response set: Strongly Agree (SA), Agree (A), Neutral (N), Disagree (D), Strongly Disagree (SD)

1. I feel that students in this course care about each other
2. I feel that I am encouraged to ask questions
3. I feel connected to others in this course
4. I feel that it is hard to get help when I have a question
5. I do not feel a spirit of community
6. I feel that I receive timely feedback
7. I feel that this course is like a family
8. I feel isolated in this course
9. I feel that I can rely on others in this course

10. I feel uncertain about others in this course

11. I feel that my educational needs are not being met

12. I feel confident that others will support me

Notes:

Items are scored as follows: SA = 4, A = 3, N = 2, D = 1, SD = 0. To obtain the overall Classroom Community Index score, one must add the weights of all 12 items. Total raw scores range from a maximum of 48 to a minimum of 0. Items 4, 5, 8, 10, and 11 are reversed scored.

Task: Use the Excel file Community Index.xlsx located at http://www.watertreepress.com/stats if you want to follow along with the analysis. The Data tab contains the data and the Cronbach's Alpha Reliability tab contains the Cronbach's alpha reliability analysis described below.

1.   Open the *Community Index.xlsx file using Excel.*

2.   Copy variables q01 through q12 from the Excel workbook Data tab to columns A through L on an empty sheet. Copy all 346 cases.

3.   Enter labels n, Sum, Means, and Variance in cells M1:P1. Enter formulas =COUNT(A2:L2), =SUM(A2:L2), =AVERAGE(A2:L2), and =VAR.S(A2:L2) in cells M2:P2 and Fill Down to cells M347:P347.

	M	N	O	P
1	n	Sum	Means	Variance
2	=COUNT(A2:L2)	=SUM(A2:L2)	=AVERAGE(A2:L2)	=VAR.S(A2:L2)
3	=COUNT(A3:L3)	=SUM(A3:L3)	=AVERAGE(A3:L3)	=VAR.S(A3:L3)
4	=COUNT(A4:L4)	=SUM(A4:L4)	=AVERAGE(A4:L4)	=VAR.S(A4:L4)
5	=COUNT(A5:L5)	=SUM(A5:L5)	=AVERAGE(A5:L5)	=VAR.S(A5:L5)

	M	N	O	P
1	n	Sum	Means	Variance
2	12	45	3.75	0.204545
3	12	37	3.0833333	0.44697
4	12	36	3	0
5	12	36	3	0.363636

4. Enter labels q01 through q12 in cells R2:R13 and n and Sum in cells S1:T1. Enter formulas =COUNT(A$2:A$347) and =SUM(A$2:A$347) in cells S2:T2 and Fill Down to cells S13:T13.

	R	S	T
1		n	Sum
2	q01	=COUNT(A$2:A$347)	=SUM(A$2:A$347)
3	q02	=COUNT(B$2:B$347)	=SUM(B$2:B$347)
4	q03	=COUNT(C$2:C$347)	=SUM(C$2:C$347)
5	q04	=COUNT(D$2:D$347)	=SUM(D$2:D$347)

	R	S	T
1		n	Sum
2	q01	346	1072
3	q02	346	1124
4	q03	346	930
5	q04	346	1052

5. Enter labels Means and Variance in cells U1:V1. Enter formulas =AVERAGE(A$2:A$347) and =VAR.S(A$2:A$347) in cells U2:V2 and Fill Down to cells U13:V13.

	U	V
1	Means	Variance
2	=AVERAGE(A$2:A$347)	=VAR.S(A$2:A$347)
3	=AVERAGE(B$2:B$347)	=VAR.S(B$2:B$347)
4	=AVERAGE(C$2:C$347)	=VAR.S(C$2:C$347)
5	=AVERAGE(D$2:D$347)	=VAR.S(D$2:D$347)

6. Enter labels N and #items in cells R15:R16 and Sources of Variation in cell R18. Enter formulas =COUNT(A2:A347 and =COUNTA(A1:L1) in cells S15:S16.

	R	S
15	N	=COUNT(A2:A347)
16	# items	=COUNTA(A1:L1)
17		
18	Sources of Variation	

	R	S
15	N	346
16	# items	12
17		
18	Sources of Variation	

7. Enter labels People Between, People Within, Error, and Total in cells R20:R23 and SS, df, MS, F, and p-level in cells S19:T19. Enter formulas =S16*DEVSQ(O2:O347), S15*DEVSG(U2:U13), =S23-S20-S21, and =DEVSQ(A2:L347) in cells S20:S23, =S15-1, =S16-1, =T23-T20-T21, and =S15*S16-1 in cells T20:T23, =S20/T20, =S21/T21, and =S22/T22 in cells U20:U22, =U21/U22 in cell V21, and =F.DIST.RT(V21, T21, T22) in cell W21.

	R	S	T
19		SS	df
20	People Between	=S16*DEVSQ(O2:O347)	=S15-1
21	People Within	=S15*DEVSQ(U2:U13)	=S16-1
22	Error	=S23-S20-S21	=T23-T20-T21
23	Total	=DEVSQ(A2:L347)	=S15*S16-1

	U	V	W
19	MS	F	p-level
20	=S20/T20		
21	=S21/T21	=U21/U22	=F.DIST.RT(V21,T21,T22)
22	=S22/T22		
23			

	R	S	T	U	V	W
19		SS	df	MS	F	p-level
20	People Between	1967.557	345	5.7031		
21	People Within	336.5614	11	30.596	55.3004	0.000000
22	Error	2099.689	3795	0.5533		
23	Total	4403.807	4151			

8. Finally, enter the label Cronbach's Alpha in cell R25 and formula =1-U22/U20 in cell S25.

	R	S
25	Cronbach's Alpha	=1-U22/U20

	R	S
25	Cronbach's Alpha	0.9029859

Formatted Cronbach's alpha internal consistency reliability analysis output summarizing test results:

	R	S	T
27	Cronbach's Alpha		
28	Alpha	N of Items	p-level
29	0.9029859	12	0.000000

The above Excel outputs shows that the Sense of

Classroom Community Index possesses a very high internal consistency reliability as measured by Cronbach's alpha, alpha = .90, p < .001.

Cronbach's Alpha Internal Consistency Reliability Analysis Reporting

As a minimum, the following information should be reported in the results section of any report to confirm the reliability characteristics of an existing scale: identification of instrument, model used (e.g., Cronbach's alpha), and reliability coefficient. For example, one might report results as follows for a research study that used an existing, unmodified instrument.

The present research, which used the Sense of Classroom Community Index to operationalize classroom community, confirmed the very high internal consistency reliability of this instrument, Cronbach's alpha = .90, *p* < .001.

SPEARMAN RANK ORDER CORRELATION TEST

The Spearman Rank Order Correlation Test (also known as Spearman rho) is a nonparametric symmetric procedure that determines the monotonic strength and direction of the relationship between two ranked variables. Either the Greek letter ρ (rho) or r_s is used as the symbol for this correlation coefficient. It has a value in the range $-1 \leq r_s \leq 1$. If there are no repeated data values, a perfect Spearman correlation of +1 or −1 occurs when each of the variables is a perfect monotone function of the other. The absolute value of r_s can be interpreted as follows (Hinkle, Wiersma, & Jurs, 1998):

Little if any relationship < .30
Low relationship = .30 to < .50
Moderate relationship = .50 to < .70
High relationship = .70 to < .90
Very high relationship = .90 and above

This test is not based on the concordance pair concept. It can be used for any type of data, except categories that cannot be ordered. The Spearman rank order correlation coefficient can be used instead of Pearson *r* if Pearson *r* parametric assumptions cannot be met. The formula for Spearman rho is:

$$\rho = 1 - \frac{6 \sum d_i^2}{n(n^2 - 1)}$$

where n is the number of pairs of ranks and d is the difference between the two ranks in each pair.

The p-level for this correlation coefficient can be calculated using the t-distribution and the following t-value.

$$t = \frac{r_s \sqrt{N - 2}}{\sqrt{1 - r_s^2}}$$

Key Assumptions & Requirements

Random selection of sample (probability sample) to allow for generalization of results to a target population.

Variables. Two ranked variables (ordinal, interval, or ratio data can be used). Absence of restricted range (data range is not truncated for any variable).

Independence of observations.

Monotonicity. Monotonic relationship between variables.

Excel Functions Used

CORREL(array1,array2). Returns the correlation coefficient, where the two arrays identify the cell range of values for two variables.

COUNT(value1,value2,...). Counts the numbers in the range of numbers.

F.DIST.RT(x,deg_freedom1,deg_freedom2). Returns the right-tailed F-distribution probability, where x is the F-value to be evaluated, deg_freedom1 is the between groups df, and deg_freedom2 is the within groups df.

MEDIAN(number1,number2,...). Returns the median of a range of numbers.

RANK.AVG(number,ref,order). Returns the rank of a number in a list, where number = the number to be ranked, ref = the list of numbers upon which the rankings are based, and 0 indicates the reference list is sorted in descending order.

Spearman Rank Order Correlation Test Procedures

Research question and null hypothesis:

Is there a relationship between grade point average and sense of classroom community?

H_0: There is no relationship between grade point average and sense of classroom community.

Alternatively, H_0: Grade point average and sense of classroom community are independent of each other or H_0: The ranks of grade point average are not related to the ranks of classroom community.

Note: Each of the above null hypotheses are statistically equivalent.

Task: Use the Excel file Motivation.xlsx located at http:// www.watertreepress.com/stats if you want to follow along with the analysis. The Data tab contains the data and the Spearman rho tab contains the Spearman rho test analysis described below.

1. Open the *Motivation.xlsx file using Excel.*

2. Copy variables gpa (grade point average) and c_community (classroom community) from the Excel workbook Data tab to columns A and B on an empty sheet. Copy all 169 variable pairs.

	A	B
1	gpa	c_community
2	1.58	23
3	1.87	22
4	2	23
5	2	23

3. Enter the labels Ranks (gpa) and Ranks (c_community) in cells C1:D1. Enter formulas =RANK.AVG(A2,$A$2:$A$170,1) and =RANK.AVG(B2,$B$2:$B$170,1) in cells C2:D2

and Fill Down to cells C170:D170.

	C
1	Ranks (gpa)
2	=RANK.AVG(A2,$A$2:$A$170,0)
3	=RANK.AVG(A3,$A$2:$A$170,0)
4	=RANK.AVG(A4,$A$2:$A$170,0)
5	=RANK.AVG(A5,$A$2:$A$170,0)

	D
1	Ranks (c_community)
2	=RANK.AVG(B2,$B$2:$B$170,0)
3	=RANK.AVG(B3,$B$2:$B$170,0)
4	=RANK.AVG(B4,$B$2:$B$170,0)
5	=RANK.AVG(B5,$B$2:$B$170,0)

	C	D
1	Ranks (gpa)	Ranks (c_community)
2	3	39
3	5	28.5
4	7	39
5	7	39

4. Enter label Median in cell F1 and gpa and c_community in cells E2:E3. Also enter labels N, df, rho, rho squared, t, and p-level (2-tailed) in cells E5:E10. Enter formulas =MEDIAN(A2:A170) and =MEDIAN(B2:B170) in cells F2:F3. Also enter formulas =COUNT(A2:A170), =F5-2, =CORREL(C2:C170,D2:D170), =POWER(F7,2), =F7*SQRT(F5-2)/SQRT(1-F8), and =T.DIST.2T(F9,F6) in cells F5:F10.

	E	F
1		Median
2	gpa	=MEDIAN(A2:A170)
3	c_community	=MEDIAN(B2:B170)
4		
5	N	=COUNT(A2:A170)
6	df	=F5-2
7	rho	=CORREL(C2:C170,D2:D170)
8	rho squared	=POWER(F7,2)
9	t	=F7*SQRT(F5-2)/SQRT(1-F8)
10	p-level (2-tailed)	=T.DIST.2T(F9,F6)

	E	F
1		Median
2	gpa	3.5
3	c_community	29
4		
5	N	169
6	df	167
7	rho	0.382344129
8	rho squared	0.146187033
9	t	5.347259846
10	p-level (2-tailed)	0.000000290

Formatted Spearman Rank Order Correlation Test output summarizing test results:

	E	F	G	H
12	Spearman Rank Order Correlation Test			
13		Value	df	p-level (2-tailed)
14	rho	0.3823441	167	0.000000290

The above output shows that the results of the Spearman Rank Order Correlation Test are statistically significant since the *p*-level <= .05 (the assumed *à priori* significance level).

Automated Procedures

Use the following procedures for StatPlus Pro.

1. Launch Microsoft Excel and open the Motivation.xlsx file. Go to the Spearman rho sheet.

2. Launch StatPlus Pro and select Statistics > Nonparametric Statistics > Rank Correlations (Spearman R, Kendall Tau, Gamma) from the StatPlus menu bar.

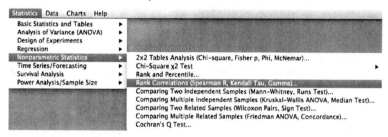

3. Select the Variable #1 range by highlighting gpa (grade point average) data in cells A1:A170 and c_community (classroom community) data in cells A1:B170. Select Labels in first row.

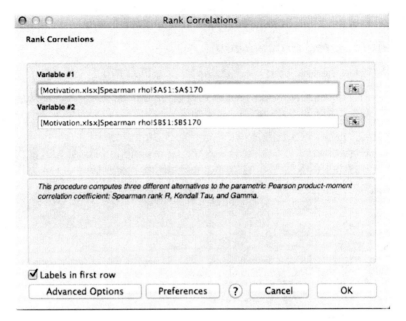

4. Click the Advances Options button, select Scatter Diagram (i.e., scatterplot), and click OK.

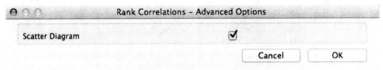

5. Click the OK button to run the procedure.

	A	B	C	D	E	F
1		Rank Correlations				
2		gpa	Rank	gpa	Rank	Difference
3	1	1.58	3.	23.	39.	-36.
4	2	1.87	5.	22.	28.5	-23.5
5	3	2.	7.	23.	39.	-32.
6	4	2.	7.	23.	39.	-32.
7	5	2.1	9.	22.	28.5	-19.5
8	6	2.4	11.	32.	110.	-99.
9	7	2.5	14.5	24.	47.5	-33.
10	8	2.5	14.5	22.	28.5	-14.

Output includes raw scores for each variable together with ranks.

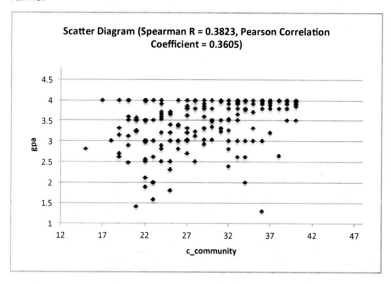

The scatterplot shows a low relationship between grade point average and classroom community because of the spread of the plots.

	G	H
1		
2	Spearman R	0.38234
3	Rank Difference Squares Sum	492,952.
4	t-test value for hypothesis r = 0	5.34726
5	p-level	0.
6	Kendall Tau	0.28035
7	Inversions Count	4419
8	Z	5.41068
9	p-level	0.
10	Gamma	0.29857
11	Pearson Correlation Coefficient	0.36047

The results show Spearman rho = .38, $p < .001$.

Kendall tau is a nonparametric test that determines monotonic symmetric relationship between two ordinal variables, used when the number of rows and number of columns are equal, adjusts for tied pairs, based on concordant-discordant pairs.

Gamma is a nonparametric test that determines symmetric relationship between ordinal and dichotomous nominal variables, ignores ties, based on concordant-discordant pairs.

Spearman Rank Order Correlation Test Reporting

As a minimum, the following information should be reported in the results section of any report: null hypothesis that is being evaluated, descriptive statistics (e.g., *M, SD, N* for interval/ratio scale variables; *Mdn, range, N* for ordinal scale variables), statistical test used (i.e., Spearman Rank Order Correlation Test), results of evaluation of test assumptions, and test results. For example, one might report test results as follows.

The Spearman Rank Order Correlation Test was used to evaluate the null hypothesis that there is no relationship between sense of classroom community and grade point average. The test showed a significant but low monotonic relationship between sense of classroom community and grade point average, $r_s(167)$

= .38, $p < .001$. Consequently, there was sufficient evidence to reject the null hypothesis. The coefficient of determination was $r_s^2 = .15$, which indicates that sense of classroom community and grade point average share 14 percent of variance in common.

PHI (Φ) AND CRAMÉR'S *V*

Phi (Φ) (also known as Cramér's Phi) and Cramér's *V* are nonparametric symmetric procedures based on the chi-square statistic used to determine if there is an association between columns and rows in contingency tables. The values range between 0 and 1. Both coefficients are measures of nominal by nominal association based on the chi-square statistic. Phi is used for 2 x 2 contingency tables and is the equivalent of Pearson *r* for dichotomous variables. When Phi is used in larger tables, it may be greater than 1.0, making it difficult to interpret. However, Cramér's *V* can be used for larger tables and corrects for table size. For 2 x 2 tables, Cramér's *V* equals Phi. The tests are not sensitive to sample size.

Both tests are typically used to assess effect size following a significant chi-square test.

Formulas for the two test statistics are given below

$$\phi = \sqrt{\frac{\chi^2}{N}}$$

$$V = \sqrt{\chi^2 \Big/ N(k-1)}$$

where *N* is the total number of cases and *k* is the lesser of number of rows or number of columns.

Both statistics are symmetric, so they will produce the same value regardless of how the variables are designated IV and DV. They are primarily used as post-hoc tests to determine strengths of association (effect size) after the chi-square test has determined significance in a contingency table analysis. Strength of relationship for Φ and Cramér's *V* are interpreted as follows (Rea & Parker, 2005):

Under .10, negligible association
.10 and under .20, weak association
.20 and under .40, moderate association
.40 and under .60, relatively strong association
.60 and under .80, strong association
above .80, very strong association

Key Assumptions & Requirements

Random selection of sample (probability sample) to allow for generalization of results to a target population.

Variables. Variables are categorical variables that generate a contingency table. Variables must be reported in raw frequencies (not percentages). Values/categories on the IV and DV must be mutually exclusive and exhaustive.

Independence of observations.

Excel Functions Used

CHISQ.DIST.RT(x,deg_freedom). Returns the right-tailed probability of the chi-square distribution, where x is the value that is evaluated and deg_freedom is the number of degrees of freedom.

IF(logical_test,value_if_true,value_if_false). Returns one value if the condition is TRUE and a different value if the condition is FALSE.

POWER(number,power). Returns a number raised to the specified power, where number is the base number and power is the exponent.

SQRT(number). Returns the square root of a number.

SUM(number1,number2,...). Adds the range of numbers.

Phi (Φ) and Cramér's V Test Procedures

Research question and null hypothesis:

Are student outcomes on the candidacy examination (pass, fail) the same for traditional on-campus and distance students?

H_0: Student outcomes on the candidacy examination (pass, fail) are independent of student program (traditional on-campus, distance).

Task: Use the Excel file Community.xlsx located at http://www.watertreepress.com/stats if you want to follow along with the analysis. The Data tab contains the data and the Phi & Cramér's V tab contains the Phi and Cramér's V analysis described below.

1. Open the *Community.xlsx* file using Excel.

2. Copy variables mode (0 = traditional, 1 = distance) and grade (0 = fail, 1 = pass) from the Excel workbook Data tab to columns A and B on an empty sheet. Copy all 117 cases.

	A	B
1	mode	grade
2	1	0
3	1	0
4	1	1
5	1	1

3. Sort cases by mode in ascending order.

4. Enter the following formulas in columns C through F:

   a. traditional, fail: Enter =IF(B2=1,0,1) in cell C2. Fill Down to cell C20 (all cases where mode = 0).

   b. traditional, pass: Enter =IF(B2=1,1,0) in cell D2. Fill Down to cell D20 (all cases where mode = 0).

   c. distance, fail: Enter =IF(B21=1,0,1) in cell E21. Fill Down to cell E118 (all cases where mode = 1).

   d. Enter =IF(B21=1,1,0) in cell F21. Fill Down to cell F118.

	C	D
1	traditional, fail	traditional, pass
2	=IF(B2=1,0,1)	=IF(B2=1,1,0)
3	=IF(B3=1,0,1)	=IF(B3=1,1,0)
4	=IF(B4=1,0,1)	=IF(B4=1,1,0)
5	=IF(B5=1,0,1)	=IF(B5=1,1,0)

Statistical Fundamentals

	E	F
1	distance, fail	distance, pass

	E	F
21	=IF(B21=1,0,1)	=IF(B21=1,1,0)
22	=IF(B22=1,0,1)	=IF(B22=1,1,0)
23	=IF(B23=1,0,1)	=IF(B23=1,1,0)
24	=IF(B24=1,0,1)	=IF(B24=1,1,0)
25	=IF(B25=1,0,1)	=IF(B25=1,1,0)

	C	D
1	traditional, fail	traditional, pass
2	0	1
3	0	1
4	0	1
5	1	0

	E	F
21	1	0
22	1	0
23	0	1
24	0	1
25	0	1

5. Enter labels Fail, Pass, and Totals in cells G2:G4 and Traditional, Distance, and Totals in cells H1:J1. Enter formulas =SUM(C2:C20), =SUM(D2:D20), and =SUM(H2:H3) in cells H2:H4, =SUM(E21:E118), =SUM(F21:F118), and =SUM(I2:I3) in cells I2:I4, and =SUM(H2:I2), =SUM(H3:I3), and =SUM(J2:J3) in cells J2:J4 to create a crosstabulation.

	G	H	I	J
1		Traditional	Distance	Totals
2	Fail	=SUM(C2:C20)	=SUM(E21:E118)	=SUM(H2:I2)
3	Pass	=SUM(D2:D20)	=SUM(F21:F118)	=SUM(H3:I3)
4	Totals	=SUM(H2:H3)	=SUM(I2:I3)	=SUM(J2:J3)

	G	H	I	J
1		Traditional	Distance	Totals
2	Fail	2	18	20
3	Pass	17	80	97
4	Totals	19	98	117

6. Enter labels Fail and Pass in cells G7:G8 and Traditional Expected and Distance Expected in cells H1:I1. Enter formulas =$J2*H$4/$J$4 and =$J3*H$4/$J$4 in cells H7:H8 and =$J2*I$4/$J$4 and =$J3*I$4/$J$4 in cells I7:I8 to create an expected frequencies table.

	G	H	I
6		Traditional Expected	Distance Expected
7	Fail	=$J2*H$4/$J$4	=$J2*I$4/$J$4
8	Pass	=$J3*H$4/$J$4	=$J3*I$4/$J$4

	G	H	I
6		Traditional Expected	Distance Expected
7	Fail	3.247863248	16.75213675
8	Pass	15.75213675	81.24786325

7. Enter label (Observed - Expected)-squared/Expected in cell J6. Enter formulas =POWER((H2-H7),2)/H7 and =POWER((H3-H8),2)/H8 in cells J7:J8 and =POWER((I2-I7),2)/I7 and =POWER((I3-I8),2)/I8 in cells K7:K8 to create a calculation table.

⊿	J	K
6	(Observed - Expected)-squared/Expected	
7	=POWER((H2-H7),2)/H7	=POWER((I2-I7),2)/I7
8	=POWER((H3-H8),2)/H8	=POWER((I3-I8),2)/I8

⊿	J	K
6	(Observed - Expected)-squared/Expected	
7	0.479442195	0.092953079
8	0.098854061	0.019165583

8. Finally, enter labels Rows, Columns, Chi-square, Phi, Cramer's V, df, and p-level in cells G10:G16. Enter formulas 2, 2, =SUM(J7:K8), =SQRT(H12/J4), =SQRT(H12/J4*(MAX(H10,H11)-1)), =(H10-1)*(H11-1), and =CHISQ.DIST.RT(H12,H15) in cells H10:H16.

⊿	G	H
10	Rows	2
11	Columns	2
12	Chi-square	=SUM(J7:K8)
13	Phi	=SQRT(H12/J4)
14	Cramer's V	=SQRT(H12/J4*(MAX(H10,H11)-1))
15	df	=(H10-1)*(H11-1)
16	p-level	=CHISQ.DIST.RT(H12,H15)

	G	H
10	Rows	2
11	Columns	2
12	Chi-square	0.690414918
13	Phi	0.076817851
14	Cramer's V	0.076817851
15	df	1
16	p-level	0.406023288

Formatted Phi and Cramér's *V* output summarizing test results:

	G	H	I
18	Phi (Φ) and Cramér's V		
19		Value	p-level
20	Phi	0.076817851	0.406023
21	Cramér's V	0.076817851	0.406023
22	N	117	

The above output shows that both Phi and Cramér's *V* are not significant since the *p*-level > .05 (the assumed *à priori* significance level).

Automated Procedures

Use the following procedures for StatPlus Pro.

1. Launch Microsoft Excel and open the Community.xlsx file. Go to the Phi & Cramér's *V* sheet.

2. Launch StatPlus Pro and select Statistics > Nonparametric Statistics > 2x2 Tables Analysis (Chi-square, Fisher p, Phi, McNemar) from the StatPlus menu bar.

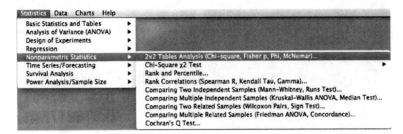

3. Enter cell values based on data contained in cells G1:I3.
    A (Exposed x Disease) = 18 (Distance x Fail), B (Exposed x
    No disease) = 80 (Distance x Pass), C (Not exposed x
    Disease) = 2 (Traditional x Fail), and D (Not exposed x No
    disease) = 17 (Traditional x Pass).

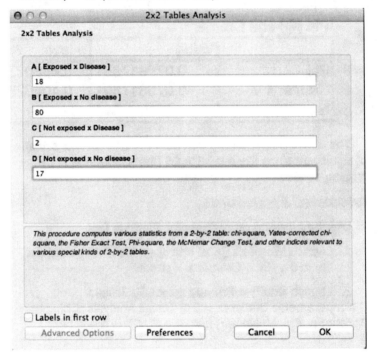

4. Click the OK button to run the procedure.

	A	B	C	D
1		2x2 Tables Analysis		
2	Alpha value (for confidence interval)	0.05		
3				
4		Column 1	Column 2	Row totals
5	Frequencies, row 1	18.	2.	20.
6	Percent of total	0.15385	0.01709	0.17094
7	Frequencies, row 2	80.	17.	97.
8	Percent of total	0.68376	0.1453	0.82906
9	Column totals	98.	19.	117.
10	Percent of total	0.83761	0.16239	

Output includes descriptive statistics for the crosstabulation table.

	A	B	C
12	**Statistics**	**Value**	**p-level**
13	Chi-square (df=1)	0.69041	0.40602
14	Yates corrected Chi-square	0.24798	0.6185
15	Mantel-Haenszel	0.68451	0.40804
16	McNemar Test (d.f.=1)	74.19512	0.E+0
17			
18	Fisher exact p		
19	Fisher exact p	0.88281	

Statistics	Value
Phi-square	0.07682
Cramer's V	0.07682
Pearson's Contingency	0.07659
Adjusted Pearson's Contingency	0.10832
Odds Ratio	42.35294
Relative Risk	0.74227
Kappa	0.02954
Yule's Q	0.3133
Equitable threat score	0.01499
Percent correct (Overall fraction correct)	0.29915

The results show Phi (results should identify Phi, not Phi-square) and Cramér's $V = .08$, $p = .41$. For 2 x 2 tables, Cramér's V equals Phi. Other statistics reported are not relevant to Phi and Cramér's V.

Phi (Φ) and Cramér's V Test Reporting

As a minimum, the following information should be reported in the results section of any report: null hypothesis that is being evaluated, descriptive statistics (e.g., observed frequency counts, N), statistical test used (i.e., Phi or Cramér's V), results of evaluation of test assumptions, and test results. For example, one might report results as follows.

A 2x2 contingency table was analyzed using the Phi test to evaluate the null hypothesis that student outcomes on the candidacy examination were independent of mode of student program delivery. The two variables are candidacy examination grade (fail = 20, pass = 97) and mode of student program (traditional = 19, distance = 98), $N = 117$. The proportions of students who passed the examination were reported as follows: traditional students = 89.47%, distance students = 81.63%, overall = 82.91%. The test was not significant, Phi = −.08, $p = .41$. Therefore, there was insufficient evidence to reject the null hypothesis. Consequently, test results provide evidence that candidacy examination grade is independent of type of student program.

(Note: Cramér's V is reported for contingency tables larger than 2x2.)

4.8: Linear Regression

INTRODUCTION

Regression uses the relationship between variables in making predictions. If there is a relationship between two variables, it is possible to predict a person's score on one variable (y) on the basis of their score on the other variable (x). One can say "regress x on y" to indicate using the variation in the data on x to explain the variation in y.

When one looks at a scatterplot of two variables that are associated, one can imagine a curve or line running through the data points that characterizes the general pattern of the data. A straight line reflects the pattern of a linear relationship. The Pearson correlation summarizes how tightly clustered the points are around this imaginary line. The process of placing a best fit line onto a scatterplot is called bivariate linear regression.

Typically no single straight line will align with each data point (that is, one cannot draw a single line through all of the data points in a scatterplot). What one desires is the line that fits the best and minimizes error. In other words, one seeks the line that differs the least from all of the data points as the best fitting line. To do this one finds the least-squares solution, that is, the line that generates the least value if one adds the squares of all errors. Such a straight line is called the *line of best fit*. See Figure 4.5 below.

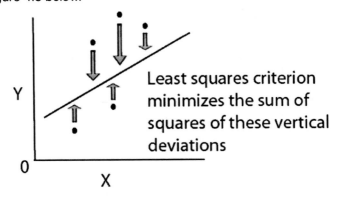

Least squares criterion minimizes the sum of squares of these vertical deviations

FIGURE 4.5
Least squares criterion for line of best fit.

Characteristics of the best fit line:

- Line minimizes the sum of the squared distances between the data points and the line.

- Line goes through the mean scores for both the dependent (y) and the independent (x) variable.

- If one squares the vertical distance of each data point from the line, and then sums these values, the resulting value is smaller than the value obtained with any other line. This is known as the *ordinary least squares (OLS) criterion.*

Statisticians use the adjusted coefficient of multiple determination (R^2) as a measure of the goodness of fit of the model. It is interpreted as the percent of variance in the DV explained collectively by multiple IVs. It represents the ratio of explained variation to total variation. R^2 is used as a measure of effect size (Cohen, 1988):

Small effect = .0196
Medium Effect = .1300
Large effect = .2600

BIVARIATE REGRESSION

Bivariate regression is a parametric procedure that predicts individual scores on a continuous DV based on scores of a continuous IV. Bivariate regression refers to the situation where there are only two distributions of scores, X and Y. By convention, X is the predictor variable (IV), and Y is the criterion (predicted) variable (DV). Bivariate regression analysis determines the fit of the best line to the bivariate scatterplot. That line represents the predicted relationship between two variables. Bivariate regression is a special case of the multiple regression procedure that uses only one IV instead of multiple IVs. The linear relationship between the two variables is shown by the following equation:

$$Y' = a + bx$$

where a = the y-axis intercept and b = the slope of the regression line.

Bivariate regression can incorporate a dichotomous variable as the IV that is coded using 1 and 0 and treated as a continuous variable. One codes this dummy variable with 1 if the characteristic is present and with 0 if the characteristic is absent. For example, maleness would be coded as 1 if present and 0 if absent. Conversely, femaleness could be coded as 1 if present and 0 if absent.

Important bivariate regression statistics:

• b is the unstandardized regression coefficient, that is, the slope of the regression or best fit line. It signifies the amount of change in y associated with one unit change in x.

$$b = \frac{n\sum XY - \sum X \sum Y}{n\sum X^2 - (\sum X)^2}$$

• a is the y-axis intercept, that is, the predicted value of y when x is zero. This is the point at which the regression line intersects with the vertical y-axis.

$$a = \frac{\sum Y - b\sum X}{n}$$

• The standard error of the estimate (SEE) is the standard deviation of the prediction errors. Approximately 68% of actual scores will fall between ±1 standard error of their predicted values. It is also referred to as the root mean square error.

$$SEE = \sqrt{\frac{\sum (Y - \bar{Y})^2}{(N - 2)}}$$

• R is the coefficient of multiple correlation. It reflects the relationship between the DV and the IV. In bivariate regression this statistic is the same as the absolute value of Pearson r.

• R^2 is the coefficient of multiple determination. It identifies the portion of variance in the DV explained by variance in the IV.

• The unstandardized residual (RES) is the difference between the observed value of the DV and the predicted value. The residual and its plot are useful for checking how well the regression line fits the data and, in particular, if there is any systematic lack of fit.

• The standardized residual (ZRE) is a residual divided by the standard error of the estimate. Standardized residuals should behave like a sample from a normal distribution with a mean of 0 and a standard deviation of 1. The standardized residual can be viewed as a z-score. So any observation with a standardized residual greater than |2| would be viewed as an outlier or an extreme observation.

• The studentized residual (SRE) is a type of standardized residual in which the residual is divided by its estimated standard deviation. It recognizes that the error associated with predicting values far from the mean of x is larger than the error associated with predicting values closer to the mean of x. The studentized residual increases the size of residuals for points distant from the mean of x.

• A significant *t*-test is evidence that the b coefficient is significantly different from zero.

• A significant *F*-test is evidence that the linear regression model is statistically significant.

The unstandardized regression line derived from the regression of y on x (i.e., the bivariate regression prediction equation) takes the following form:

$$Y' = a + bx$$

where Y' = predicted value of the DV, a = y-axis intercept, b = unstandardized regression coefficient.

The more linear the relationship, the more accurate the prediction. Since a relationship between two variables can be approximately linear over a certain range, then change, one should be very cautious about predictions beyond the range of observed data that produces a regression equation. This practice of extrapolation may yield inaccurate answers.

Key Assumptions & Requirements

Random selection of samples (probability samples) to allow for generalization of results to a target population.

Independence of observations. Residuals should be independent and not correlated serially from one observation to the next. This assumption is important for time-series data.

Variables. All variables are at least interval scale. Data range is not truncated (i.e., variables have unrestricted variance).

Measurement without error. Measurement errors in the DV do not lead to estimation bias in the correlation coefficients, but they do lead to an increase in the standard error of the estimate, thereby weakening the test of statistical significance. Additionally, measurement errors in the IVs may lead to either an upward or a downward bias in the regression coefficients (Pedhazur, 1997).

Normality. Residuals (predicted minus observed values) are distributed normally.

Absence of extreme outliers. Regression analysis is strongly influenced by outliers, especially extreme outliers. This means that a single extreme observation can have an excessive influence on the regression solution and make the results very misleading.

Absence of restricted range (i.e., data range is not truncated in any variable).

Homoscedasticity. Homoscedasticity means that the variance of errors (residuals) is the same across all levels of the IV. This assumption is checked with a scatterplot of observed y and predicted y. When this assumption is violated, heteroscedasticity is indicated. Slight heteroscedasticity has minimal effect on significance tests; however, larger heteroscedasticity can lead to serious distortion of findings and seriously weaken the analysis and increase the possibility of a Type I error (Tabachnick & Fidell, 2007). In particular, the standard errors are biased, which means the test statistics, confidence intervals, and the standard error of the estimate are not reliable and may produce incorrect conclusions.

Linearity. If the relationship between IVs and the criterion variable is not linear, the results of the regression analysis will under-estimate the true relationship. This under-estimation carries an increased chance of a Type II error.

Proper specification of the model. If relevant variables are omitted from the model, the common variance they share with included variables may be wrongly attributed to those variables, and the error term is inflated. If causally irrelevant variables are included in the model, the common variance they share with included variables may be wrongly attributed to the irrelevant variables. The more the correlation of the irrelevant variable(s) with other independents, the greater the standard errors of the regression coefficients for these independents. Omission and irrelevancy can both affect substantially the size of the b and beta coefficients. The specification problem in regression is similar to the problem of spuriousness in correlation, where a given bivariate correlation may be inflated because one has not yet introduced control variables into the model by way of partial correlation.

When the omitted variable has a suppressing effect, coefficients in the model may underestimate rather than overestimate the effect of those variables on the dependent. Suppression occurs when the omitted variable has a positive causal influence on the included independent and a negative influence on the included dependent (or vice versa), thereby masking the impact the independent would have on the dependent if the third variable did not exist.

Sample size. Various rules of thumb have been suggested regarding sample size, but much depends on the amount of noise in the data and the nature of the phenomena being investigated. Tabachnick and Fidell (2007) suggest researchers have 104 cases plus the number of independent variables if one wishes to test regression coefficients. Stevens (2002) suggests regression analysis must include at least 15 cases per predictor variable.

Excel Functions Used

AVERAGE(number1,number2,...). Returns the arithmetic mean, where numbers represent the range of numbers.

COUNT(value1,value2,...). Counts the numbers in the range of numbers.

F.DIST.RT(x,deg_freedom1,deg_freedom2). Returns the right-tailed F-distribution probability, where x is the F-value to be evaluated, deg_freedom1 is the between groups df, and deg_freedom2 is the within groups df.

INTERCEPT(known y's, known x's). Returns the y-intercept based on the best-fit regression line.

POWER(number,power). Returns a number raised to the specified power, where number is the base number and power is the exponent.

RSQ (known y's, known x's). Returns the coefficient of multiple determination.

SLOPE (known y's, known x's). Returns the slope of the linear regression line.

SQRT(number). Returns the square root of a number.

STDEV.S(number1,number2,...). Returns the unbiased estimate of population standard deviation deviation, where numbers represent the range of numbers.

STEYX (known y's, known x's). Returns the standard error of the estimate.

SUM(number1,number2,...). Adds the range of numbers.

T.INV.2T(probability,deg_freedom). Returns the inverse of the t-distribution (2-tailed), where probability is the significance level and deg_freedom is a number representing degrees of freedom.

Bivariate Regression Procedures

Research question and null hypothesis:

Can perceived learning predict sense of classroom community among university students, $b \neq 0$?

H_0: perceived learning cannot predict classroom community among university students, $b = 0$.

Task: Use the Excel file Motivation.xlsx located at http:// www.watertreepress.com/stats if you want to follow along with the analysis. The Data tab contains the data and the Bivariate Regression Analysis tab contains the bivariate regression analysis described below.

1.　Open the *Motivation.xlsx file using Excel.*

2.　Copy variables p_learning (perceived learning) and c_community (classroom community) from the Excel

workbook Data tab to columns A and B on an empty sheet.
Copy 169 cases.

	A	B
1	p_learning	c_community
2	7	23
3	7	22
4	5	23
5	7	23

3.   Delete case #93 because of missing datum. There are
now 168 cases.

4.   Enter labels N, M p-learning (x), M c_community (y), SD
p_learning, and SD c_community in cells C1:C5. Enter
formulas =COUNT(A2:A169), =AVERAGE(A2:A169),
=AVERAGE(B2:B169), =STDEV.S(A2:A169), and
STDEV.S(B2:B169) in cells D1:D5.

	C	D
1	N	=COUNT(A2:A169)
2	M p_learning (x)	=AVERAGE(A2:A169)
3	M c_community (y)	=AVERAGE(B2:B169)
4	SD p_learning	=STDEV.S(A2:A169)
5	SD c_community	=STDEV.S(B2:B169)

	C	D
1	N	168
2	M p_learning (x)	6.514880952
3	M c_community (y)	28.82142857
4	SD p_learning	1.760703448
5	SD c_community	6.255365533

5.   Create a scatterplot of p-learning and c_community in
order to visually evaluate the bivariate relationship, presence
of outliers, and linearity of the two variables.

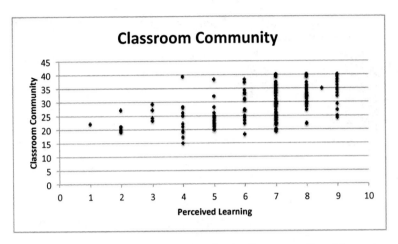

The scatterplot suggests a moderate linear relationship and the absence of extreme outliers.

6.   Enter labels a (constant), b, SEE, r-squared, and R in cells C6:C10. Enter formulas
=INTERCEPT(B2:B169,A2:A169),
=SLOPE(B2:B169,A2:A169), =STEYX(B2:B169,A2:A169),
=RSQ(B2:B169,A2:A169), and =SQRT(D9) in cells D6:D10.

	C	D
6	a (constant)	=INTERCEPT(B2:B169,A2:A169)
7	b	=SLOPE(B2:B169,A2:A169)
8	SEE	=STEYX(B2:B169,A2:A169)
9	R-squared	=RSQ(B2:B169,A2:A169)
10	R	=SQRT(D9)

	C	D
6	a (constant)	16.64711428
7	b	1.868693285
8	SEE	5.336158884
9	R-squared	0.276657911
10	R	0.525982805

The constant term of the prediction equation is a, b is the unstandardized coefficient of x, SEE is the standard error of the estimate, and R^2 is the coefficient of multiple determination. Based on these results, the prediction equation is y = 16.65 + 1.87x, where y = sense of classroom community and x = perceived learning.

7. Enter labels Predicted y, RES, ZRE, and SRE in cells E1:H1. Enter formulas =$D$6+$D$7*A2, =B2-E2, =F2/$D$8, and =F2/STDEV.S($F$2:$F$169) in cells E2:H2 and Fill Down to cells E169:H169.

	E	F	G	H
1	Predicted y	RES	ZRE	SRE
2	=$D$6+$D$7*A2	=B2-E2	=F2/$D$8	=F2/STDEV.S($F$2:$F$169)
3	=$D$6+$D$7*A3	=B3-E3	=F3/$D$8	=F3/STDEV.S($F$2:$F$169)
4	=$D$6+$D$7*A4	=B4-E4	=F4/$D$8	=F4/STDEV.S($F$2:$F$169)
5	=$D$6+$D$7*A5	=B5-E5	=F5/$D$8	=F5/STDEV.S($F$2:$F$169)

	E	F	G	H
1	Predicted y	RES	ZRE	SRE
2	29.727967	-6.727967	-1.2608	-1.2646179
3	29.727967	-7.727967	-1.4482	-1.4525822
4	25.990581	-2.990581	-0.5604	-0.5621225
5	29.727967	-6.727967	-1.2608	-1.2646179

8. Create a scatterplot of p-learning and p_learning residuals in order to visually evaluate the accuracy of predicted values. Perfect accuracy would produce a chart where all predicted values are plotted on the zero-axis.

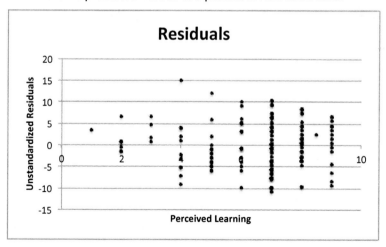

9. Enter label x-xbar squared in cell I1. Enter formula
=POWER(A2=$D2$2,2) in cell I2 and Fill Down to cell I169.

	I
1	x-xbar squared
2	=POWER(A2-$D$2,2)
3	=POWER(A3-$D$2,2)
4	=POWER(A4-$D$2,2)
5	=POWER(A5-$D$2,2)

	I
1	x-xbar squared
2	0.23534049
3	0.23534049
4	2.2948643
5	0.23534049

10. Finally, enter labels SSX, SSb, t(p-learning), #
predictors, df, Upper critical value (2-tailed), Lower critical
value (2-tailed), F, and p-value in cells J1:J9. Enter formulas
=SUM(I2:I169), =D8/SQRT(K1), =D7/K2, 1, =D1-(K4+1),
=T.INV.2T(0.05,K5), =-K6, = K5*D9/(K4*(1-D9)), and
=F.DIST.RT(K8,K4,K5) in cells K1:K9.

	J	K
1	SSX	=SUM(I2:I169)
2	Sb	=D8/SQRT(K1)
3	t (p_learning)	=D7/K2
4	# predictors	1
5	df	=D1-(K4+1)
6	Upper critical value (2-tailed)	=T.INV.2T(0.05,K5)
7	Lower critical value (2-tailed)	=-K6
8	F	=K5*D9/(K4*(1-D9))
9	p-value	=F.DIST.RT(K8,K4,K5)

	J	K
1	SSX	517.712798
2	Sb	0.23452238
3	t (p_learning)	7.96808069
4	# predictors	1
5	df	166
6	Upper critical value (2-tailed)	1.97435776
7	Lower critical value (2-tailed)	-1.97435776
8	F	63.4903098
9	p-value	2.4506E-13

Note: The upper and lower critical values pertain to the *t*-value at the .05 significance level.

Formatted bivariate regression output summarizing test results:

	J	K
12	Bivariate Regression	
13	R	0.525982805
14	R-squared	0.276657911
15	SEE	5.336158884
16	a (constant)	16.64711428
17	b	1.868693285
18	t (p-learning)	7.968080685
19	Upper critical value (2-tailed)	1.974357764
20	Lower critical value (2-tailed)	-1.974357764
21	F	63.49030981
22	p-value	2.4506E-13

The above output also shows that the regression model is statistically significant since the *t*-test significance level <= .05 (the assumed *à priori* significance level). In particular, 27.67% of the variance in classroom community in the sample is accounted for by perceived learning based on the R^2. The standard error of the estimate indicates that 68% of actual scores will fall between ±1 5.34 of their predicted values.

Automated Procedures

Use the following procedures for Analysis ToolPak.

1. Launch Microsoft Excel for Windows and open the Motivation.xlsx file. Go to the Bivariate Regression sheet.

2. Select the Data tab and click the Data Analysis icon to open the Data Analysis dialog. Select Regression and click OK to open the Regression dialog.

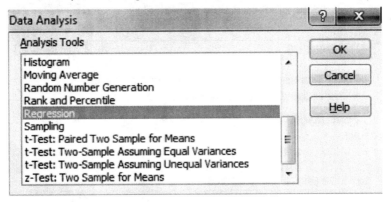

3. Select the Input Y Range by highlighting c_community (classroom community) data in cells B1:B169. Select the Input X Range by highlighting p_learning (perceived learning) data in cells A1:A169. Check Labels, Residuals, and Residual Plots.

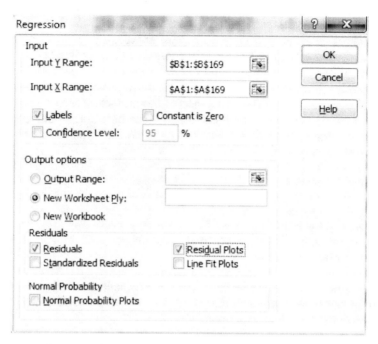

4. Click the OK button to run the procedure. Excel places the following output in a new sheet.

	A	B
1	SUMMARY OUTPUT	
2		
3	Regression Statistics	
4	Multiple R	0.525982805
5	R Square	0.276657911
6	Adjusted R Square	0.272300429
7	Standard Error	5.336158884
8	Observations	168

In bivariate regression analysis, Multiple R represents the absolute value of the Pearson r product-moment correlation coefficient between the DV and the IV. R square is the coefficient of determination. It identifies the portion of variance in the DV explained by variance in the IV. Adjusted R^2 (coefficient of multiple determination) is a downward adjustment to R^2 because it becomes artificially high simply because of the addition of more IVs. At the extreme, when there are as many IVs as cases in the sample, R^2 equals 1.0. The standard error (standard error of the estimate) is the standard deviation of the prediction errors. Approximately 68% of actual scores will fall between ±1 standard error of their predicted values. It is also referred to as the root mean square error.

	A	B	C	D	E	F
11		df	SS	MS	F	Significance F
12	Regression	1	1807.861	1807.861	63.49031	2.45E-13
13	Residual	166	4726.782	28.47459		
14	Total	167	6534.643			

The ANOVA table tests the overall significance of the model (that is, of the regression equation). The null hypothesis tested by the ANOVA procedure is $R = 0$.

	A	B	C	D	E
16		Coefficients	Standard Error	t Stat	P-value
17	Intercept	16.647114	1.58238	10.5203	3.73E-20
18	p_learning	1.8686933	0.234522	7.968081	2.45E-13

These coefficients provide the values needed to write the regression equation where the intercept coefficient is the constant (y-intercept) and p_learning is the x-coefficient (the slope of the least squares regression line). The unstandardized coefficients are used to create an unstandardized prediction equation. A significant t-test is evidence that the coefficient is significantly different from zero

	F	G	H	I
16	Lower 95%	Upper 95%	Lower 95.0%	Upper 95.0%
17	13.522931	19.7712979	13.5229307	19.7712979
18	1.4056622	2.33172438	1.40566219	2.33172438

The results indicate that perceived learning can reliably predict classroom community among university students, $t(166) = 7.97$, $p < .001$. The constant term is 16.65 and the x-coefficient is 1.87. The unstandardized regression equation for predicting classroom community is:

$$Y' = 16.65 + 1.87x$$

where Y' = classroom community and x = perceived learning.

	A	B	C
22	RESIDUAL OUTPUT		
23			
24	Observation	Predicted c_community	Residuals
25	1	29.72796728	-6.727967
26	2	29.72796728	-7.727967
27	3	25.99058071	-2.990581
28	4	29.72796728	-6.727967
29	5	25.99058071	-3.990581

An unstandardized residual is the difference between the observed value and the predicted value.

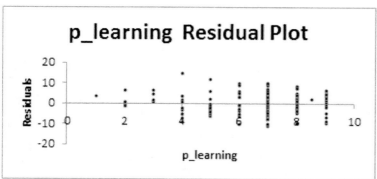

The p_learning residual plot shows a random pattern, suggesting a good fit for a linear model. Plot patterns that appear non-random, e.g., U or inverted U shaped, suggest a non-linear model.

Use the following procedures for StatPlus LE.

1. Launch Microsoft Excel and open the Motivation.xlsx file. Go to the Bivariate Regression sheet.

2. Launch StatPlus LE and select Statistics > Regression > Linear Regression from the StatPlus menu bar.

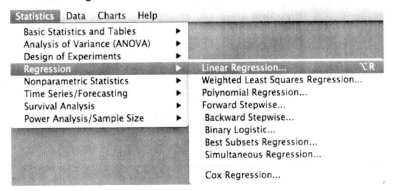

3. Select the Dependent variable range by highlighting c_community (classroom community) data in cells B1:B169. Select the Independent variables range by highlighting p_learning (perceived learning) data in cells A1:A169. Check Labels in first row.

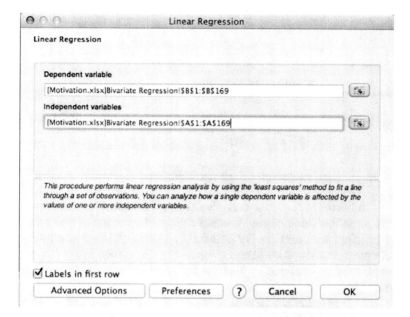

4. Click the Advanced Options button. Check Residual Plots. Click the OK button.

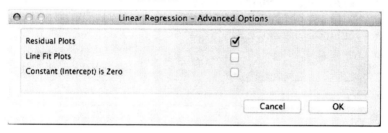

5. Click the OK button to run the procedure.

	A	B
1	**Linear Regression**	
2		
3	**Regression Statistics**	
4	R	0.52598
5	R Square	0.27666
6	Adjusted R Square	0.2723
7	S	5.33616
8	Total number of observations	168

In bivariate regression analysis, R or Multiple R represents the absolute value of the Pearson r product-moment correlation coefficient between the DV and the IV. R square is the coefficient of determination. It identifies the portion of variance in the DV explained by variance in the IV. Adjusted R^2 (coefficient of multiple determination) is a downward adjustment to R^2 because it becomes artificially high simply because of the addition of more IVs. S represents the standard error (standard error of the estimate), which is the standard deviation of the prediction errors. Approximately 68% of actual scores will fall between ±1 standard error of their predicted values. It is also referred to as the root mean square error.

	A	B	C	D	E	F
9		c_community = 16.6471 + 1.8687 * p_learning				
10						
11	**ANOVA**					
12		d.f.	SS	MS	F	p-level
13	Regression	1.	1,807.86064	1,807.86064	63.49031	2.45026E-13
14	Residual	166.	4,726.78221	28.47459		
15	Total	167.	6,534.64286			

The ANOVA table tests the overall significance of the model (that is, of the regression equation). The null hypothesis tested by the ANOVA procedure is $R = 0$.

	A	B	C	D	E
17		Coefficients	Standard Error	LCL	UCL
18	**Intercept**	16.64711	1.58238	13.52293	19.7713
19	**p_learning**	1.86869	0.23452	1.40566	2.33172
20	T (5%)	1.97436			
21	LCL - Lower value of a reliable interval (LCL)				
22	UCL - Upper value of a reliable interval (UCL)				

These coefficients provide the values needed to write the regression equation where the intercept coefficient is the constant (y-intercept) and p_learning is the x-coefficient (the slope of the least squares regression line). The unstandardized coefficients are used to create an unstandardized prediction equation.

	F	G	H
17	t Stat	p-level	H0 (5%) rejected?
18	10.5203	0.E+0	Yes
19	7.96808	2.45026E-13	Yes
20			
21			
22			

A significant t-test is evidence that the coefficient is significantly different from zero

	A	B	C	D
24	**Residuals**			
25	Observation	Predicted Y	Residual	Standard Residuals
26	1	29.72797	-6.72797	-1.26462
27	2	29.72797	-7.72797	-1.45258
28	3	25.99058	-2.99058	-0.56212
29	4	29.72797	-6.72797	-1.26462
30	5	25.99058	-3.99058	-0.75009

A standardized residual is the difference between the observed value and the predicted standardized value.

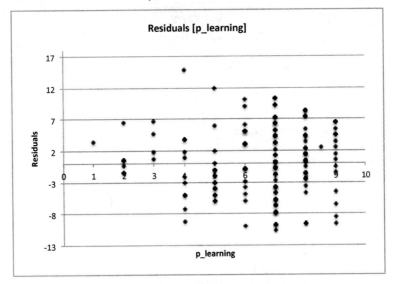

The p_learning residual plot shows a random pattern, suggesting a good fit for a linear model. Plot patterns that appear non-random, e.g., U or inverted U shaped, suggest a non-linear model.

Bivariate Regression Reporting

As a minimum, the following information should be reported in the results section of any report: null hypothesis that is being evaluated, descriptive statistics (e.g., M, SD, N), correlations, statistical test used (i.e., bivariate regression), results of evaluation of regression assumptions, and bivariate regression test results, to include the amount of variance explained by the model (i.e., R^2), the significance of the model, and identification of the predictor variable. For a significant bivariate regression model one should also report the regression equation and the standard error of the estimate. For example, one might report test results as follows.

Bivariate regression was used to evaluate the null hypothesis that perceived learning cannot predict classroom community among university students. A bivariate linear regression analysis indicated that perceived learning ($M = 6.51$,

$SD = 1.76$) can reliably predict classroom community ($M = 28.82$, $SD = 6.26$) among university students, $N = 168$, $F(1,166) = 63.49$, $p < .001$. Consequently, there was sufficient evidence to reject the null hypothesis that perceived learning cannot predict classroom community. 27.7% of the variance in classroom community in the sample is accounted for by perceived learning. The standard error of the estimate was 5.34 indicating that 68% of actual scores fall within ± 5.34 points of their predicted values. The unstandardized regression equation for predicting classroom community was:

$$Y' = 16.65 + 1.87x$$

where Y' = classroom community and x = perceived learning.

4.9: Chapter 4 Review

The answer key is at the end of this section.

1. Which of the following tests is a parametric test?

    A. One-sample *t*-test

    B. Binomial test

    C. Kolmogorov-Smirnov test

    D. Spearman rank order correlation test

2. What is the best inferential test for normality?

    A. One-sample *t*-test

    B. Kolmogorov-Smirnov test

    C. McNemar test

    D. F-test for equality of variance

3. What is the best test to address the following null hypothesis: H_0: Online college students are equally likely to report low, medium, or high sense of classroom community.

    A. Chi-Square (χ^2) goodness-of-fit test

    B. Binomial test

    C. One sample *t*-test

    D. Kolmogorov-Smirnov test

4. What is the best test to answer the following research question: Is the proportion of college students who prefer online courses different from the proportion of college students who prefer traditional on-campus courses?

    A. McNemar test

    B. Chi-square (χ^2) goodness-of-fit test

    C. Kolmogorov-Smirnov test

    D. Binomial test

5. What test determines if the proportion of individuals in one of two categories is different from a specified test proportion?

A. Chi-square goodness-of-fit test

B. Binomial test

C. One-sample *t*-test

D. Kolmogorov-Smirnov test

6. What test assumes normality?

A. Binomial test

B. Kolmogorov-Smirnov test

C. One-sample *t*-test

D. Pearson chi-square (χ^2) contingency table analysis

7. What does b represent in the prediction equation, $\dot{Y}= a + bX$?

A. Slope of the best-fit line

B. Y-intercept

C. Residual

D. Correlation coefficient

8. What does a represent in the prediction equation, $\dot{Y}= a + bX$?

A. Slope of the best-fit line

B. Y-intercept

C. Residual

D. Correlation coefficient

9. What does Pearson *r* measure?

A. Direction of relationship

B. Strength of relationship

C. Shape of relationship

D. Choices A and B

10. What correlation coefficient shows the strongest strength of relationship?

A. .15

B. .65

C. −.30

D. −.70

11. What statistic provides a measure of internal consistency reliability??

A. F-ratio

B. Pearson r

C. Cronbach's alpha

D. Spearman rho

12. What is the generally accepted minimum reliability standard for a measurement instrument?

A. .40

B. .60

C. .70

D. .80

13. What is internal consistency reliability?

A. The degree to which the same raters/observers give consistent estimates of the same phenomenon over time

B. The ability of each item on an instrument to measure a single construct or dimension

C. An estimation of the stability of scores generated by a measurement instrument over time

D. The degree to which different raters/observers give consistent estimates of the same phenomenon

14. What is the equivalent nonparametric test for the independent t-teat?

A. Mann-Whitney U test

B. Wilcoxon matched-pair signed ranks test

C. Kruskal-Wallis H test

D. Friedman test

15. What is the equivalent nonparametric test for the dependent *t*-teat?

    A. Mann-Whitney *U* test

    B. Wilcoxon matched-pair signed ranks test

    C. Kruskal-Wallis *H* test

    D. Friedman test

16. What is the equivalent nonparametric test for the one-way between subjects ANOVA?

    A. Binomial test

    B. McNemar test

    C. Kruskal-Wallis *H* test

    D. Friedman test

17. What is the equivalent nonparametric test for the one-way within subjects ANOVA?

    A. Binomial test

    B. McNemar test

    C. Kruskal-Wallis *H* test

    D. Friedman test

18. What test is used to determine the strength and direction of relationship between two ranked variables?

    A. Phi

    B. Pearson *r*

    C. Spearman rho

    D. Cramér's *V*

19. What test is used to determine the strength and direction of relationship between two interval scale variables variables?

    A. Phi

    B. Pearson *r*

    C. Spearman rho

    D. Cramér's *V*

20. What test is used to determine the strength and direction of relationship between two nominal scale variables variables in a 2x3 crosstabulation table?

    A. Phi

    B. Pearson *r*

    C. Spearman rho

    D. Cramér's *V*

Chapter 4 Answers

1A, 2C, 3A, 4D, 5B, 6C, 7A, 8A, 9D, 10D, 11C, 12C, 13B, 14A, 15B, 16C, 17D, 18C, 19B, 20D

Chapter 5: Research Reports

Research reports, to include scholarly research articles, theses, and dissertations, communicate information that was compiled as a result of research and analysis of data. "Rightly or wrongly, the quality and worth of that work are judged by the quality of the written report - its clarity, organization and content" (Blake & Bly, 1993, p. 119).

Chapter 5 Learning Objectives

• Explain the purpose of a research report.

• Understand the organization, format, and content of a research report.

• Write the results section of a research report using APA style.

• Use rhetorical and stylistic elements necessary to communicate concisely and precisely statistical outcomes.

5.1: The Research Report

The purpose of a dissertation, according to Lovitts and Wert (2009), is to prepare the student to be a professional in the discipline. Consequently, a dissertation is a credential for a doctoral degree. The student learns and demonstrates the ability to conduct independent, original, and significant research (Lovitts & Wert, p. 1). Based on the results of a faculty survey, Lovitts and Wert (2009) define originality as follows:

> An original contribution offers a novel or new perspective. The faculty in the social sciences who participated in the study described an original contribution as 'something that has not been done, found, proved, or seen before. It is publishable because it adds to knowledge, changes the way people think, informs policy, moves the field forward, or advances the state of the art (p. 4).

Similarly, scholarly journal articles report on original research to scholars worldwide. This is in contrast to trade journal articles that disseminate news to people in a specific discipline or industry and to popular press articles that are meant to entertain, persuade, and promote specific products and services. Scholarly articles, according to *Webster's Third International Dictionary*, focus on academic study, especially academic research; exhibit the methods and attitudes of a scholar; and reflect the manner and appearance of a scholar. Additionally, most scholarly articles are peer reviewed (i.e., refereed) by experts in the field before they are accepted for publication.

Typically, institutions do not impose length limitations on dissertations although all manuscripts are expected to be concise. The nature of the research will determine manuscript length. Qualitative research manuscripts tend to be longer than quantitative research manuscripts. However, journals do impose length limitations, often 3,000 words (not including abstract and references), on manuscripts submitted for publication.

Dissertations, theses, scholarly journal articles, and other types of research reports often consist of front matter, the following five chapters or major sections, and end matter:

1. Introduction
2. Literature review
3. Methodology
4. Results
5. Discussion

A research proposal typically consists of the first three chapters/sections outlined above, double spaced, and with 12-point Times font. Some institutions and book publishers require a research proposal or prospectus, which is a preliminary plan for conducting a study. The length of a proposal varies and can consist of dozens of pages. A prospectus is often limited to 12-15 double-spaced pages and up to 7-10 additional pages for references and exhibits. The proposal or prospectus enables interested parties (including funding agencies and university dissertation committees) to obtain information about the proposed study, offer suggestions for improvement, and render a judgment. The proposal addresses four major questions:

1. What problem is to be studied?
2. Why is it worth studying?
3. How will it be studied?

4. How will the proposed book, dissertation, research report, or journal article be different from others?

Once the proposal or prospectus is approved, the researcher then conducts the study, refines the first three chapters/sections, and adds the final two chapters/sections and end matter to complete the report.

Key Point

Each institution and book and journal publisher has its own style guide for research manuscripts, so it is important to obtain and follow the appropriate guideline for authors. What is provided in this chapter is a sampling of the contents and organization of typical research proposals and reports.

5.2: Research Report Organization

FRONT MATTER

Content of the front matter of the manuscript will vary depending on the purpose of the research, e.g., a doctoral dissertation versus a scholarly journal article.

- Title page. The title page should show the title of the study, identification of the researcher(s), and date of submission. The title should include the following:
  - Precise identification of the problem area, including specification of IVs, DVs, and target population.
  - Sufficient clarity and conciseness for data base indexing purposes.

- Copyright page. Typically a copyright page is only required from doctoral and masters students for their dissertations and theses.

- Abstract. The abstract is a condensed, one paragraph summary of the manuscript that is normally limited to 350 words or less for dissertations. This is the length preferred by Dissertation Abstracts, University Microfilms International Publications. Scholarly journals often limit an abstract to between 100 and 150 words. It should be accurate, self-contained, and readable and includes the purpose of the research as well as a summary of findings. Do not include tables or illustrations.

- Dissertation or thesis committee signature/approval page.

- Acknowledgements. One should remain positive and write the acknowledgements section in a conversational tone unlike the more formal tone used in the rest of the report. One should thank those who made a meaningful contribution to the dissertation or thesis and acknowledge any funding sources used to support the research. It is better not to distribute the acknowledgements page to dissertation or thesis committees until after the final oral defense.

- Table of contents.

- List of tables.

- List of figures.

- Other materials as required by the institution or publisher. Short lists of keywords and highlights are examples of additional material that may be required.

INTRODUCTION

The introduction provides readers with background information for the study. Its purpose is to establish a framework for the research. The researcher should accomplish the following:

- Create reader interest in the topic.

- Lay the broad foundation for the problem that leads to the study.

- Place the study within the context of the scholarly professional literature.

Introductions to scholarly research articles should be short, often not exceeding two pages. An introduction to a more comprehensive research report, such as a doctoral dissertation, is longer and often includes the following sections:

- Background. A concise description of the background and need organized from the general to the specific. Includes an explanation of the theoretical framework for the research by identifying the broad theoretical concepts and principles underpinning the research. The background logically leads to the problem statement.

- Problem statement. A problem is a situation that, left alone, produces a documented negative consequence for a target population. There are two types of problem statements:

  - Practical problems are the result of some condition in the world that needs to be changed. Practical problems are ultimately solved by changing professional practice.

  - Conceptual problems arise due to an inadequate understanding of a phenomenon. Conceptual problems are addressed by answering a question that helps us better understand the phenomenon.

Some common mistakes in problem-formulation (Isaac & Michael, 1990) include the following:

- Collecting data without a well-defined plan or purpose, hoping to make some sense out of it afterward.

- Taking a "batch of data" that already exists and attempting to fit meaningful research questions to it.

- Defining questions in such general or ambiguous terms that one's interpretations and conclusions will be arbitrary and invalid.

- Formulating a problem without first reviewing the existing professional literature on the topic.

- Ad hoc research that is unique to a given situation and makes no contribution to the general body of research.

- Failure to base research on a sound theoretical or conceptual framework, which would tie together the divergent masses of research into a systematic and comparative scheme.

- Failure to make explicit and clear the underlying assumptions within the research so that it can be evaluated in terms of these foundations.

- Failure to recognize the limitations of the research approach, implied or explicit, that place restrictions on the conclusions and how they apply to other situations.

- Failure to anticipate alternative rival hypotheses that would also account for a given set of findings and that challenge the interpretations and conclusions reached by the investigator.

• Significance of the problem. This section is a statement that addresses why the problem merits investigation and the importance of the study.

• Purpose. A one or two sentence description of the methodological direction of the study

• Research question(s). Research questions flow from the problem statement and specify precise relations or differences between identified constructs that the study will address. Below are examples of quantitative research questions and identification of the hypothesis tests they imply:

- Is there a difference in sense of classroom community among university students enrolled in fully online programs and the national norm for university students, $\mu \neq$ [test value]?

    [Implies a one-sample t-test]

- Is there a difference in mean sense of classroom community between online and traditional on-campus university students, $\mu_1 \neq \mu_2$?

    [Implies an independent t-test]

- Is there a difference between sense of classroom community pretest and sense of classroom community posttest among university students, $D \neq 0$? (Note: D represents the mean difference between paired observations.)

    [Implies a dependent t-test]

- Is there a difference in sense of classroom community between graduate students based on program type (fully online, blended, traditional), $\mu_1 \neq \mu_2 \neq \mu_3$?

    [Implies a one-way between subjects analysis of variance (ANOVA)]

- Is there a difference in sense of classroom community over time (observation 1, observation 2, observation 3, observation 4) among undergraduate students, $\mu_1 \neq \mu_2 \neq \mu_3 \neq \mu_4$?

    [Implies a one-way within subjects analysis of variance (ANOVA)]

- Is there a relationship between sense of classroom community and grade point average among freshmen students?

    [Implies a Pearson product-moment correlation test]

- Is there a relationship between sense of classroom community and grade point average in online students after controlling for student age?

[Implies a partial correlation test]

- Can sense of classroom community predict grade point average among university students?

[Implies a bivariate regression test]

- Delimitations and limitations. A delimitation is a self-imposed reduction in the study's scope. For example, a school study may be delimited to public schools and not address private schools. A limitation is a potential weakness to the generalizability of the study due to a delimitation. For example, a limitation of a study could be that because the sample was drawn from a single state (i.e., a delimitation), the results may not generalize to all states.

- Assumptions. Assumptions are premises and propositions that the researcher accepts as true within the context of the research study. Assumptions influence study results. For example, an important assumption for survey research would be that respondents answered survey questions honestly.

- Definition of terms. Constitutive definitions (i.e., dictionary-like definitions) are provided for all important terms and concepts used in the manuscript. References should be cited as appropriate.

- Organization of the study. This section summarizes the main chapters/sections of the report (e.g., the introduction, literature review, and methodology if a proposal) so that readers will know where to find specific information.

LITERATURE REVIEW

This part of the research report or proposal expands on the information provided in the introduction, identifies important threads from the literature that is relevant to the research, places the research study in a theoretical context, and enables the reader to understand and appreciate the research. It emphasizes recent developments and avoids the researcher's personal opinions. Consequently, citations to the professional literature are required throughout this section but citations should only be included that inform the present study

The literature review need not be lengthy; however, it should be comprehensive and critical (i.e., identify strengths and weaknesses). It is organized (often under headings) to facilitate understanding, starts with a short paragraph outlining the organization of the chapter, forms a connected argument, and has a conclusion at the end in which the researcher does the following:

- Provides a summary of the main issues and findings of the review.

- Discusses the existing scientific knowledge base related to the research problem.

- Describes and supports the problem statement.

Poor reviews lose the reader in details and give the impression the researcher is meandering. The literature review describes important threads rather than simply providing summaries of prior research. Good reviews also relate the professional literature to the research problem.

Key Point
An acceptable structure for the literature review provides a funnel effect, which goes from general to more specific, ending with the research problem.

METHODOLOGY

The methodology chapter or section usually contains the following parts:

- Introduction. A concise description of the contents and organization of the chapter or section.

- Population and sample. Identification of the target population, sample, sample size, and sampling methodology.

- Setting. A description of the research setting.

- Instrumentation. A description of all instruments and apparatus used in the research. Includes reliability and validity characteristics.

- Procedures. Identification of the process used by the researcher to conduct the study. Details should be sufficient for study replication. If lengthy, the details can be provided in an appendix.

- Research question(s). The researcher repeats the research question(s) from the introduction. There should be a null hypothesis following each quantitative research question.

- Variables. The researcher identifies the constructs to be measured and their operational definitions (should be consistent with any previous definitions provided in the manuscript). For example, an operational definition of intelligence could be "intelligence quotient as measured by the Wechsler Intelligence Scale for Children (WISC-III)."

- Design. Identification of the type of study and design. For example, the study might use a true experimental pretest-posttest with a control group design. The design must be appropriate for the problem and allow for adequate controls.

- Data Analysis. It is often useful to organize this section according to each hypothesis, explaining how one will analyze the data to respond to the hypothesis.

- Threats to validity. List the major threats to the internal and external validity of the study and how they will be controlled. Note that the threats are not restricted to the limitations created by the delimitations as discussed in the Introduction; however, threats not adequately controlled do become study limitations.

- Summary.

RESULTS

This chapter or section is limited to statistical results and should be objective. All relevant results should be included, including nonsignificant findings and findings that are counter to the study's hypothesis(es). It is not a place for interpretations, opinions, conclusions, or recommendations. Often it will include tables and figures. It is often divided into the following sections:

- Introduction. A brief description of the purpose and organization of the chapter or section. It is a good idea to restate the research question and null hypothesis(es), since the purpose of the results section is to respond to the research question and evaluate the null hypothis(es) based on the analysis of data.

- Background information. Briefly include demographic information and data collection response rates, as appropriate.

- Descriptive statistics. Consider, as a minimum, reporting the following, as appropriate:

  - Sample (N) and sub-sample (n) sizes

  - Best measures of central tendency and dispersion for pooled and grouped data

If the study includes many variables and groups, a table is normally the best way of presenting these statistics. "Statistical and mathematical copy can be presented in text, in tables, and in figures... Select the mode of presentation that optimizes understanding of the data by the reader" (APA, 2010, p. 116). If descriptive statistics are presented in a table or figure, they need not be repeated in the text although one should "(a) mention the table in which the statistics can be found and (b) emphasize particular data in the narrative when they help in interpretation" (APA, 2010, p. 117).

Figure 5.1 below is an example of an APA-style table. Note the first line identifies the table by number (i.e., Table 1), the second line is a concise and explanatory title, each column has a descriptive heading, and there are no vertical rules.

Table 1

Descriptive Statistics for Classroom Community (N = 168)

	Male			Female			Total		
Student age	M	SD	n	M	SD	n	M	SD	n
18-20	26.40	6.66	5	24.21	4.05	19	24.67	4.62	24
21-30	26.33	6.09	6	27.32	5.56	60	27.23	5.57	66
31-40	29.00	6.57	8	30.86	6.15	44	30.58	6.19	52
41-50	34.67	4.73	3	32.69	5.58	16	33.00	5.39	19
Over 50	37.00	2.83	2	34.60	5.46	5	35.29	4.75	7
Total	29.17	6.65	24	28.84	6.18	144	28.89	6.23	168

Note: Classroom community raw scores can range from a maximum of 40 to a minimum of zero. Higher classroom community scores reflect a stronger sense of classroom community.

FIGURE 5.1

Example of an APA-style table.

Text should complement any tables, not repeat the same information. If few groups and variables are included in the study, one should present descriptive statistics in the text instead of a table. Below is an example of descriptive statistics included in the text that is based on the *Publication Manual of the American Psychological Association* (2010):

> The means (with standard deviations in parentheses) for classroom community and the two subscales of connectedness and learning for the entire sample ($N = 262$) were 55.75 (10.82), 26.85 (6.96), and 28.90 (5.05), respectively. These scores were higher for females ($n = 177$), 56.83 (10.89), 27.62 (6.87), and 29.21 (5.17), than for males ($n = 85$), 53.51 (10.40), 25.25 (6.90), and 28.26 (4.77).

For basic statistical tests, such as a *t*-test, one can combine some of the descriptive statistics with the hypothesis test results. For example:

For the treatment group, as predicted, research participants ($M = 8.19$, $SD = 7.12$, $n = 30$) reported higher levels of perceived learning than did the other participants ($M = 5.26$, $SD = 4.25$, $n = 32$), $t(60) = 1.99$, $p = .03$ (one tailed), $d = .50$.

The reporting format for a bivariate correlation test is very similar:

The relationship between classroom community ($M = 57.42$, $SD = 12.53$) and perceived cognitive learning ($M = 7.02$, $SD = 1.65$) was significant, $r(312) = .63$, $p = .01$.

- Hypothesis tests. This section should be organized by each hypothesis that is tested. Results of evaluating test assumptions should be included. For example:

The assumption of normality for each of the two populations defined by the grouping variable (i.e., males and females) was tested using the Kolmogorov-Smirnov test for normality and was found tenable for males, $p = .10$, and for females, $p = .24$. Homogeneity of variance across the two populations was evaluated using the *F*-test for equality of variances and was also found to be tenable, $p = .31$.

If a major assumption of a parametric test is not tenable, one has three choices:

- Report the violation and continue with the parametric test.
- Report the violation and transform one or more variables.
- Use an equivalent nonparametric test in which assumptions are tenable.

The results of a one-way ANOVA, which evaluates one null hypotheses, might look as follows:

The student age main effect was significant, $F(4,163) = 10.88$, $p < .001$, $\eta^2 = .21$. Consequently, there is significant evidence to reject the null hypothesis and conclude there is a difference between the classroom community means by student age. The strength of relationship between student and classroom community was strong, accounting for 21% of the variance of the dependent variable. Post hoc comparisons to evaluate pairwise differences among group means were conducted with the use of Bonferroni test since equal variances were tenable. Tests revealed significant pairwise differences in the group means between the following student age categories: ages 18-20 was less than ages 31-40, 41-50, and over 50; ages 21-30 was less than ages 31-40, 41-50, and over 50. Remaining pairwise differences were not statistically significant: ages 18-20 and 21-30, 31-40 and 41-50, and 31-40 and over 50.

Some things to note:

- Present results clearly and concisely.

- Report he direction of the difference (e.g., the highly hypnotizable group scored significantly higher).

- Report the best measures of central tendency and dispersion (e.g., *M* and *SD* in the above example). It's a good idea to also include group sizes.

- Statistical symbols are italicized (e.g., *M, SD, t, r, p,* and *d*). Parametric symbols (e.g., η^2) use the Greek alphabet and are not italicized.

- Test results include the test-statistic, degrees of freedom, *p*-value, and effect size (e.g., Cohen's *d* and η^2 in the above examples). One must report effect size with any significant effect.

Some things to avoid:

- Do not include tables and figures unless there is a need to do so. If the results can be effectively described in the text, do not use tables and/or figures.

- Do not present the same data in both a table and figure. Use the format that best shows the result.

- Do not report raw data values when they can be summarized as means, percentages, etc.

- Avoid using tables or figures to report the results of tests of assumptions unless the assumption is not tenable and the table or figure conveys important information about the data that one cannot convey effectively in the text.

- Summary. The results are summarized in this section to include identification of null hypotheses that were rejected as well as those that were not rejected.

Report the research results concisely and objectively. Use the active voice as much as possible as well as the past tense. Avoid repetitive paragraph structures. Consider the following principles when writing this part:

- Do not write the results as a tutorial on statistics. Assume the readers understand statistics. Economy of expression and clarity are important principles.

- Round to two decimal places.

- The results should tell a story. Compose this part of the research report as if writing a descriptive essay. Start with the research question and null hypothesis(es) followed by descriptive statistics. Next, identify the major statistical test and provide the results of the evaluation of major test assumptions. Then provide the results of the statistical test. Provide informationally adequate statistics. Finally, provide a statistical conclusion in terms of rejecting or failing to reject the null hypothesis(es).

- Although it is tempting, do not discuss the problem statement or statistical results in the results section; this is left to the Discussion section, which follows.

DISCUSSION

This part of the research report is the place to evaluate and interpret the results and provide conclusions and recommendations. This is the place to suggest why results came out as they did. Dissertation discussions often consists of the following sections; however, it is a good idea to restrict journal article discussions to four pages or less:

- Introduction. Addresses the organization of this chapter or section.

- Study summary. Summarizes the entire study. Includes a clear statement of support or nonsupport for the research hypotheses.

- Conclusions. Findings from the results chapter or section are not restated. Instead, the researcher draws from the results chapter to formulate conclusions. References should be made to the problem statement in the Introduction.

- Discussion. The researcher organizes this section by research question. Links are provided to the literature review. The researcher compares and contrasts findings from previous studies and describes how the present study's findings advance knowledge in the field. The researcher's personal ideas and interpretations are expected in this section.

- Threats to validity. Threats to validity that have not been fully controlled are listed here.

- Recommendations. Recommendations should be prescriptive in nature. If appropriate, recommendations for further study are included.

END MATTER

End matter typically includes the following:

- References or Bibliography. The references format is preferred in scientific fields. Most references should be no older than five years. Only works actually cited in the manuscript are to be included. The bibliography format, which includes works not actually cited in the manuscript, is often acceptable in nonscientific fields.

- Appendices. Appendices should contain copies of documents that have been used in the research such as copies of instruments used, transcripts of interviews, informed consent form used in the research, cover letters, permission letters, Institutional Review Board approval letter, photographs, etc.

- Vita. A curriculum vitae (CV) or simply vita is a summary of a person's experiences and other professional qualifications. Although the term is frequently used synonymously with resumé, the two are different. A typical resumé consists of name and contact Information, education, and work experience. A vita includes these elements plus it can also include academic interests; grants, honors and awards; publications and presentations; and professional memberships.

5.3: Chapter 5 Review

The answer key is at the end of this section.

1. What section of a research report includes the constitutive definitions for important terms or concepts used in the study?

    A. Introduction

    B. Literature review

    C. Methodology

    D. Results

    E. Discussion

2. What section of a research report includes the operational definitions for important constructs used in the study?

    A. Introduction

    B. Literature review

    C. Methodology

    D. Results

    E. Discussion

3. What section of a research report includes the research questions?

    A. Introduction

    B. Literature review

    C. Methodology

    D. Choices A and C

4. What section of a research report includes a description of all instruments and apparatus used in the research?

    A. Introduction

    B. Literature review

    C. Methodology

    D. Results

E. Discussion

5. What section of a research report discusses the existing scientific knowledge base related to the research problem?

 A. Introduction

 B. Literature review

 C. Methodology

 D. Results

 E. Discussion

6. What sections are typically part of a research proposal?

 A. Introduction

 B. Literature review

 C. Methodology

 D. Discussion

 E. Choices A, B, and C

 F. Choices A, B, C, and D

7. What section is used to evaluate and interpret the results?

 A. Introduction

 B. Methodology

 C. Results

 D. Discussion

 E. Choices C and D

8. Where would one include a copy of a survey used to collect data for the research study?

 A. Introduction

 B. Methodology

 C. Results

 D. Discussion

 E. End Matter

9. What section would one use to describe the significance of the study?

    A. Front Matter

    B. Introduction

    C. Literature review

    D. Methodology

    E. Results

    F. Discussion

10. What statistical test does the following research question imply: Is there a difference in sense of classroom community between graduate students based on type program (fully online, blended, traditional), $\mu 1 \neq \mu 2 \neq \mu 3$?

    A. Independent t-test

    B. Dependent t-test

    C. Between subjects ANOVA

    D. Within subjects ANOVA

    E. Linear Regression

    F. Spearman rho

11. What statistical test does the following research question imply: Is there a difference in sense of classroom community over time (observation 1, observation 2, observation 3, observation 4) among undergraduate students, $\mu_1 \neq \mu_2 \neq \mu_3 \neq \mu_4$?

    A. Independent t-test

    B. Dependent t-test

    C. Between subjects ANOVA

    D. Within subjects ANOVA

    E. Linear Regression

    F. Spearman rho

12. What statistical test does the following research question imply: Is there a difference in mean sense of classroom

community between online and traditional on-campus university students, $\mu_1 \neq \mu_2$?

A. Independent *t*-test

B. Dependent *t*-test

C. Between subjects ANOVA

D. Within subjects ANOVA

E. Linear Regression

F. Spearman rho

13. What section of the research report contains the statistical findings?

A. Methodology

B. Results

C. Discussion

D. End matter

E. Choices B and C

14. What section of the research report identifies the target population, sample, sample size, and sampling methodology?

A. Introduction

B. Literature review

C. Methodology

D. Results

E. Discussion

F. Choices B and C

15. What section of the research report describes the research problem?

A. Introduction

B. Literature review

C. Methodology

D. Results

E. Discussion

F. Choices A and B

16. What topic is typically included in a resumé?

A. Work experience

B. Academic interests

C. Grants, honors and awards

D. Publications and presentations

E. Professional memberships

F. All of the above

Chapter 5 Answers

1A, 2C, 3D, 4C, 5B, 6E, 7D, 8E, 9B, 10C, 11D, 12A, 13E, 14C, 15F, 16A

Appendix A: Statistical Abbreviations and Symbols

Abbreviations and symbols using Latin letters should be italicized while abbreviations and symbols using Greek letters should not be italicized.

≠, <>	not equal
>	greater than
≥	greater than or equal
<	less than
≤	less than or equal
±	plus and minus
*	asterisk; multiplication, interaction
ANOVA	analysis of variance
CI	confidence interval
d	Cohen's measure of effect size
D	decile; Kolmogorov-Smirnov test statistic
df	degrees of freedom
DV	dependent variable
E	event
ES	effect size
f	frequency

f_e	expected frequency
f_o	observed frequency
F	Fisher's F-ratio, F distribution
g_1	coefficient of skewness
g_2	coefficient of kurtosis
GLM	general linear model
H_0	null hypothesis
H_1 or H_A	alternative or research hypothesis
IQR	interquartile range
IV	independent variable
k	cardinal number
k^2	coefficient of nondetermination
M	sample mean, arithmetic average
m	slope of a line
Mdn	median
MLE	maximum likelihood estimation
Mo	mode
MS	mean square
MSE	mean square error
n	sample size, subsample size
N	total number of cases

$N(\mu,\sigma)$	normal distribution
ns	not statistically significant
OLS	ordinary least squares
$p(E)$	probability of event E
P	percentage, percentile; probability
PDF	probability density function
Q	quartile
Q_1	first quartile
Q_2	second quartile
Q_3	third quartile
r	Pearson correlation coefficient
$r_{12.3}$	partial correlation
r_s	Spearman rank order correlation
r^2	Pearson coefficient of determination
R	coefficient of multiple correlation
R^2	coefficient of multiple determination
RES	unstandardized residual
s	sample standard deviation
s^2	sample variance
SD	standard deviation

SEM	standard error of the mean
SRE	studentized residual
SS	sum of squares
t	*t*-test statistic, *t* distribution
U	Mann-Witney *U* statistic
V	Cramér's *V*
z	standard score
ZRE	standardized residual
α	alpha, Type I error
β	beta, Type II error; regression coefficient
Δ	delta, increment of change
η	eta, correlation coefficient
η^2	eta squared, effect size
η_p^2	partial eta squared, effect size
ε	epsilon, measure of sphericity departure
μ	mu, population mean
ω^2	lowercase omega, measure of effect size
Φ	phi correlation coefficient
Σ	sigma (capitalized), summation

σ	sigma, population standard deviation
σ^2	sigma squared, population variance
χ^2	chi-square test statistic

Appendix B: Glossary

Analysis of Variance

Analysis of variance (ANOVA) is a parametric procedure that assesses whether the means of multiple groups are statistically different from each other.

Autocorrelation

Autocorrelation (also called serial correlation) refers to the correlation of numbers in a series of numbers. It is present when observations are not independent of each other.

Bar Chart

A bar chart is made up of horizontal columns positioned over a label that represents a categorical variable. The length of the column represents the size of the group defined by the column label.

Behavioral Measurement

Behavioral measurement is the measurement of behaviors through observation; e.g. recording reaction times, reading speed, disruptive behavior, etc.

Between Subjects Design

Between Subjects designs are quantitative research designs in which the researcher is comparing different groups of research participants who experience different interventions.

Binomial Distribution

Binomial distributions model discrete random variables. A binomial random variable represents the number of successes in a series of trials in which the outcome is either success or failure.

Binomial Test

The binomial test is a nonparametric procedure that determines if the proportion of individuals in one of two categories is different from a specified test proportion, e.g., different from .5.

Bivariate Regression

Bivariate regression is a parametric procedure that predicts individual scores on a continuous DV based on the scores of one continuous IV.

Bonferroni Correction

The Bonferroni correction is a procedure for controlling familywise Type I error for multiple pairwise comparisons by dividing the p-value to be achieved for significance by the number of paired comparisons to be made.

Case

A case represents one unit of analysis in a research study. Cases can be research participants or subjects, classes of students, countries, states, provinces, etc. One case represents one row in an Excel spreadsheet.

Categorical Variable

A categorical variable, also called a discrete or qualitative variable, has values that differ from each other in terms of quality or category (e.g., gender, political party affiliation, etc.).

Cause and Effect

A cause is an explanation for some phenomenon that involves the belief that variation in an IV will be followed by variation in the DV when all other possible explanations are held constant. Social researchers often explore possible causal relationships – e.g., correlation and causal-comparative studies – or attempt to generate evidence to support a specific causal relationship, as in experimental studies in which specific hypotheses are tested. One must address several factors to obtain evidence of a cause and effect relationship:

- temporal precedence of the cause over the effect
- covariation of the cause and effect
- no plausible alternative explanations for the effect
- theoretical basis for the cause and effect relationship

Ceiling Effect

A ceiling effect is a type of range effect that causes the clustering of scores at the high end of a measurement scale.

Central Limit Theorem

According to the central limit theorem, the sampling distribution of any statistic will be normal or nearly normal, if the sample size is large enough. The Central Limit Theorem is useful to inferential statistics. Assuming a large sample, it allows one to use hypothesis tests that assume normality, even if the data appear non-normal. This is because the tests use the sample mean, which the Central Limit Theorem posits is approximately normally distributed.

Chi-Square Goodness-of-Fit Test

The chi-square (χ^2) goodness-of-fit test is a nonparametric procedure that determines if a sample of data for one categorical variable comes from a population with a specific distribution. The researcher compares observed values with theoretical or expected values.

Cluster Random Sample

A cluster random sample is a probability sample in which existing clusters or groups are randomly selected and then each member of the cluster is used in the research. For example, if classes of students are selected at random and then the students in each class become participants in the research study, the classes are the clusters.

Coefficient of Determination

The coefficient of determination is the percentage of the variability among scores on one variable that can be attributed to differences in the scores on the other variable (or multiple variables in multiple regression). To compute the coefficient of determination one simply squares the correlation coefficient. For example, if the bivariate correlation is $r = .7$ (a high relationship), $r^2 = .7 * .7 = .49$. Therefore, 49% of the variation in the criterion variable is related to the predictor variable. In other words, the IV is said to explain 49% of the variance in the DV.

Coefficient of Nondetermination

The coefficient of nondetermination (k^2) is the proportion of total variance in one variable that is not predictable by another variable. It is calculated by subtracting the coefficient of determination from 1.

Cohen's *d*

Cohen's *d* is a measure of effect size used to show the standardized difference between two means.

Collapsed Ordinal Data

Collapsed ordinal data are ordinal data displayed as categories.

Concurrent Validity

Concurrent validity is the effectiveness of an instrument to predict present behavior by comparing it to the results of a different instrument that has been shown to predict the behavior.

Confidence Interval

A confidence interval is an estimated range of values that is likely to include an unknown population parameter. Confidence intervals are constructed at a confidence level, such as 95%, selected by the statistician. It means that if a population is sampled repeatedly and interval estimates are made on each occasion, the resulting intervals would reflect the true population parameter in approximately 95% of the cases. This example corresponds to hypothesis testing with $p = .05$.

Confidence Level

The confidence level is the probability that a true null hypothesis (H_0) is not rejected ($1 - \alpha$).

Confounding Variable

A confounding variable, also called a lurking variable, is an extraneous variable relevant to a research study that the researcher fails to control, thereby adversely affecting the internal validity of a study.

Constitutive Definition

A constitutive definition is a dictionary-like definition using terms commonly understood within the discipline. Constitutive definitions provide a general understanding of the characteristics or concepts that are going to be studied, but these definitions must be changed into operational definitions before the study can actually be implemented. For example, Howard Gardner's constitutive definition of intelligence is an ability to solve a problem or fashion a product which is valued in one or more cultural settings.

Construct

A construct is a concept for a set of related behaviors or characteristics of an individual that cannot be directly observed or measured (Gall, Gall, & Borg, 2007).

Construct Validity

Construct validity refers to whether an instrument actually reflects the true theoretical meaning of a construct, to include the instrument's dimensionality (i.e., existence of subscales). Construct validity also refers to the degree to which inferences can be made from the operationalizations in a study to the theoretical constructs on which these operationalizations are based. Construct validity includes convergent and discriminant validity.

Content Validity

Content validity is based on the extent to which a measurement reflects the specific intended domain of content based on the professional expertise of experts in the field (Anastasi, 1988).

Contingency Table Analysis

Contingency table analysis is a chi-square nonparametric procedure that determines the association between two categorical variables. It is a test of independence that compares the frequencies of one nominal variable variable to those of a second nominal variable. The dataset produces a R x C table, where R is the number of rows (categories of one variable) and C is the number of columns (categories of the second variable).

Continuous Variable

A continuous variable is a type of random variable that can take on any value between two specified values.

Control

Control is a characteristic of a true experiment. Campbell and Stanley (1963) observed that obtaining scientific evidence requires at least one comparison. Control groups are used for this purpose.

Control Group

Control group refers to the participants who do not receive the experimental intervention and their performance on the DV serves as a basis for evaluating the performance of the experimental group (the group who received the experimental intervention) on the same DV.

Convenience Sample

A convenience sample is a non-probability sample where the researcher relies on readily available participants. While this is the most convenient method, a major risk will be to generalize the results to a known target population.

Convergent Validity

Convergent validity is the degree to which scores on one test correlate with scores on other tests that are designed to measure the same construct.

Correlation

Correlation is a statistical technique that measures and describes the strength and direction of relationship (i.e., association, correlation) between two or more variables.

Count Coding System

A count coding system is used in behavioral measurement to count the number of instances and/or duration of all instances of each key behavior.

Cramér's *V*

The Cramér's *V* test is a nonparametric procedure used to determine if there is an association between columns and rows in contingency tables. It is a measure of nominal by nominal association based on the chi square statistic. Cramér's V can be used for tables larger than 2 x 2. The test is symmetric, so it will produce the same value regardless of how the variables are designated IV and DV. Cramér's V is frequently used to calculate effect size in conjunction with contingency table analysis.

Criterion Validity

Criterion validity relates to how adequately a test score can be used to infer an individual's most probable standing on an accepted criterion (Hopkins, 1998). Criterion validity includes predictive validity, concurrent validity, and retrospective validity.

Cronbach's Alpha

Cronbach's alpha is a model of internal consistency reliability based on the average inter-item correlation of an instrument.

Crosstabulation

Crosstabulation is a procedure that cross-tabulates two categorical variables in order to determine their relationship. It represents the number of cases in a category of one variable divided into the categories of another variable. From a crosstabulation, a number of statistics can be calculated, such as Pearson chi-square, phi, and Cramér's V.

Decile

A decile (D) divides the data into ten equal parts based on their statistical ranks and position from the bottom, where $D_1 = P_{10}$ and $D_5 = P_{50} = Q_2$.

Degrees of Freedom

Degrees of freedom (*df*) represent the number of independent pieces of information that go into the estimate of a parameter. The higher the degrees of freedom, the more representative the sample is of the population.

Delimitation

A delimitation addresses how a study is narrowed in scope; i.e., how it is bounded.

Density Curve

A density curve is a smooth curve (rather than a frequency curve as one sees in the histogram of a small sample) that is on or above the x-axis and displays the overall shape of a distribution. The area under any density curve sums to 1. Since the density curve represents the entire distribution, the area under the curve on any interval represents the proportion of observations in that interval. Since a density curve represents the distribution of a specific dataset, it can take on different shapes. The normal distribution is an example of a density curve.

Dependent *t*-test

The dependent *t*-test (also called a paired-samples *t*-test) is a parametric procedure that compares mean scores obtained from two dependent (related) samples. Dependent or related data are obtained by:

- Measuring participants from the same sample on two different occasions (i.e., using repeated-measures or within subjects design).

- Using a matching procedure by pairing research participants and dividing them so one member of the pair is assigned to each group.

Dependent Variable

Dependent variables (DVs) are outcome variables or those that one expects to be affected by IVs. They are measured variables in a research study.

Descriptive Statistics

Descriptive statistics are used to describe what the data shows regarding a dataset. They summarize datasets and are used to detect patterns in the data in order to convey their essence to others and/or to allow for further analysis using inferential statistics.

Dichotomous Variable

A dichotomous variable is a nominal variable that has two categories or levels; e.g., gender (male, female).

Discrete Variable

A discrete variable, also known as a categorical or qualitative variable, is one that cannot take on all values within the limits of the variable. For example, consider responses to a five-point rating scale that can only take on the values of 1, 2, 3, 4, and 5. The variable cannot have the value of 2.5. Therefore, data generated by this rating scale represent a discrete variable.

Discriminant Validity

Discriminant validity is the degree to which scores on one test do not correlate with scores on other tests that are not designed to assess the same construct. For example, one would not expect scores on a trait anxiety test to correlate with scores on a state anxiety test.

Distribution

The distribution of a variable refers to the set of observed or theoretical values of a variable to include associated frequencies of occurrence or probabilities.

Dummy Variable

A dummy variable is one that takes the values 0 or 1 to indicate the absence or presence of some categorical effect. It is used as a numeric stand-in for a categorical IV in regression analysis.

Effect Size

Effect size is a measure of the magnitude of a treatment effect. It is the degree to which H_0 is false and is indexed by the discrepancy between the null hypothesis and the alternate hypothesis. It is frequently used to assess the practical significance of an effect.

Estimation

Estimation is a way to estimate a population parameter based on measuring a sample. It can be expressed in two ways:

• A point estimate of a population parameter is a single value of a statistic.

• An interval estimate is defined by two numbers, between which a population parameter is said to lie.

Experimentally Accessible Population

The experimentally accessible population are all those in the target population accessible to be studied or included in the sample.

External Validity

External validity is the generalizability of study findings to the target population (i.e., can the experiment be replicated with the same results?; Campbell & Stanley, 1963). It is the ability to generalize across categories or classes of individuals and across settings within the same target population. It includes population validity and ecological validity.

Extraneous Variable

An extraneous variable is an additional variable relevant to a research study that the researcher needs to control. An extraneous variable becomes a confounding variable when the researcher cannot or does not control for it, thereby adversely affecting the internal validity of a study by increasing error.

Extrapolation

Extrapolation occurs when one uses a regression equation to predict values outside the range of values used to produce the equation. Since a relationship between two variables can be approximately linear over a certain range, then change, one should be very cautious about predictions beyond the range of observed data that produced a regression equation.

Extreme Outlier

Extreme outliers are extreme values that are greater than 3 standard deviations from the mean.

Face Validity

Face validity is an evaluation of the degree to which an instrument appears to measure what it purports to measure.

Factor

A factor is a categorical variable with two or more values, referred to as levels; e.g., gender (male, female). For example, the IVs in the ANOVA procedure is referred to as a factor.

Factorial Design

Intervention studies with two or more categorical explanatory variables (IVs) that influence a DV are referred to as factorial designs.

Floor Effect

A floor effect is a type of range effect that causes the clustering of scores at the low end of a measurement scale.

Forced-Choice Scale

A forced-choice scale is a measurement scale missing the middle or neutral option, thereby forcing the participant to take a position.

Friedman Test

The Friedman test is a nonparametric procedure that compares medians between multiple dependent groups when the DV is either ordinal or interval/ratio. It is an extension of the Wilcoxon matched-pair signed ranks test. The test uses the ranks of the data rather than their raw values to calculate the statistic. If there are only two groups for this test, it is equivalent to the related samples sign test.

Gaussian Distribution

The Gaussian distribution is the normal distribution.

General Linear Model

The general linear model (GLM) is the underlying mathematical model for relational parametric tests covering the range of procedures used to analyze one continuous DV and one or more IVs (continuous or categorical).

Geometric Distribution

Geometric distributions model discrete random variables. A geometric random variable typically represents the number of trials required to obtain the first failure.

Guttman Scale

The Guttman scale is a cumulative design approach to scaling. The purpose is to establish a one-dimensional continuum for a concept one wishes to measure. Essentially, the items are ordered so that if a respondent agrees with any specific item in the list, he or she will also agree with all previous items.

Heavy-Tailedness

A heavy-tailed distribution is one in which the extreme portion of the distribution spreads out further relative to the center of the distribution when compared to the normal distribution. Heavy-tailedness can be detected using histograms and boxplots.

Histogram

A histogram is a graphical representation of a univariate dataset of a variable measured on the interval or ratio scales. It is constructed by dividing the range of data into equal-sized bins (classes or groups) and plotting each bin on a chart.

Holm's Sequential Bonferroni Correction

The Holm's sequential Bonferroni correction is a less conservative variant of the Bonferroni correction for controlling familywise Type I error when there are multiple comparisons.

Homogeneity of Variance

Homogeneity of variance (or error variance) is the assumption that two or more groups have equal or similar variances. The assumption is that the variability in the DV is expected to be about the same at all levels of the IV.

Homoscedasticity

The assumption of homoscedasticity is that the variability in scores for one variable is roughly the same at all values of a second variable.

Hypothesis Testing

Hypothesis testing is the use of statistics to determine the probability that a given hypothesis is true.

Independence of Observations

Independence of observations means that multiple observations are not acted on by an outside influence common to the observations. It would be violated, for example, if one participant's response to a measurement item was influenced by another's response. Generally, implementation of a survey questionnaire excludes any possibility of dependence among the observations provided the researcher implements controls to prevent respondents for discussing their responses prior to completing the survey.

Independent *t*-Test

The independent *t*-test is a parametric procedure that assesses whether the means of two independent groups are statistically different from each other. This analysis is appropriate whenever one wants to compare the means of two independent groups.

Independent Variable

Independent variables (IVs) are the predictor variables that one expects to influence other variables. In an experiment, the researcher manipulates the IV(s), which typically involve an intervention of some type.

Inferential Statistics

Inferential statistics are used to reach conclusions that extend beyond the sample measured to a target population. It is divided into estimation and hypothesis testing.

Inter-Rater Reliability

Inter-rater or inter-observer reliability (rater agreement) is used to assess the degree to which different raters/observers give consistent estimates of the same phenomenon.

Internal Consistency Reliability

Internal consistency reliability addresses how consistently individuals respond to the items within a scale that are measuring the same construct or dimension.

Internal Validity

Internal validity is the extent to which one can accurately state that the IV produced the observed effect (Campbell & Stanley, 1963). It reflects the extent of control over confounding variables (possible rival hypotheses) in a research study.

Interquartile Range

The interquartile range (IQR) is used with continuous variables and reflects the distance between the 75th percentile and the 25th percentile. In other words, the IQR is the range of the middle 50% of the data.

Interval Estimate

An interval estimate is defined by two numbers, between which a population parameter is said to lie.

Interval Scale

Interval scale intervals, like ratio scale intervals, are equal to each other. However, unlike ratio scale variables, interval scales have an arbitrary zero (i.e., negative values are permissible).

Intra-Rater Reliability

Intra-rater or intra-observer reliability is used to assess the degree to which the same raters/observers give consistent estimates of the same phenomenon over time.

Kolmogorov-Smirnov Test

The Kolmogorov-Smirnov test is a nonparametric procedure that determines whether a sample of data comes from a specific distribution. The test can evaluate goodness-of-fit against many theoretical distributions, to include the normal distribution.

Kruskal-Wallis *H* Test

The Kruskal-Wallis *H* test is a nonparametric procedure that compares medians between multiple independent groups when the DV is either ordinal or interval/ratio. It is an extension of the Mann-Whitney *U* test.

Kurtosis

Kurtosis measures heavy-tailedness or light-tailedness relative to the normal distribution. A heavy-tailed distribution has more values in the tails (away from the center of the distribution) than the normal distribution, and will have negative kurtosis.

- Platykurtic – flat shape, kurtosis statistic below 0, large SD.

- Mesokurtic – normal shape, between extremes, normal shape, kurtosis statistic around 0.

- Leptokurtic – peaked shape, kurtosis statistic above 0, small SD.

Light-Tailedness

A light-tailed distribution is one in which the extreme portion of the distribution spreads out less far relative to the center of the distribution when compared to the normal distribution. Light-tailedness can be detected using histograms and boxplots.

Likert Scale

The Likert scale is a unidimensional, summative design approach to scaling. It consists of responses to a series of statements, based on the attitudes/opinions to be assessed, that are typically expressed in terms of a five- or seven-point scale. For example, the choices of a five-point Likert scale might be strongly disagree, somewhat disagree, neither agree nor disagree, somewhat agree, and strongly agree.

Limitation

A limitation is a potential weakness of a research study (i.e., threats to validity that were not adequately controlled).

Line Chart

A line chart allows one to visually examine the mean (or other statistic) of a continuous variable across the various levels of a categorical variable. Line charts are ideally suited to show trends for data over time in longitudinal studies.

Linearity

Linearity means that the amount of change, or rate of change, between scores on two variables are constant for the entire range of scores for the two variables. The graph representing a linear relationship is a straight line.

Mann-Whitney U Test

The Mann-Whitney U test is a nonparametric procedure that compares medians between two independent groups when the DV is either ordinal or interval/ratio.

Matched Pairs Design

A matched pairs design is achieved when participants are matched on known extraneous variable(s) and then one member of each matched pair is randomly assigned to each group. The researcher is thus assured that the groups are initially equivalent on the variables used in the matching procedure.

McNemar Test

The McNemar test is a nonparametric chi-square procedure that compares proportions obtained from a 2 x 2 contingency table where the row variable (A) is the DV and the column variable (B) is the IV. The McNemar test can be used to test if there is a statistically significant difference between the probability of a (0,1) pair and the probability of a (1,0) pair.

Mean

The mean or arithmetic average is a statistic such that the sum of deviations from it is zero. That is, it is based on the sum of the deviation scores raised to the first power, or what is known as the first moment of the distribution, and captures the central location of the distribution.

Mean Square (MS)

The mean square (MS) is an estimate of variance across groups. MS is used in analysis of variance and regression analysis. It equals sum of squares divided by its appropriate degrees of freedom.

Mean Square Error (MSE)

The mean square error (MSE) is used to evaluate the performance of a predictor or an estimator.

Measure of Central Tendency

A measure of central tendency is a descriptive statistic that tells one where the middle of a distribution lies. Researchers typically report the best measures of central tendency and dispersion for each variable in research reports.

Measure of Dispersion

A measure of dispersion is a descriptive statistic that indicates the variability of a distribution. Researchers typically report the best measures of central tendency and dispersion for each variable in research reports.

Measure of Relative Position

A measure of relative position is a descriptive statistic that indicates where a score is in relation to all other scores in a distribution.

Measurement

Measurement is the process of representing a construct with numbers in order to depict the amount of a phenomenon that is present at a given point in time. The purpose of this process is to differentiate between people, objects, or events that possess varying degrees of the phenomenon of interest.

Measurement Error

Measurement error is a type of non-sampling error that occurs when data collection is not reliable. Instrument reliability as well as inter- and intra-rater reliability are ways to help protect against measurement error. Measurement Error = True Score – Observed Score.

Measurement Validity

Measurement validity refers the relative correctness of a measurement. In other words, it evaluates how well an instrument measures a construct and refers to the degree to which evidence and theory support the interpretations of test scores.

Measurement Without Error

The assumption of measurement without error refers to the need for error-free measurement when using the general linear model.

Median

The median divides the distribution into two equal halves. It is the midpoint of a distribution when the distribution has an odd number of scores. It is the number halfway between the two middle scores when the distribution has an even number of scores.

Mediating Variable

A given variable may be said to function as a mediator to the extent that it accounts for the relationship between the predictor and the criterion.

Mode

The mode is the most frequently occurring score(s) in a distribution.

Moderating Variable

A moderator is a qualitative or quantitative variable that affects the direction and/or strength of the relationship between an independent or predictor variable and a dependent or criterion variable.

Monotonicity

A monotonic relationship is one where the value of one variable increases as the value of the other variable increases or the value of one variable increases as the value of the other variable decreases, but not necessarily in a linear fashion.

Multinomial Distribution

A multinomial distribution deals with events that have multiple discrete outcomes, in contrast to a binomial distribution, which has two discrete outcomes.

Nominal Scale

Nominal scale variables are unordered categories. Also called categorical or discrete variables, they allow for only qualitative classification. That is, they can be measured only in terms of whether individual units of analysis belong to some distinctively different categories, but one cannot rank order those categories.

Non-Probability Sampling

Non-probability sampling (purposeful or theoretical sampling) is a type of sampling that does not involve the use of randomization to select research participants. Consequently, research participants are not selected according to probability or mathematical rules, but by other means (e.g., convenience or access). It occurs when random sampling is too costly, where nonrandom sampling is the only feasible alternative, or when the sampling frame is not known.

Non-Sampling Error

Non-sampling error is an error caused by human error that effects a specific statistical analysis. These errors can include data entry errors and biased questions.

Nonparametric Test

A nonparametric test does not make any assumptions regarding the distribution or scales of measurement. Consequently, a nonparametric test is considered a distribution-free method because it does not rely on any underlying mathematical distribution. Nonparametric tests do, however, have various assumptions that must be met and are less powerful than parametric tests.

Nonresponse Bias

Nonresponse bias occurs when some individuals selected for the sample are unwilling or unable to participate in the study. It results when respondents differ in meaningful ways from nonrespondents.

Nonresponse Error

Nonresponse error is a type of non-sampling error that occurs when some members of the sample don't respond. A high response rate is essential to reliable statistical inference.

Norm

A norm is a standard average performance on a particular characteristic by a specific population with a given background or age. It can also refer to normative data that are standards of comparison based on the results of a test administered to a specific population.

Normal Curve Equivalent (NCE) Score

NCE scores are normalized standard scores with a mean of 50 and a standard deviation of 21.06. The standard deviation of 21.06 was chosen so that NCE scores of 1 and 99 are equivalent to the 1st (P_1) and 99th (P_{99}) percentiles.

Normal Distribution

The normal or Gaussian distribution is a special type of density curve. It is shaped like a bell curve. Its importance flows from the fact that any sum of normally distributed variables is itself a normally distributed variable. Sums of variables that, individually, are not normally distributed tend to become normally distributed.

Normality

Normality refers to the shape of a variable's distribution. The variable of interest is distributed normally, which means it is symmetrical and shaped like a bell-curve.

Null Hypothesis

The null hypothesis, denoted by H_0, is the hypothesis of no difference or no relationship.

One-Sample *t*-Test

The one-sample *t*-test is a parametric procedure that compares a calculated sample mean to a known population mean or a previously reported value in order to determine if the difference is statistically significant.

One-Tailed Hypothesis

A one-tailed hypothesis is directional (i.e., the direction of difference or association is predicted); e.g., H_0: $\mu_1 \gtrless \mu_2$, H_a: $\mu_1 > \mu_2$. For example, sense of classroom community in graduate students is higher in face-to-face courses than online courses. Here the DV is sense of classroom community and the IV is type course (face-to-face, online).

Operational Definition

An operational definition of a construct is a procedure for measuring and defining a construct and provides an indirect method of measuring something that cannot be measured directly.

Ordinal Scale

Ordinal scale variables allow one to rank order the items one measures in terms of which has less and which has more of the quality represented by the variable, but they do not provide information regarding much more. In other words, the values simply express an order of magnitude.

Outlier

Outliers are extreme values. There are regular or mild outliers and extreme outliers. Extreme outliers are any data values that lie more or less than 3.0 standard deviations from the mean.

p-value (*p*-level)

See significance level.

Parallel Forms Reliability

Parallel forms reliability is used to measure consistency over two forms of an instrument. Parallel or alternate forms of an instrument are two forms that have similar kinds of items so that they can be interchanged.

Parametric Test

A parametric test is a statistical test that assumes that the data come from a probability distribution and makes inferences about the parameters of the distribution. It also assumes the data are normally distributed and the DV(s) are measured on the interval or ratio scales.

Partial Correlation

Partial correlation is the relationship between two variables after removing the overlap of a third or more other variables from both variables.

Pearson Product-Moment Correlation Test

The Pearson product-moment correlation test (Pearson *r*) is a parametric procedure that determines the strength and direction of the linear relationship between two continuous variables. Pearson *r* is symmetric, with the same coefficient value obtained regardless of which variable is the IV and which is the DV.

Percentile

A percentile (or percentile rank) is a number between 0 and 100 that shows the percent of cases falling at or below that score.

Phi Coefficient

The phi (Φ) test is a nonparametric procedure used to determine if there is an association between columns and rows in 2 x 2 contingency tables. It measures nominal by nominal association based on the chi square statistic. The coefficient is symmetric, so it will produce the same value regardless of how the variables are designated IV and DV. Phi is frequently used to calculate effect size in conjunction with contingency table analysis.

Pie Chart

A pie chart is a circular chart divided into sectors that illustrate numerical proportions.

Pivot Table

A pivot table is a data summarization tool that is used to sort, reorganize, and perform arithmetic operations on data stored in one table.

Point Estimate

A point estimate of a population parameter is a single value of a statistic.

Poisson Distribution

Poisson distributions model discrete random variables. A Poisson random variable typically is the count of the number of events that occur in a given time period when the events occur at a constant average rate.

Post Hoc Multiple Comparison Tests

Post hoc (or follow-up) multiple comparison tests are used following a significant test involving over two groups in order to determine which groups differ from each other. For example, a significant ANOVA only provides evidence to the researcher that the groups differ, not where the groups differ. In a three group test the researcher does not know if group A differs significantly from group B and group C or if group B differs significantly from group C. Hence there is a need to conduct post hoc multiple comparison tests to determine where the pairwise differences lie.

Practical Significance

Researchers frequently refer to effect size as practical significance in contrast to statistical significance (α). There is no practical significance without statistical significance. While statistical significance is concerned with whether a statistical result is due to chance, practical significance is concerned with whether the result is useful in the real world.

Predictive Validity

Predictive validity is the effectiveness of an instrument to predict the outcome of future behavior. Examples of predictor measures related to academic success in college include the Scholastic Aptitude Test (SAT) scores, the Graduate Record Exam (GRE) scores, and high school grade point average (GPA).

Predictor Variable

Predictor variable (or explanatory variable) is another name for the IV in regression analysis.

Probability

Probability is the chance that something random will occur. The basic rules of probability are:

- Any probability of any event, $p(E)$, is a number between 0 and 1.

- The probability that all possible outcomes can occur is 1.

- If there are k possible outcomes for a phenomenon and each is equally likely, then each individual outcome has probability 1/k.

- The chance of any (one or more) of two or more events occurring is the union of the events. The probability of the union of events is the sum of their individual probabilities.

- The probability that any event E does not occur is $1 - p(E)$.

- If two events E_1 and E_2 are independent, then the probability of both events is the product of the probabilities for each event, $p(E_1 \text{ and } E_2) = p(E_1)p(E_2)$.

Probability Distribution

A probability distribution is a function that describes the probability of a random variable taking on certain values.

Probability Sampling

Probability sampling uses some form of random selection of research participants from the experimentally accessible population. Only random samples permit true statistical inference and foster external validity.

Processing Error

Processing error is a type of non-sampling error that occurs as a result of editing errors, coding errors, data entry errors, programming errors, etc. during data analysis.

Purposive Sample

A purposive sample is a non-probability sample selected on the basis of the researcher's knowledge of the target population. The researcher then chooses research participants who are similar to this population in attributes of interest.

Qualitative Variable

A qualitative variable, also known as categorical variable or discrete variable, have values that differs from each other in terms of quality or category (e.g., gender, political party affiliation, etc.).

Quantitative Research

A quantitative approach to research is one in which the investigator uses scientific inquiry. It involves the analysis of numerical data using statistical procedures in order to test a hypothesis.

Quantitative Variable

Quantitative variables have values that differ from each other by amount or quantity (e.g., test scores). Ratio and interval scale variable are quantitative variables.

Quartile

A quartile is one of the four divisions of observations that have been grouped into four equal-sized sets based on their statistical rank. $Q_1 = P_{25}$, $Q_2 = P_{50} = Mdn$, $Q_3 = P_{75}$.

Quartile Deviation

Quartile deviation (or semi-interquartile range) is half the IQR. It is sometimes preferred over the range as a measure of dispersion because it is not affected by extreme scores.

Quota Sample

A quota sample is a stratified, non-probability convenience sampling strategy. The sample is formed by selecting research participants that reflect the proportions of the target population on key attributes; e.g., gender, race, socioeconomic status, education level, etc.

Random Assignment

Random assignment is the random allocation of research participants from the sample to groups; e.g., treatment group and control group.

Random Error

Random error is caused by any factors that randomly affect measurement of the variable across the sample. For example, in a particular testing situation, some individuals may be tired while others are alert. If mood affects their performance on a measure, it may artificially inflate the observed scores for some individuals and artificially weaken them for others. Random error does not have consistent effects across the entire sample.

Random Sample

A random sample is a subset of research participants that are randomly selected from a target population.

Random Selection

Random selection deals with how one draws the sample of people for a study from a target population. To be random, everyone in the target population must have an equal and independent chance of being chosen.

Random Variable

A random variable is a variable whose value is determined by chance. For example, if a coin is tossed 30 times, the random variable X is the number of tails that come up. There are two types of random variables: discrete and continuous.

Randomization

Randomization is the random assignment of research participants to groups.

Range

The range of a distribution is a measure of dispersion calculated by subtracting the minimum score from the maximum score.

Range Effect

Range effects are typically a consequence of using a measure that is inappropriate for a specific group (i.e., too easy, too difficult, not age appropriate, etc.).

Ratio Scale

Ratio scale variables allow one to quantify and compare the sizes of differences between individual values. They also feature an identifiable absolute zero, thus they allow for statements such as x is two times more than y.

Reactive Measure

A measurement is reactive whenever the participant is directly involved in a study and he or she is reacting to the measurement process itself.

Regression

Regression analysis consists of techniques for modeling and analyzing multiple variables for the purpose of prediction and forecasting.

Reliability

Reliability refers to the consistency of measurement. For example, instrument reliability is the extent to which an item, scale, or instrument will yield the same score when administered at different times, locations, or populations, assuming the two administrations do not differ on relevant variables.

Research Design

A research design is a logical blueprint for research that focuses on the logical structure of the research and identifies how research participants are grouped and when data are to be collected.

Research Hypothesis

The research or alternative hypothesis, denoted by H_1 or H_a or H_A, is the hypothesis that sample observations are influenced by a nonrandom cause; i.e., the intervention.

Research Question

A research question is a question that seeks an answer to a researchable problem using quantitative or qualitative research methodologies. A good research question is concise, identifies relevant variables or phenomena, implies a research design and, in the case of quantitative designs, also implies a research hypothesis and statistical procedure. Additionally, a good research question is grounded in current theory and knowledge.

Residual

A residual is the difference between a predicted and observed value.

Response Bias

Response bias occurs when some individuals selected for the sample are unwilling or unable to respond in a truthful manner to questions or items on a survey.

Retrospective Self-Report

A retrospective self-report is a self-report in which a person is asked to look back in time and remember details of a behavior or experience.

Retrospective Validity

Retrospective validity refers to administering an instrument to a sample and then going back to others, e.g., former teachers of the respondents in the sample, and asking them to rate the respondents on the construct that was measured by the instrument. A significant relationship between test score and retrospective ratings would be evidence of retrospective validity.

Sample

A sample consists of a individuals drawn from the experimentally accessible population who participate in a research study.

Sampling

Sampling involves the collection, analysis, and interpretation of data gathered from random samples of a population under study. It is concerned with the selection of a subset of individuals from a population to participate in a research study whose results can be generalized to the population.

Sampling Distribution

A sampling distribution is the resultant probability distribution of a statistic created by drawing all possible samples of size N from a given population and computing a statistic – e.g., mean – for each sample.

Sampling Error

Sampling error is an error because the researcher is working with sample data rather than population data. When one takes a sample from a population, as opposed to collecting information from the entire population, there is a probability that one's sample will not precisely reflect the characteristics of the population because of chance error.

Sampling Frame

The sampling frame is the list of ultimate sampling entities, which may be people, organizations, or other units of analysis, from the experimentally accessible population. The list of registered students may be the sampling frame for a survey of the student body at a university. Problems can arise in sampling frame bias. Telephone directories are often used as sampling frames, for example, but tend to under-represent the poor (who have no phones) and the wealthy (who may have unlisted numbers).

Scale of Measurement

The scale of measurement categorizes variables according to the amount of information they convey. The four scales of measurement commonly used in statistical analysis are nominal, ordinal, interval, and ratio scales.

Scaling

Scaling is the branch of measurement that involves the construction of an instrument. Three unidimensional scaling methods frequently used in social science measurement are Likert, Guttman, and Thurstone scalings.

Scatterplot

Scatterplots (also called scattergrams) show the relationship between two variables. For each case, scatterplots depict the value of the IV on the *x*-axis and the value of the DV on the *y*-axis. Each dot on a scatterplot is a case. The dot is placed at the intersection of each case's scores on *x* and *y*. Scatterplots are often used to evaluate linearity between two continuous variables as well as to display strength of relationship.

Self-Report Measurement

Self-report measurement is a type of measurement in which the researcher asks participants to describe their behavior, to express their opinions, or to engage in interviews or focus groups in order to express their views. Alternatively, study participants can be asked to complete a survey, either face-to-face or online using the Internet. The self-report is the least accurate and most unreliable of the three types of measurements.

Semantic Differential Scale

A semantic differential scale (a type of Likert scale) asks a person to rate a statement based upon a rating scale anchored at each end by opposites. For example,

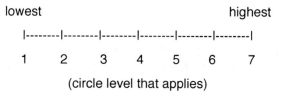

(circle level that applies)

Semi-Interquartile Range

The semi-interquartile range is half the IQR. It is sometimes preferred over the range as a measure of dispersion because it is not affected by extreme scores.

Semi-Structured Interviews

Semi-structured interviews use some pre-formulated questions, but there is no strict adherence to them. New questions might emerge during the interview process.

Semipartial Correlation

Semipartial correlation is the relationship between two variables after removing a third variable from just one of the two variables.

Significance Level

The significance level (also called statistical significance level or p-value) is the probability of making a Type I error. The criterion for any hypothesis test is established by the researcher. Normally set at .05 for social science research (.10 is sometimes used for exploratory research and .01 or .001 is sometimes used when greater confidence in the results is required). The significance level is set prior to analyzing data.

Simple Random Sample

A simple random sample is a probability sample that is selected from a population in such a manner that all members of the population have an equal and independent chance of being selected.

Simpson's Paradox

Simpson's paradox (also known as the Yule–Simpson effect) is a type of confounding that occurs in which a relationship that appears in different groups of data disappears when these groups are combined and the reverse trend appears for the aggregated data.

Singularity

Singularity refers to perfect correlation where the correlation coefficient equals 1 or -1. It represents an extreme case of multicollinearity.

Skewness

Skewness is a measure of the lack of symmetry. A distribution, or dataset, is symmetric if it is the same to the left and right of the center point. If the data are not distributed symmetrically, the distribution is said to be skewed.

Social Desirability Bias

Social desirability bias occurs during testing or observation when individuals respond or behave in a way they believe is socially acceptable and desirable as opposed to being truthful. It can manifest itself in a number of ways, including being political correct.

Spearman Rank Order Correlation Test

The Spearman rank order correlation test is a nonparametric procedure that determines the strength and direction of the linear relationship between two variables. It can be used for any type of data, except categories that cannot be ordered. It can be used instead of Pearson r if the parametric assumptions cannot be met. The symbol for the correlation coefficient is r_s.

Specification Error

Specification error is non-sampling error that occurs when the measurement instrument is not properly aligned with the construct that is measured. In other words, the construct validity of the instrument is weak.

Sphericity

Sphericity is an assumption in repeated measures ANOVA/MANOVA designs. In a repeated measures design, the univariate ANOVA tables will not be interpreted properly unless the variance/covariance matrix of the DVs is circular in form. In other words, sphericity means that the variance of the difference between all pairs of means is constant across all combinations of related groups.

Split-Half Reliability

Split-half is a model of internal consistency reliability that splits the scale into two parts and examines the correlation between the two parts.

Spurious Relationship

A spurious relationship exists between two variables that are significantly related to each other when there is no direct causal connection due to the presence of a third (or more) variable, often referred to as a confounding or lurking variable, which is related to each of the original variables. The spurious relationship between the original two variables becomes evident when the original relationship becomes insignificant after controlling (i.e., removing) the effects of the third (or more) variable.

Standard Deviation

Standard deviation (*SD*) is a measure of variability or dispersion of a set of data. It is calculated from the deviations between each data value and the sample mean. It is also the square root of the variance.

Standard Error of Measurement

The standard error of measurement (SEm) is used to determine the range of certainty around an individual's reported score. If one SEm is added to an observed score and one SEm is subtracted from it, one can be 68% sure that the true score falls within the created range.

Standard Error of the Estimate

The standard error of the estimate is the standard deviation of the prediction errors. Approximately 68% of actual scores will fall between ±1 standard error of their predicted values.

Standard Error of the Mean

The standard error of the mean is the standard deviation of the sampling distribution of the mean.

Standard Normal Distribution

The standard normal distribution is a normal distribution that has a mean of 0 and a standard deviation of 1. *Z*-scores are used to represent the standard normal distribution.

Standard Score

A standard score is a general term referring to a score that has been transformed for reasons of convenience, comparability, etc. The basic type of standard score, known as a z-score, is an expression of the deviation of a score from the mean score of the group in relation to the standard deviation of the scores of the group.

Standardized Residual

A standardized residual (ZRE) is a residual divided by the standard error of the estimate. Standardized residuals should behave like a sample from a normal distribution with a mean of 0 and a standard deviation of 1. The standardized residual is essentially a z-score. So any observation with a standardized residual greater than |2| would be viewed as an outlier or an extreme observation. Standardized residuals are useful in detecting anomalous observations or outliers.

Stanine Score

Stanine scores are groups of percentile ranks consisting of nine specific bands, with the 5th stanine centered on the mean, the first stanine being the lowest, and the ninth stanine being the highest. Each stanine is one-half standard deviation wide.

Statistical Power

Statistical power or observed power of a statistical test is the probability that a false H_0 is rejected. It is equal to 1 minus the probability of accepting a false H_0 $(1 - \beta)$.

Stratified Random Sample

A stratified random sample is a probability sample in which the accessible population is first divided into subsets or strata; e.g., a population of college students can first be divided into freshman, sophomores, juniors, and seniors, and then individuals are selected at random from each stratum.

Studentized Residual

A studentized residual (SRE) is a type of standardized residual in which the residual is divided by its estimated standard deviation. It recognizes that the error associated with predicting values far from the mean of x is larger than the error associated with predicting values closer to the mean of x. The studentized residual increases the size of residuals for points distant from the mean of x.

484   Statistical Foundations

Sum of Squares

Sum of squares (SS) is the sum of squared differences from the mean.

Suppressor Variable

A suppressor variable is a variable that appears to be positively related to the DV but when included in the regression model has a negative regression coefficient. This is due to the fact that an IV (the suppressor variable) is highly related to another IV and any variability that is explained in the DV by the suppressor variable is explained by the other IV. Conger (1974) provides the following definition of a suppressor variable: "...a variable which increases the predictive validity of another variable (or set of variables) by its inclusion in a regression equation" (pp. 36-37).

Systematic Error

Systematic error is caused by any factors that systematically affect measurement of the variable across the entire sample.

T-Score

A *T*-score is standard score with a mean of 50 and a standard deviation of 10.

Target Population

The target population refers to the group of individuals or objects to which researchers are interested in generalizing research study conclusions.

Test-Retest Reliability

Test-retest reliability is a method of estimating the stability of scores generated by a measurement instrument over time. It involves administering the same instrument to the same individuals at two different times. The test-retest method should only be used when the variables being measured are considered to be stable over the test-retest period.

Thurstone Scale

The Thurstone scale consists of a series of items. Respondents rate each item on a 1- to-11 scale in terms of how much each statement elicits a favorable attitude representing the entire range of attitudes from extremely favorable to extremely unfavorable. A middle rating is for items in which participants hold neither a favorable nor unfavorable opinion.

Triangulation

Triangulation is the use of more than one measurement technique to measure a single construct in order to enhance the confidence in and reliability of research findings.

Two-Tailed Hypothesis

A two-tailed hypothesis is non-directional (i.e., the direction of difference or association is not predicted); e.g., $H_0: \mu_1 = \mu_2$, $H_a: \mu_1 \neq \mu_2$. For example, a two-tailed test determines whether or not the mean of the sample group is either less than or greater than the mean of the control group.

Type I Error

Type I error (α) is the probability of deciding that a significant effect is present when it is not. That is, it is the probability of rejecting a true null hypothesis.

Type II Error

Type II error (β) is the probability of not detecting a significant effect when one exists. That is, it is the probability of not rejecting a false null hypothesis.

Uniform Distribution

Uniform distributions model both continuous random variables and discrete random variables. The values of a uniform random variable are uniformly distributed over an interval.

Unstandardized Residual

An unstandardized residual (RES) is the difference between the observed value of the DV and the predicted value. The residual and its plot are useful for checking how well the regression line fits the data and, in particular if there is any systematic lack of fit.

Validity

Validity deals with the accuracy of a test (measurement validity) or study (experimental validity). A common topology is provided below:
- Measurement validity
  - Face validity
  - Construct validity
    - Convergent validity
    - Discriminant validity
  - Content validity
  - Criterion validity
    - Predictive validity
    - Concurrent validity
    - Retrospective validity
- Experimental validity
  - Internal validity
  - External validity
    - Population validity
    - Ecological validity

Variable

A variable is anything that is measured – e.g., characteristic, attitude, behavior, weight, height, etc. – that possesses a value that changes within the scope of a given research study. Variables appear as columns in an Excel spreadsheet.

Variance

Variance is a measure of variability derived from the sum of the deviation scores from the mean raised to the second power (i.e., the second moment of the distribution). It is the square of the standard deviation.

Wilcoxon Matched-Pair Signed Ranks Test

The Wilcoxon matched-pair signed-ranks test is a nonparametric procedure that compares median scores obtained from two dependent (related) samples. The test factors in the size as well as the sign of the paired differences. It assesses the null hypothesis that the medians of two samples do not differ, or that the median of one sample does not differ from a known value.

Within Subjects Design

Within subjects or repeated measures designs are quantitative research designs in which the researcher is comparing the same participants repeatedly over time.

z-Score

A *z*-score distribution is the standard normal distribution, $N(0,1)$, with mean = 0 and standard deviation = 1.

Zero Order Correlation

Zero-order correlation is the relationship between two variables, while ignoring the influence of other variables.

Appendix C: About the Author

Alfred P. (Fred) Rovai

Fred, a native of San Jose, California, received a BA degree (mathematics) from San Jose State University, a MA degree (public administration) from the University of Northern Colorado, and a MS degree (education) and PhD degree (academic leadership) from Old Dominion University. He also completed postgraduate work in systems management at the University of Southern California and possesses a postgraduate professional license in mathematics from the Commonwealth of Virginia. Following his retirement from the U.S. Army as Dean at the Armed Forces Staff College in Norfolk, VA, he served as Visiting Assistant Professor at Old Dominion University and then as Assistant Professor through tenured Professor at Regent University. He retired in December 2011 as Associate Vice President for Academic Affairs. During his career in academe he authored or co-authored six textbooks and more than 50 articles in scholarly journals and served on four editorial review boards. He presently writes, consults, and serves as an adjunct professor teaching research and statistics courses online.

Appendix D: References

American Psychological Association. (2010). *Publication manual of the American Psychological Association* (6th ed.). Washington, DC: Author.

Anastasi, A. (1988). *Psychological testing.* New York, NY: Macmillan.

Baron, R. M., & Kenny, D. A. (1986). The moderator-mediator variable distinction in social psychological research: Conceptual, strategic, and statistical considerations. *Journal of Personality and Social Psychology, 51,* 1173-1182.

Bartos, R. B. (1992). *Educational research.* Shippensburg, PA: Shippensburg University.

Biemer, P. P., & Lyberg, L. E. (2003). *Introduction to survey quality: Wiley series in survey methodology.* Hoboken, NJ: Wiley.

Blake, G., & Bly, R. W. (1993). *The elements of technical writing.* New York: Macmillan.

Campbell, D. T., & Stanley, J. C. (1963). Experimental and quasi-experimental designs for research on teaching. In N. L. Gage (Ed.), *Handbook of research on teaching.* Chicago, IL: Rand McNally.

Chakravarti, I. M., Laha, R. G., & Roy, J. (1967). *Handbook of methods of applied statistics, Volume I.* New York: John Wiley & Sons.

Chatterjee, S., & Hadi, A. S. (1988). *Sensitivity analysis in linear regression.* New York, NY: John Wiley & Sons.

Cohen, J. (1988). *Statistical power analysis for the behavioral sciences* (2nd ed.). Hillsdale, NJ: Lawrence-Erlbaum.

Cohen, J. (1992). A power primer. *Psychological Bulletin, 112*(1), 155–159.

Cohen, B. H. (2001). *Explaining psychological statistics* (2nd ed.). New York: Wiley.

Conger, A. J. (1974). A revised definition for suppressor variables: A guide to their identification and interpretation. *Educational and Psychological Measurement, 34,* 35-46.

Creswell, J. W. (2012). *Educational research: Planning, conducting, and evaluating quantitative and qualitative research* (4th ed.). Boston, MA: Pearson.

Cronbach, L. J., & Furby, L. (1970) How should we measure change – or should we? *Psychological Bulletin, 74,* 68.

Diekhoff, G. (1992). *Statistics for the social and behavioral sciences: Univariate, bivariate, multivariate.* Dubuque, IA: Wm. C. Brown.

Fagerland, M. W., & Sandvik. L. (2009). The Wilcoxon-Mann-Whitney test under scrutiny. *Statistics in Medicine, 28*(10), 1487-1497.

Field, A. (2000). *Discovering statistics using SPSS for windows.* Thousand Oaks, CA: Sage.

Fink, A. (Ed.). (1995). *How to measure survey reliability and validity,* Vol. 7. Thousand Oaks, CA: Sage.

Gall, M. D., Gall, J. P., & Borg, W. R. (2007). *Educational research: An introduction* (8th ed.). White Plains, NY: Longman.

George, D., & Mallery, P. (2003). *SPSS for Windows step by step: A simple guide and reference. 11.0 update* (4th ed.). Boston: Allyn & Bacon.

Glass, G. V., & Hopkins, K. D. (1996). *Statistical methods in education and psychology.* Needham Heights, MA: Allyn & Bacon.

Glenberg, A. M. (1996). *Learning from data: An introduction to statistical reasoning.* Mahwah, NJ: Erlbaum.

Green, S. B., & Salkind, N. J. (2008). *Using SPSS for Windows and Macintosh* (5th ed.). Upper Saddle River, NJ: Pearson,

Hinkle, D. E., Wiersma, W., & Jurs, S. G. (1998). *Applied statistics for the behavioral sciences* (4th ed.). Chicago, IL: Rand McNally College Publishing.

Holm, S. (1979). A simple sequentially rejective multiple test procedure. *Scandinavian Journal of Statistics, 6*, 65-70.

Hopkins, J. D. (1998). *Educational and psychological measurement and evaluation.* Needham Heights, MA: Allyn & Bacon.

Isaac, S., & Michael, W. B. (1990). *Handbook in research and evaluation for education and the behavioral sciences* (2d ed.). San Diego, CA: EdITS.

Johnson, C. E., Wood, R., & Blinkhorn, S. F. (1988). Spuriouser and spuriouser: The use of ipsative personality tests. *Journal of Occupational Psychology, 61*, 153-162.

Keppel, G. (2004). *Design and analysis: A researcher's handbook* (4th ed.). Upper Saddle River, NJ: Prentice-Hall.

Kline, R. B. (2004). *Beyond significance testing.* Washington, DC: American Psychological Association.

Leech, N. L., & Onwuegbuzie, A. J. (2002). A call for greater use of nonparametric statistics. *Paper presented at the Annual Meeting of the Mid-South Educational Research Association,* Chattanooga, TN, November 6-8.

Lovitts, B., & Wert, E. (2009). *Developing quality dissertations in the social sciences: A graduate student's guide to achieving excellence.* Sterling VA: Stylus.

Nunnally, J. C. (1975). *Introduction to statistics for psychology and education.* New York, NY: McGraw Hill.

Nunnally, J. C., & Bernstein, I. H. (1994). *Psychometric theory* (3rd ed.). New York, NY: McGraw-Hill.

Pedhazur, E. J., (1997). *Multiple regression in behavioral research* (3rd ed.). Orlando, FL: Harcourt Brace.

Rea, L. M., & Parker, R. A. (2005). *Designing and conducting survey research* (3rd ed.). San Francisco, CA: Jossey-Bass.

Rosenthal, R. (1991). *Meta-analytic procedures for social research* (2d ed.). Newbury Park, CA: Sage.

Rosnow, R. L., & Rosenthal, R. (2005). *Beginning behavioural research: A conceptual primer* (5th ed.). Englewood Cliffs, NJ: Pearson/Prentice/Hall.

Rovai, A. P. (2002). Development of an instrument to measure classroom community. *Internet & Higher Education, 5*(3), 197-211. (ERIC Document Reproduction Service No. EJ663068)

Scariano, S. M., & Davenport, J. M. (1987). The effects of violations of independence in the one-way ANOVA. *The American Statistician, 41*(2), 123-129.

Shapiro, S. S., & Wilk, M. B. (1965). An analysis of variance test for normality (complete samples). *Biometrika 52*(3-4): 591–611.

Snedecor, G. W., & Cochran, W. G. (1989). *Statistical methods* (8th ed.). Ames, IA: Iowa State University Press.

Stevens, J. (2002). *Applied multivariate statistics for the social sciences* (4th ed.). Mahwah, NJ: Lawrence Erlbaum.

Tabachnick, B., & Fidell, L. (2007). *Using multivariate statistics* (5th ed.). Needham Heights, MA: Allyn & Bacon.

Tiku, M. L. (1971). Power function of the F-test under non-normal situations. *Journal of the American Statistical Association, 66*, 913-915.

Triola, M. (2010). *Elementary statistics* (11th ed.). Boston, MA: Addison-Wesley/Pearson Education.

Vogt, W. P. (1993). *Dictionary of statistics and methodology: A nontechnical guide for the social sciences.* Newbury Park, CA: Sage.

Weinberg, A. (1978). The obligations of citizenship in the republic of science. *Minerva, 16*:1-3.

Williams, R. H., & Zimmerman, D. W. (1996). Are simple gain scores obsolete? *Applied Psychological Measurement, 20*(1), 59-69.

Index
